Delivering Internet
Connections over Cable
Breaking the Access Barrier

Delivering Internet Connections over Cable
Breaking the Access Barrier

Mark E. Laubach
David J. Farber
Stephen D. Dukes

Wiley Computer Publishing

John Wiley & Sons, Inc.
NEW YORK · CHICHESTER · WEINHEIM · BRISBANE · SINGAPORE · TORONTO

Publisher: Robert Ipsen

Editor: Carol A. Long

Managing Editor: Micheline Frederick

Production Assistant: Kerstin Nasdeo

Text Design & Composition: Thomark Design

Designations used by companies to distinguish their products are often claimed as trade-marks. In all instances where John Wiley & Sons, Inc., is aware of a claim, the product names appear in initial capital or ALL CAPITAL LETTERS. Readers, however, should contact the appropriate companies for more complete information regarding trademarks and registration.

This book is printed on acid-free paper. ∞

This publication is designed to provide accurate and authoritative information in regard to the subject matter covered. It is sold with the understanding that the publisher is not engaged in professional services. If professional advice or other expert assistance is required, the services of a competent professional person should be sought.

Library of Congress Cataloging-in-Publication Data:

Laubach, Mark.
    Delivering Internet connections over cable : breaking the accerss barrier / Mark Laubach, David Farber, Stephen Dukes.
       p. cm. -- (Wiley Networking Council series)
    ISBN 0-471-38950-1 (pbk. : alk. paper)
    1. Broadband communication systems. 2. Cable television. 3. Internet 4. Data transmission systems. I. Farber, Dave. II. Dukes, Stephen. III. Title. IV. Series.

TK5103.4.L38 2001
384.3'3--dc21

                                                  98-51575

Printed in the United States of America.

10 9 8 7 6 5 4 3 2 1

Wiley Networking Council Series

Series Editors:

Scott Bradner
Senior Technical Consultant, Harvard University

Vinton Cerf
Senior Vice President, MCI WorldCom

Lyman Chapin
Chief Scientist, BBN/GTE

Books in series:

- *ISP Survival Guide: Strategies for Running a Competitive ISP*
  Geoff Huston
  ISBN: 0-471-31499-4

- *Implementing IPsec: Making Security Work on VPN's, Intranets, and Extranets*
  Elizabeth Kaufman, Andrew Newman
  ISBN: 0-471-34467-2

- *Internet Performance Survival Guide: QoS Strategies for Multiservice Networks*
  Geoff Huston
  ISBN: 0-471-37808-9

- *ISP Liability Survival Guide: Strategies for Managing Copyright, Spam, Cache, and Privacy Regulations*
  Tim Casey
  ISBN: 0-471-37748-1

- *VPN Applications Guide: Real Solutions for Enterprise Networks*
  Dave McDysan
  ISBN: 0-471-37175-0

- *Converged Networks and Services: Internetworking IP and the PSTN*
  Igor Faynberg, Hui-Lan Lu, and Lawrence Gabuzda
  ISBN: 0-471-35644-1

(continues)

Books in series: (*Continued*)

- *WAN Survival Guide: Strategies for VPNs and Multiservice Networks*
  Howard C. Berkowitz
  ISBN: 0-471-38428-3

- *The NAT Handbook: Implementing and Managing Network Address Translation*
  Bill Dutcher
  ISBN: 0-471-39089-5

For more information, please visit the Networking Council Web site at www.wiley.com/networking council

This book is dedicated to:

*Dame Sieglinde Gann Laubach, aka, Lindy,
the 11-year-old floppy-eared female
wonder Doberman, my best companion,
who was very patient but persistent in
reminding me that walks in the park are a
good way to step back and think about
what to write. She was a very special
companion to me and will be missed.*

*Ward Laubach, my father, who finds
himself amazed at some of the things I do.
He was especially helpful in my moments
of procrastination by always asking me
how the book was going.*

Contents

Networking Council Foreword

The Networking Council Series was created in 1998 within Wiley's Computer Publishing group to fill an important gap in networking literature. Many current technical books are long on details but short on understanding. They do not give the reader a sense of where, in the universe of practical and theoretical knowledge, the technology might be useful in a particular organization. The Networking Council Series is concerned more with helping readers to think clearly about networking issues than with promoting the virtues of a particular technology—how to relate new information to the rest of what the reader knows and needs, so that he or she can develop a customized strategy for vendor and product selection, outsourcing, and design.

In *Delivering Internet Connections over Cable: Breaking the Access Barrier*, you'll see the hallmarks of Networking Council books: examination of the advantages and disadvantages, strengths and weaknesses of market-ready technology, useful ways to think about options pragmatically, and direct links to business practices and needs. Disclosure of pertinent background issues needed to understand who supports a technology and how it was developed is another goal of all Networking Council books.

The Networking Council Series is aimed at satisfying the need for perspective in an evolving data and telecommunications world filled with hyperbole, speculation, and unearned optimism. In *Delivering Internet Connections over Cable: Breaking the Access Barrier*, you'll get clear information from experienced practitioners.

We hope you enjoy the read. Let us know what you think. Feel free to visit the Networking Council Web site at www.wiley.com/networkingcouncil.

Scott Bradner
Senior Technical Consultant, Harvard University

Vinton Cerf
Senior Vice President, MCI WorldCom

Lyman Chapin
Chief Scientist, BBN/GTE

Acknowledgments

I would like to thank David Farber and Stephen Dukes, my co-authors, for their substantive help with filling out the content of this book to include important views concerning the future of broadband communications.

Thanks also go to our two reviewers: George Abe, from Palomar Ventures in Santa Monica, California, and Dan Pike, from Prime Management, in Austin, Texas. George was instrumental in focusing the book on up-to-date issues, while Dan helped to put those issues in the context of the history of cable networks. During the process, he quoted Yogi Berra: "It's déjà vu all over again."

Thanks also to:

John Pickens, from Com21, who gave us some valuable pointers along the way, and who coined the phrase, "Oops, there goes the neighborhood."

Fred Wilkenloh from CommScope, and Walter Ciciora, from EnCamera, helped fill in some of the gaps in the technical history area. We also thank Walter for his book *Modern Cable Television Technology* (co-authored with James Farmer and David Large) which was a very useful reference during the preparation of this book.

Mary Woodard, from United Pan-Europe Communications, N.V., for reviewing the book as a prospective reader.

Chuck House for enlightening me that *Cindy and the Cheese Soufflé: Immersive Family Communications* tells of a very important future evolution for the home network.

Finally, we thank Paul Baran, who founded Com21, and all the folks at Com21 who helped build the business. The past several years have been an incredible experience, giving us great insight to the broadband data and voice technologies. We are also grateful for the opportunity to work with so many people in the cable industry.

Preface

Collectively, our experience with high-speed data over broadband cable started in July 1994 with the initial funding and hiring at Com21, following in the footsteps of Paul Baran, who invented packet switching in 1964, and Retired Vice Admiral RSN Bill Hauser. They had started working with the company as early at 1991 with the focus of providing packet voice services over cable. The World Wide Web was still in its infancy, and the only money-making opportunity at the time looked like telephony over cable.

In early 1994, Com21 had developed a symmetric 1.44Mbps-based prototype, which was targeted for voice. But the company switched gears that year and focused on high-speed data, though always keeping packet voice as a requirement for its system. By late 1994, it became apparent that the World Wide Web was the wunderkind of the technological world, and many in the cable industry shifted their interests to high-speed data and telephony. In 1995 @Home was launched; this accelerated the focus and drive to provide Internet services over cable.

In late 1995, the North American cable industry started the DOCSIS (Data Over Cable Service Interface Specifications) project under the auspices of MCNS Holdings, which consisted of Comcast, Cox, TCI, and Time Warner Cable, but later consigned to CableLabs. CableLabs formally took over the project later in 1997 after the selection of LANCity (later bought by Bay Networks, again later bought by Nortel Networks; the broadband cable activities were transferred to Arris Interactive in December 1998, the joint venture of Nortel Networks and Antec), General Instruments (which merged with Motorola in January 2000 under the name Motorola's Broadband Communications Sector), and Broadcom as the vendor authors.

DOCSIS was initiated in part due to the slow progress being made by the IEEE 802.14 Cable TV MAC and PHY Working Group. In time, however, the IEEE group did make substantial progress, and some of that group's achievements were implemented to the DOCSIS specifications, and vice versa. The vendors, however, clearly chose DOCSIS as the preferred specification for the North American market. This fueled DOCSIS development to its current status.

It was during this time period that the collective wisdom said to switch from symmetric systems to asymmetric systems with an intelligent head-end controller. In April 1997, Com21 delivered such a system, and entered the market behind Motorola and LANCity. The Com21 and Motorola systems demonstrated that intelligent controllers were the way to go. Com21 added bandwidth allocation for multi-tier services, along with the promise of QoS for voice telephony via a simple cable modem expansion card. DOCSIS later added similar capabilities for supporting QoS for packet voice services with the Version 1.1 update.

This book is a direct outcome of the development of the Com21 product family and the IEEE and DOCSIS standards, which gave the industry the insight to build high-speed two-way packet data and packet voice systems over cable.

Cable networks are a gold mine for broadband access to the home, with a virtual motherload of capability, and a very strong vein of ongoing opportunity to scale for the future. This book attempts to communicate the depth and breadth of this opportunity for cable networks.

Overview of the Book and Technology

The goal of this book is to help readers understand cable networks and high-speed data-over-cable networks, as well as the basic architecture and capabilities of the physical cable plant and high-speed data and emerging voice services. To that end, it tracks current trends, in high-speed packet data and packet voice-over-broadband access networks, specifically detailing cable networks.

Cable networks have always been regarded as a kind of dark horse in the data networking world, primarily because of their focus on television and their anecdotal reputation for poor customer service. All that is changing rapidly. Cable networks today have a highly scalable broadband infrastructure that can deliver many different kinds of service to the home, beginning with high-speed Internet access, followed closely by Internet plus telephony.

How This Book Is Organized

The history, topology, and capabilities of cable networks is not as well known as it should be. To remedy that situation, Chapter 1 presents an overview of the significant events in the regulatory and technical history of cable networks. Chapter 2 is devoted to illuminating how cable networks support high-speed data. The history of two-way cable modem products and services is two decades long, and in that time, much has been learned and subsequently applied, resulting in more capable modem networks. Chapter 3 is devoted to a discussion of the old and the new cable modem architectures. Chapter 4 addresses issues the cable operator and Internet service provider must face when deploying and scaling their networks and services.

Only one cable standard exists in North America. The DOCSIS suite of specifications define how cable modems must operate to comply with this standard. Chapter 5 delves into these specifications, to convey a high level understanding of the operation of the DOCSIS protocol, and to act as a guide for subsequent reading of the specifications themselves. Chapter 6 describes another, early-stage set of specifications, called PacketCable, which targets packet voice and video services. When enabling Ethernet-over-cable networks it is important to recognize that the residential access network is not a local area network. It is a public access network, and as such embodies public privacy protection issues. Chapter 7 discusses this important distinction.

Later chapters in the book explore issues that are shaping the way broadband data is today and will be in the future. In particular, network open access has ignited public controversy, as well as several lawsuits filed municipalities and groups of citizens against cable companies. Therefore, we have dedicated Chapter 8 to exploring and explaining the technical underpinnings of network open access. Chapter 9 takes on the issues of home computer vulnerability. With millions of homes coming online with broadband always-on access, the home computer and electronic commerce are now more vulnerable to compromise by hackers and viruses. Chapter 10 discusses several hot topics shaping the broadband infrastructure in the home. A tug of war is developing between cable modems and next-generation two-way set-top terminals for controlling access to high-speed data and packet telephony. And residential gateways may move the network side of the multimedia interactive network to just outside or just inside the house, taking cable modems and much of the set-top terminal functions with it. Furthermore, the home network is about to explode with capabilities and interactive services, and the industry will have to move quickly beyond the IPv4 addressing and routing architecture if it is to keep pace with consumer demand.

As cable networks take on more and more services, these new services will need to use a common shared infrastructure, shared fabric, in the cable operator's backend networks. That is the topic of Chapter 11, the final chapter of the book.

Who Should Read This Book

This book has been written as an introductory text. However, some experience or understanding of Ethernet and IP protocols is recommended to gain a full understanding of the content. Probably though, a basic understanding of the systems can be gleaned without this background.

The intended audience is managers, implementers, policymakers, and regulators who want or need more knowledge of the current technologies implemented in high-speed data and voice-over-cable networks. The book is also written for anyone who wants to understand the basics of cable modem systems.

The Future Is Now

It is relevant to note that this book was prepared on a Macintosh Powerbook which uses an Airport (IEEE 802.11b) wireless interface to connect to the home network. On occasion, the Powerbook was located at the "new house," which is part of the Com21 Silicon Valley wireless testbed. There, the Airport hub was directly connected to a normal Com21 cable modem, which in turn was connected to the wireless network. This created a wireless LAN-to-wireless WAN network. In addition, the wireless Com21 modem had a voice telephony card, which was connected an ordinary phone used for making calls while writing the book. Both old home and new home networks were protected with a Sonicwall firewall appliance, to ensure that this book was written using safe networking practices. The point is, broadband communications capabilities are possible now; they await only deployment. (For more information about this home network, send email to laubach@inconvenient.net.)

Introduction

A fascinating aspect of high-speed data over cable networks is that though the foundations for creating two-way interactive services in the United States began over 30 years ago, in the late sixties and early seventies, it is only recently that consumers began to savor the fruits of widespread cable modem deployment. The promise of high-speed data over cable has been met; it works, and it is affordable.

In the race for supplying multimedia broadband services to the home, cable networks outdistance the competitors of digital subscriber line (DSL), fixed-point wireless, and fiber optic to the home systems. In addition to having a very high aggregate bandwidth delivery capability, cable networks today are already delivering a mixture of analog and digital television, toll-quality telephony, and high-speed data services. Moreover, the cable network itself is evolving into a highly scalable distribution system. The race is ongoing and for the foreseeable future it appears likely that cable will lead the race to the home for supplying television, telephony, and high-speed data services.

This book is about the implementation of today's modern high-speed digital interactive services over cable. It focuses not just on cable modems, rather on the entire cable network system and its potential for creating the highly pervasive broadband access network of the future. The chapters comprise a systematic discussion of cable network technology, beginning with cable plant topology.

All modern two-way interactive services, specifically modern cable modem systems, share common architectural aspects that were honed from the lessons taught by early cable modem deployments in the 1990s. A cable modem is part of a larger system, which includes the cable operator's network and the cable Internet service provider's (ISP's) network. While cable modems themselves bear much similarity to an Ethernet local area network (LAN), in reality, supplying that service requires substantial backend network services in a cable operator's facility. To make this all work for the benefit of the consumer, the North American cable operators developed a standard for cable modems that is being widely implemented by many manufacturers. Following close on the heels of the establishment of cable modems standards were various approaches for supplying telephone services over cable. The deployment of high-speed data services carries with it many aspects of socialization that are part of the education process of both the consumer and the cable operator. These include various security, service availability, and vulnerability issues. Eventually, the cable services we know today—video, data, and voice—will undergo an evolution.

Before launching the discussion of cable plant topology, it is important to review the past 30 years of cable network development, as well as the impact that government regulation and technology advances have had on the industry.

The Original Motivation for Cable Networks

The popular label for cable television networks is CATV, which stands for Community Antenna Television. CATV's roots in America date back to 1948, when twin-lead wires were strung from roof to roof in the town of Astoria, Oregon. The first use of coaxial cable appeared in 1950, in Lansford, Pennsylvania. Beginning in the late forties and continuing through the fifties, America was in the throes of a television frenzy; everyone wanted to own a TV. The problem was, not everyone could receive TV signals. Over-the-air broadcast was the only means available to distribute network television. The motivation behind the development of CATV was to improve reception, either in areas where the television signals were too weak or where there was reception interference, such as in large cities where the tall buildings deflected signals every which way, causing multipath distortions.

CATV networks grew up around cities and municipalities chiefly because the cable operators needed access to both the utility poles to string their coaxial cables or permission to dig the holes in which to bury cables, and local governments had the power to grant such access. Having right of way is a fundamental necessity to the cable operator. The permission to provide CATV service and obtain right of way is given via a franchise agreement from the local government. Periodically, a franchise agreement needs to be renewed. The large cable operators are called Multiple System Operators (MSOs) because they own the cable operations in many cities. Each city, however, has its own franchise agreement that must be renewed separately. Historically, local municipalities granted a cable franchise to only one operator. This created an environment where MSOs did not compete with each other for the same subscribers. This unique arrangement has persisted, allowing MSOs to openly join together on various activities to improve cable television technology and deployment. This also gave MSOs a monopoly in each franchise and one could argue whether that was beneficial or not to customers.

The CATV network in any given town typically runs past dwellings, not businesses, as there is no need to run the cable where there is no potential for adequate revenue. Thus, the primary factor used to describe the size of the cable operator is households passed (HHP), also called *homes passed*. HHP is based on the number of homes physically passed by the CATV network. The other factor is called the *take rate*, for a particular service. For example, assume the HHP is 10,000 for a cable operator; therefore, a 35 percent take rate for video services would mean there are 3,500 subscribers.

Today, CATV networks have evolved far beyond their roots as the community antenna into a multiple service broadband network. Concomitantly, the term CATV has been replaced by the more appropriate term *cable network*.

Cable Chronology

Government Regulations

The success and growth of the cable television industry has been both helped and hampered by government restrictions throughout the past 40 years. To address the competitive posturing among the cable operators and the broadcast television industry, including the development market called Ultra High-Frequency (UHF), the Federal Communications Commission (FCC), Congress, the Supreme Court, and various other legal bodies all became involved in modifying the way cable television was permitted to operate. This section summarizes the more noteworthy events that shaped how cable networks function today.

1966. FCC issued its "Second Report and Order." To address arguments over competing rights from the broadcast *off-air* (over the air) television industry, the FCC imposed wide-ranging and restrictive regulations on cable television. The commission declared that cable television stations "must carry" local off-air television channels within their markets. On distant station programs, the FCC issued a nonduplication rule that required cable television operators to wait at least a day to rebroadcast a program. And cable television networks in the top 100 markets had to show evidence supporting public interest before importing a distant station. The latter regulation was imposed to protect fledgling UHF stations. In smaller markets, this restriction was not applied.

1968. The Supreme Court ruled that, based on the Copyright Act of 1909, cable operators did not have to pay royalties nor seek consent to retransmit distant television signals because the distribution process was not considered a "performance of the work." As a reaction in part to the Supreme Court ruling, the FCC reshaped its distant signal rules; the new requirements said that, within 35 miles of the top 100 markets, cable operators had to obtain permission of the originating distant station before retransmitting. In addition, cable operators located with 35 miles of an off-air station in smaller markets were required to carry signals from the nearest full network, independent, and education stations in their region or state. Cable operators outside the 35-mile zone of any station were permitted to carry distant signals as long as they did not do so in lieu of carrying a closer station of the same type. The latter rules were called *anti-leapfrogging restrictions*. These new rulings, however, caused confusion, and thus stalled evidentiary hearings. Awaiting clarification, the FCC declared that new hearings would be held, based on the new 1968 rules. This declaration greatly slowed down the process of retransmission consents, essentially freezing cable television expansion, especially in the major markets. This slowdown came to be called *the freeze*.

1969. The FCC mandated that cable operators with over 3,500 subscribers had to originate their own programming on at least one channel. This forced these cable operators to build studios, an effort that was a capital-intensive expense absent any real new revenue sources, and to dedicate a precious channel. In this year, the FCC also allowed cable operators to interconnect cable facilities.

1970. The FCC restricted telephone common carriers from providing cable television service to viewers in their operating communities, although a waiver could be issued for sufficient cause. Telephone companies were required to provide pole space if available. In this same year, the FCC also issued restrictions for cable systems that were directly or indirectly owned by national television networks or broadcast stations, and prohibited them from carrying off-air stations.

1972. The FCC issued its "Cable Television Report and Order" which was based on elements from a 1971 FCC-issued "Letter of Intent" and 1971 FCC and White House-issued "Consensus Agreement" between copyright holders, broadcast television operators, and cable television operators. In this report and order, cable systems outside all television markets had to carry all television signals assigned to the cable community, including educational stations within 35 miles and other significantly viewed[1] stations, in smaller markets, a total of three full networks stations and one independent station in combination with local and distant stations. The same must-carry rules applied to cable systems in the top 100 markets, in addition to the carriage of additional independent stations. One nonbroadcast station was allowed for every broadcast station carried on the system. This was seen as lifting distant signal importation restrictions, so the FCC required that cable systems in the top 100 markets have a minimum of 20 channels. At the time, this was pushing the limit of cable television amplifier technology, which forced some operators to deploy a dual cable system. Two-way communications capacity was required. The 1972 action was initially heralded as the thawing of the freeze (referred to as *the rules thaw*). However, the order continued to restrict the cable operator's ability to offer varied programming, as it protected the interests of broadcasters and copyright holders in the major markets. By this year, the United States had over 2,800 cable operators and

---

[1] "Significantly viewed" is a term introduced in the February 12, 1972 Code of Federal Regulation Part 76 Cable Television Service, Section 76.5 Definitions: (i) "Significantly viewed. Viewed in other than cable television households as follows: (1) For a full or partial network station–a share of viewing hours of at least 3 percent (total week hours), and a net weekly circulation of at least 25 percent; and (2) for an independent station–a share of viewing hours of at least 2 percent (total week hours), and a net weekly circulation of at least 5 percent. See § 76.54. Note: As used in this paragraph, "share of viewing hours" means the total hours that noncable television households viewed the subject station during the week, expressed as a percentage of the total hours these households viewed all stations during the period, and "net weekly circulation" means the number of noncable television households that viewed the station for 5 minutes or more during the entire week, expressed as a percentage of the total noncable television households in the survey area."

over 6 million subscribers. Unfortunately, few of these subscribers were in the top markets, due to the lack of varied programming.

1975. The FCC relaxed requirements on older systems, dropped the requirements for channel capacity and access (local origination) channels, and eliminated the two-way capacity and one-for-one requirement.

1976. FCC eliminated distant-signal anti-leapfrogging requirements. Satellites appeared in this time period. Home Box Office (HBO) launched in 1976; it was the first pay cable product delivered to cable operators via satellite. This was a milestone in the cable television industry. Also in 1976, systems with fewer than 3,500 subscribers were relieved of the two-way capacity requirement. And Congress passed the Copyright Revision Act of 1976. This required cable operators to pay royalties for the retransmission of distant signals based on the system's gross revenues.

1977. A court case involving HBO (petitioner) versus the FCC and U.S. Government (respondents) was decided in favor of HBO, forcing the FCC to abandon its pay cable restrictions. Specifically, the Court of Appeals remove all FCC pay-cable anti-siphoning[2] rules. In addition, the Court laid strict groundwork whereby current and future FCC regulation on cable had to be justified. This was a landmark case for the cable industry; it prompted the expansion of many cable systems, which henceforth began to carry more pay movie and sports channels. Subsequently, subscribership increased. Another result of the HBO decision was that the FCC now had to prove demonstrable harm to local broadcasting stations warranting federal protection. Also, now cable operators in the top 100 markets could offer compelling programming, and their subscribership, too, increased.

1980. Following a series of FCC and Supreme Court rulings, cable operators were permitted to carry as many distant signals as their viewers demanded.

1984. Congress passed the Cable Communications Policy Act ("Cable Act"), amending the Communications Act of 1934 to cover cable. Its purpose is to establish a national cable policy; establish franchise pro-

---

[2] In 1970, the FCC enacted "anti-siphoning" regulation on cable networks to prevent them from channeling programs away from over-the-air broadcast stations and from charging fees for programs that had previously been received at no charge by viewers. Cable operators were restricted from showing feature films less than two years old, any live televised sports events that had been shown on a regular basis on television within the past two years, any series programs, and any advertising on pay cable channels except those promoting other pay cable programs.

cedures that encourage cable growth and assure that cable systems are responsive to community needs and interests; outline the respective spheres of federal, state, and local authority over cable; assure that cable provides the widest possible diversity of services to the public; establish an orderly process for franchise renewal that protects cable operators against unfair denials of renewal if they meet the standards of the act; and promote competition and minimize unnecessary cable regulation. As a result of this act, franchise procedures, as well as rate-setting authorities, were put into place in local and state governments. In addition, federal procedures were established to cover leased access to cable systems, subscriber privacy, theft of cable service, and cable ownership restrictions. The act also addressed obscenity and other cable programming issues. Finally, the act amended the FCC's basic authority to include authority over cable. Cable operators gave up some rights as to freely drop, re-tier, or re-price program offerings in exchange for the franchise renewal standards and exclusion of telephone companies from offering cable services in their service areas. The act also provided that no cable system would be considered a common carrier, subjected to utility-type federal or state regulation, by virtue of its provision of cable service. However, the act did not include enhanced services such as high-speed data, telephony, or other interactive services.

1985. The Ninth Circuit Court ruled in *Preferred Communications, Inc. vs. City of Los Angeles* that, consistent with the First Amendment, cable operators could not arbitrarily restrict access to a single cable television company when the utility poles and conduits were physically capable of accepting more than one system. The court also made broad analogies between newspapers and cable, finding that cable operators exercised "substantial" editorial control of their channels.

1986. The Supreme Court ruled that cable television enjoyed First Amendment rights as a communicator of originated programming and as an editor of programming produced by others. The burden of proof was put on local municipalities to show factual basis for any restrictions on "unfettered" cable operator speech.

1992. Congress passed the Cable Television Consumer Protection and Competition Act in response to complaints from consumers about excessive rate increases. The act reintroduced rate regulation for certain services and equipment provided by most cable television systems. It noted was that competitors to cable—in Direct Broadcast Satellite (DBS), Multichannel Multipoint Distributed Service (MMDS), broadcasters, and telephone companies—backed consumers. The act required that cable operators create a basic service tier to include all local broadcast signals and all nonsatellite-delivered distant broadcast signals that the system intended to carry, as well as all public, educational, and government access programming. The act further required the FCC to develop reasonable rates for the basic tier. This requirement included the establishment of standards, based on the basis of actual cost, of charges for subscriber installation and lease of the equipment for the basic service, including a converter box and remote control unit. In addition, the FCC was directed to establish guidelines identifying unreasonable rates for higher tiers of service. The act also authorized the FCC to reduce unreasonable rates and require refunds to subscribers. The act also: required cable operators to offer their programming to future competitors, such as MMDS, Satellite Master Antenna Television (SMATV), and DBS operators at reasonable prices on a nondiscriminatory basis; barred municipalities from unreasonably refusing to grant competitive franchises; required cable operators to carry local broadcast stations ("must carry"), or at the option of the broadcaster, to compensate the broadcaster for retransmission; regulated the ownership by cable operators of other media such as MMDS and SMATV. Finally, the FCC was directed to impose new regulations in many areas that affect customer service, including "cable-ready" televisions and consumer equipment, disposition of home wiring, privacy, rates for leased access channels, and more.

1996. Congress passed the Telecommunications Act of 1996, which enabled telephone companies to become open video systems, thereby coming into direct competition with cable. Telephone companies were allowed to seek a cable franchise or to buy or build wireless MMDS, SMATV, or other wireless facilities to distribute video. The act also allowed the creation of Competitive Local Exchange Carriers (CLECs), which enabled cable operators to provide telephone services in competition to the Incumbent Local Exchange Carrier (ILEC). This prompted a renewed focus of providing telephone services over cable.

Technology Advances

Hand-in-hand with regulatory changes, numerous advances in technology were instrumental in shaping the cable industry. These events include improvements in coaxial cable, amplifiers, set-top boxes, headend equipment, satellite communications, microwave communication, use of fiber optics, use of computers, digital compression, pay-per-view, and two-way services. This section summarizes the more noteworthy technology advances and organizational events that have shaped and grown the cable industry.

1961. TelePrompTer introduced a pay TV system called KeyTV to show the second Floyd Patterson/Ingemar Johansson heavyweight fight. The pay-to-view nature of this event prompted the birth of pay-per-view.

1962. The introduction of aluminum-shielded distribution cable with foam dielectric led to major improvements in the quality reception on 12-channel systems. The range of cable bandwidth was from 50MHz to 212MHz with no specification for the FM band.

1965. Solid-state electronics were introduced to cable amplifier and headend equipment. The first patent for dual heterodyne set-top box was filed by Ronald Mandell and George Brownstein. This was the first set-top box that eliminated off-air reception interference.

1966. TelePrompTer began testing of Amplitude Modulation Link (AML) microwave technology, which enabled cable operators to import distant signals.

1967. The first dual cable system with subscriber A/B switch was deployed in San Jose, California, at Gill Cable. Jerrold introduced its Transistor Main Line amplifier, improving quality and reliability.

1969. The Society of Television Engineers (SCTE) was formed. Approximately 2,500 cable networks existed as the decade ended.

1970. Jerrold introduced the Starline One transistor amplifier. Harmonically Related Carriers (HRC) were introduced in headends, which extended the range of larger cable systems. Cable bandwidth was specified in the continuous range from 5MHz to 300MHz.

1972. SRS demonstrated the first computer-controlled interactive television at the National Cable Television Association (NCTA) convention. Cable manufacturers introduced the first bonded and laminated tape with braid-drop cable, improving handling and cable longevity.

1973. TelePrompTer, Scientific Atlanta, and HBO jointly demonstrated the first satellite delivery system. This landmark event meant that 97 percent of the homes in the United States could be served via satellite systems. HBO began satellite distribution, using 33-foot (10-meter) diameter receiver dishes. Solid-state amplifier equipment in the 50 to 300MHz range became common. This allowed distribution of 35 program channels. TelePrompTer experimented with FM-modulated fiber-optic systems to improve picture quality.

1976. Cable industry momentum builds for satellite programming.

1977. Satellite dishes of 4.5 meter were introduced. Cable manufacturers introduced low-loss polyethylene foam dielectric for trunk, distribution and drop cables, thereby effectively lowering high-frequency cable attenuation by 10 percent.

1978. A patent was issued to James Tanner for "positive tap" premium channel blocking.

1979. TRW introduced 400MHz hybrid technology, which expanded channel capacity to 55. ATC installed data transmission capabilities in four systems, providing companies with direct links between facilities.

1980. Addressable set-top converters were first implemented. The anticipation of the first two-way addressable services fueled cable and computer industry interest in an interactive age. Low-noise galium aresenide amplifiers become less expensive and more reliable, which helped to stimulate the emerging DBS industry. Backyard dishes could now tune in the satellite programs.

1982. Time Fiber Communications introduced fiber-optic Mini-Hub for Multiple Dwelling Units (MDUs). United Cable deployed fiber optics in Alameda, California.

1984–1985. Many new program channels came online, including Disney Channel, Playboy, Discovery Channel, Home Shopping Network, and others. Cable bandwidth was extended to 500MHz.

1985. Some 6,600 cable systems were serving 42 million homes, at nearly at 50 percent households passed (HHP) take rate. General Electric introduced its first compression technology for channel expansion.

1986. HBO began to scramble its signal full time, thereby preventing backyard dish owners to receive without paying.

1987. With the introduction of the 550MHz system, channel capacity rose to 80. Jim Chiddix, Chief Engineer at American Television and Communications Corporation in Denver and others, demonstrate fiber optic system to the NCTA engineering committee. Their effort laid the groundwork for the future HFC systems. Cable manufacturers extended bandwidth for trunk, feeder, distribution and drop cables to 600MHz.

1988. Cable Television Laboratories (CableLabs) was established. Stereo audio appeared on some television channels. HFC began using analog modulation, thereby successfully demonstrating compatibility with existing analog TV sets, which numbered more than a billion worldwide.

1990. General Instruments introduced its DigiCipher system at the High Definition Television (HDTV) proceedings at the FCC. The Cumulative Leakage Index (CLI) rules were put into effect by the FCC. They required cable operators to tighten their maintenance standards to protect the aeronautical industry. Pirate set-top boxes began to appear.

1991. Cable manufacturers extended bandwidth for trunk, feeder, distribution, and drop cables to 1000MHz.

1992. Tele-Communications, Inc. (TCI), Time Warner, and Viacom began building HFC systems with a target node size of fewer than 1,000 homes passed.

1993. Time Warner, with help from Silicon Graphics, launched the Full Service Network trial in Orlando, Florida. Cox Communications launched its "ring-in-ring" network, which used double, self-healing rings in the distribution plant. This greatly increased reliability and met the stricter telephone industry standards.

1994. Internationally, MPEG2 became the preferred algorithm for compressing and sending digital TV signals. Regional network designs began to include Synchronous Optical Network (SONET) and Asynchronous Transfer Mode (ATM) technology. The North American cable television industry expanded into the telecommunications industry with the formation of the Teleport Communications Group (TCG), a joint ownership of TCI, Time Warner, Continental, Comcast, and Box. The Institute of Electrical and Electronic Engineers (IEEE) 802.14 Working Group was formed, to focus on high-speed data-over-cable networks. The Digital Audio Video Council (DAVIC) consortium was formed to create video-on-demand specifications.

1995. Time Warner began experimenting with telephony over cable. In December, at the Western Cable Show, John Malone, Chairman of TCI, announced a cable modem specification initiative

1996. TCI rolled out @Home service in San Francisco. Time Warner launched Road Runner in Akron and Canton, Ohio. By end of year, 10 MSOs had launched commercial cable modem services. TCI launched Headend In The Sky (HITS) digital video programming system. The first Data Over Cable Service Interface Specifications (DOCSIS) for cable modems were released in December.

1997. CableLabs launched its Opencable project, with the objective of developing advanced digital set-top terminals for use in two-way cable networks. General Instrument announced a long-term plan to supply 15 million advanced digital set-top boxes to nine leading MSOs. This heralded the new digital video age.

1998. WebTV and WorldGate competed for Internet over-TV access. CableLabs began the DOCSIS cable modem certification program.

2000. By midyear CableLabs (www.cablemodem.com), which provides up-to-date certification status, had certified 58 DOCSIS cable modems from over two dozen vendors, and qualified Cable Modem Termination System (CMTS) products from five vendors.

The Impetus for Two-Way Services

In the original community antenna systems, signals traveled in only one direction, from the antenna to the subscriber. The direction from the cable operator is called the *forward path*, or the *downstream*. Recall from the Government Regulations chronology at the beginning of the chapter that in 1972, to end the struggle between the TV broadcasters and the CATV industry, FCC proceedings resulted in what came to be called the "rules thaw." At that time many regulations came into effect that impacted the cable industry. Among those changes was the creation of the *return path*, or *upstream spectrum allocation* for two-way cable services. This provided the frequency allocation for subscribers sending data to the *headend*

Prior to the 1972 "rules thaw," cable technology typically supported 12 channels of video programming. The 1972 actions of the FCC prompted many franchise agreements to be rewritten, forcing cable operators to carry 21 to 24 channels and requiring capital expenditures to enhance their cable plant. But because the technology at the time didn't support that capacity on a single cable, operators had to install a second cable, thereby creating the dual cable system. (A dual cable system is two separate cable systems running in a parallel topology. It requires double the length of cable, double the number of amplifiers, and double the amount of maintenance when both cable plants are active.) Subscribers were given a *switch box*, on which they selected either the "A" or "B" cable.

Later in the 1970s, an improvement in video amplifier technology permitted many more downstream channels than in previous generations.

TWO-WAY VISION

An excellent overview of the vision of two-way services in the early seventies appeared in a November 1971 *IEEE Spectrum* article, written by Ronald K. Jurgen. Entitled "Two-way Applications for Cable Television Systems in the '70s," it offers the best description of the motivation of the time:

> Now, as the '70s move ahead, there is a new impetus to further growth in cable television systems. This impetus stems from the demonstrated engineering capability to bring many more channels and new communication services to subscribers while giving them the facility to "talk back" to the system and, in some cases, to all other subscribers on the system. This two-way, or bidirectional, capability opens up a whole new realm of application possibilities. The implications of two-way cable facilities are so important to the overall communications policies of the United States that government agencies and other policy-proposing groups are taking a close look at this emerging new technology.

This, coupled with the original two-way vision, led to the development of the topology in which the A cable would be used for video programming and the B cable would be used as a mid-split system for supporting two-way commercial services. This came to be called the *A/B mid-split architecture*.

But in the seventies, the technology wasn't up to the new capabilities, so the subscriber base failed to emerge, thus the additional revenue cable operators needed to realize the vision of two-way services failed to materialize. Consequently, two-way services went by the wayside for many more years. There were trial deployments of two-way technologies throughout the 1980s but serious deployments were never realized. The market was just not ready to expand to two-way. From 1989 through 1994 several two-way data services were deployed that began to lay the groundwork and raise the awareness that the time for market deployment was nearing. In late 1994, the U.S. cable industry issued several Request for Information (RFI) documents which helped to focus vendor involvement. In December 1995, a broad-based initiative was launched by the cable industry which has led to a concentrated effort to expand the services offered over CATV networks, specifically by adding two-way high-speed data and packet-based telephony. This effort is being made in conjunction with a focus on upgrading CATV plants to combine optical fiber and coaxial cable. These are the aforementioned hybrid fiber-coaxial (HFC) plants that allow operators to grow their broadband service offerings.

In parallel with high-speed two-way data developments, a worldwide effort in the 1990s was made to move from analog signal transmission to digital signal transmission for CATV systems. The digital formats in use are based on a set of standards drafted by the Moving Pictures Experts Group (MPEG). Digitization of television signals provides compression and the capability to support enhanced quality, including high-definition TV (HDTV) and high-speed data service. But the process of moving from analog to digital CATV transmission will take time. Consequently, in 1999 many cable operators were offering digital as well as analog TV channels, and the MPEG standards also address the encoding and decoding of NTSC, PAL, and SECAM formats in support of the millions of deployed analog TV sets around the world.

Since 1995, the following heralds the progress of CATV system enhancements to support advanced television services and two-way high-speed data and voice services:

- Operators begin aggressively upgrading all-coaxial cable plants to HFC.

- Systems boast a large number of program channels, 80-plus.

- Cities begin awarding multiple franchises.

- MSOs are permitted to become CLECs and to offer telephone services.

- Operators begin to focus on high-speed data and telephony as additional services.

- Operators begin significant cable modem rollouts in 1995 with proprietary products and later in 1999 with standards based products.

- AT&T and other cable operators deploy circuit switched telephony services. CableLabs focuses on packet voice services.

- Digital TV channels based on MPEG2 standards deployed via "digital set-top boxes."

High-Speed Data over Cable Standards

Recently, numerous standards activities around the world have focused on cable modem technology. The first standards group to undertake the task was the IEEE 802.14 CATV working group, which was first chartered in November 1994. Impatient in the face of the slow-moving IEEE process, the North American cable industry began to develop its own set of specifications. Within a year, a set of specifications were in place, called the Data over Cable Service Interface Specifications (DOCSIS), which are detailed in Chapter 5.

On the international front, in September 1994, an industrial consortium called the Digital Audio Video Council (DAVIC) began its standards process, focusing initially on the video-on-demand market; it quickly switched its attention to the intelligent set-top box, digital video based on international standards, and two-way interactive services. In June 1999, DAVIC completed its task and turned its specifications over to the international standards authorities. In September 1999, DAVIC ceased to exist; many of its members moved to a new group called the TV Anytime Forum (www.tv-anytime.org).

The IEEE 802.14 committee continued its work despite the launch of the North American initiative, with the objective of creating an international, rather than national standard. A great deal of crossover, both of information and personnel, took place between the IEEE and the DOCSIS groups. IEEE 802.14 produced its draft specification in 1998. Also in 1998, in coordination with DOCSIS, the 802.14 effort started a new working group aimed at developing an advanced physical layer modulation scheme that would be suitable to both the IEEE standard and the DOCSIS specifications. But by September 1999, the joint effort was ceased, followed by the disbanding of the IEEE 802.14 working group in November 1999.

The DOCSIS Specifications

The current DOCSIS specifications are the result of a project initiated by the work of a group called Multimedia Cable Network System Partners Limited (MCNS), whose members include TCI, Time Warner, Cox, Comcast, and their partners, Continental, Rogers, and CableLabs. The goal of MCNS was to speed the development of the communications and operations support interface specifications for cable modems and associated equipment. The specifications were designed to be nonvendor-specific, allowing cross-manufacturer compatibility for high-speed data communications services over two-way hybrid fiber-coax (HFC) cable television systems.

MCNS/DOCSIS was the brainchild of John Malone, then Chairman, at TCI, in December 1995 in response to broadband access competition, vendor postures, and lack of progress in public standards process of the IEEE 802 LAN/MAN (Metropolitan Area Network) committee. Originally a closed development effort by the six MCNS cable companies and selected vendors (BayNetworks/LANCity, now Nortel, GI, Broadcom), with Cable-Labs to help with process management, today, many vendors are participating, in a nondisclosure agreement (NDA) fashion. Once completed, DOCSIS specifications were made publicly available via www.cablemodem.com, with CableLabs in charge of a strict revision and control process for updates.

The DOCSIS specifications are actually a family of coordinated specifications dealing with many aspects of a cable modem access system. The most well-known is the Radio Frequency Interface (RFI) specification, usually referred to as the DOCSIS Specification. The initial release of the RFI specification was DOCSIS RFI Version 1.0 in December, 1996. It was based on an evolved LANCity-based protocol, targeted at residential, low-cost, off-the-shelf cable modems with certified interoperability between different vendors. The architecture of the DOCSIS system is a single, large Ethernet-based bridged LAN. It has a single ISP service provider architecture. Version 1.0 is primarily a best-effort Internet access system and was not designed for Quality of Service (QoS) support. DOCSIS RFI Version 1.0 was adopted by the Society of Cable Telecommunications Engineers (SCTE) Data Standards Subcommittee (DSS) as its standard in July 1997. In the fall of 1997, it was adopted as the U.S. position, in the ITU J.112 recommendation.

In 1999, CableLabs released DOCSIS RFI Version 1.1 based upon the required needs of the PacketCable packet voice and video project (Packet-Cable is another CableLabs project). DOCSIS RFI Version 1.1 added substantial protocol support to provide dynamic QoS facilities for packet voice services, in addition to packet data services. Other enhancements include baseline privacy, multicast support, and others. Version 1.1 also has packet recognition support for IEEE 802.1p tagged Ethernet frames. The tagging supports both priority and virtual LAN (VLAN) tagging. Note that while DOCSIS RFI Version 1.1 is substantially different from Version 1.0, a DOCSIS Version 1.1 modem can operate in a fully backwards compatible DOCSIS Version 1.0 mode, also DOCSIS V1.1 continues to provide a single, large Ethernet-based bridged LAN architecture.

Today, CableLabs runs an impressive DOCSIS vendor certification process for cable modems. The acceptance of DOCSIS in the North American cable operator community is predicated on a sufficient number of vendors being certified and product being available. In October 2000, more than 90 cable modems were DOCSIS V1.0 certified from approximately 36 manufacturers. DOCSIS V1.1 certified cable modems are expected in the first quarter of 2001.

For Further Information

An excellent review of the advances in cable television from the technology perspective can be found in the book *History Between Their Ears: Recollections of Pioneer CATV Engineers* by Archer S. Taylor, available from the Cable Center at www.cablecenter.org.

Information about CableLabs is available at www.cablelabs.com and the DOCSIS project at www.cablemodem.com.

Information about the history of DAVIC and its specifications can be found at www.davic.org.

The *CED Communications Engineering and Design* magazine reports on the cable and broadband industry. Its Web site is www.cedmagazine.com.

Cable Television Network Topology

Historically, it has been straightforward to design Ethernet switches that use coaxial cable, twisted pair wires, or wireless radios, to move data from station to station over a LAN. There are also IP routers and gateways that can transmit IP packets over just about any type of point-to-point link known. The same holds true for ATM switches that transmit cells over various link technologies. All that said, marrying data networking with cable television networks has proved to be an ongoing challenge over the past two decades. It was expected that transmitting packets over a broadband RF media would be as clear-cut a process as any other link technology; it has been anything but. Many barriers have stood in the way. However, in the 1990s, the potential of high-speed data-over-cable networks grew significantly, and fueled the motivation for cable operators and vendors to overcome these access barriers and provide a viable service. This has been, and continues to be, a global undertaking.

Cable networks today are complex systems designed to deliver video, data, and telephone services to subscribers. Video content comes from the following: local broadcast *off-air* (over the air) TV stations, satellite-delivered program content, and community-based locations, such as city halls. Numerous components are required to build and operate a CATV system. We focus only on those necessary to provide a basic understanding of the

CATV network and its support of high-speed data and voice communications. We also touch on the fundamentals of video services because data and voice services must coexist with them.

The high-speed data over cable technology has been developing along two separate paths. First, the fundamental structure of the cable plant has been evolving slowly to reach its full potential for two-way broadband service delivery. Second, the traditional approaches for moving high-speed data over cable have converged on a single, consistent approach. In this chapter, we take a look at cable television technology; in Chapter 3 we turn our attention to the evolution and features of high-speed data services.

NOTE Readers who want more technical depth than is presented in this chapter are encouraged to read *Modern Cable Television Technology* by Walter Ciciora, James Farmer, and David Large, San Francisco, CA: Morgan Kaufmann Publishers, 1999.

RF Spectrum Band Plan

Television signals transmitted over a cable network or broadcast over the air use radio frequency (RF) signals. Similar to tuning into an AM or FM radio station, a television set tunes from one RF television channel to the other. The RF spectrum is allocated within cable plants following a standard called the *band plan*. In North America, National Cable Television Association (NCTA) standard analog television signals are encoded in a RF channel, which occupies 6MHz of spectrum. The band plan creates channels by laying 6MHz slices of RF spectrum and labeling them, for example, channel 2, channel 3, and so on.

The first U.S. standardized band plan was developed in the mid-1980s as a joint effort between the Electronic Industries Alliance (EIA) and the NCTA. Named IS-6, this plan specified a band plan up to 300MHz. Cable NTSC television signals are allocated starting at 52MHz and on up, skipping 88MHz through 120MHz to avoid interference with FM broadcast signals in that range, and aviation radio and navigation services in the 108MHz to 120MHz region. On a 300MHz cable system, the cable operator has about 36 channels available for television.

The band plan since has been updated to include channel frequency allocations up to 750 MHz and higher. The updated plan enables mixtures of analog and digital video channels, so, for example, a very typical and widely deployed cable configuration is a 550MHz system. Depending on individual plant conditions, this provides a cable operator with 79 to 80

NTSC video channels. And because channel allocations are standardized, set-top boxes from any manufacturer will work on the cable plant.

A single coaxial (coax) cable can simultaneously support many downstream and upstream RF transmissions because the transmissions are on different frequencies. For example, in a typical cable system, the RF region (also called a passband) from 5MHz to 40MHz today is reserved for upstream transmissions, and the region from 50MHz to the end of the usable spectrum is reserved for downstream transmissions. The regions, passbands, for downstream and upstream are selected so that they do not overlap. The area between the downstream and upstream passbands is called the *crossover region*.

There are several different spectrum plans for two-way systems. By far the most common is called the *low-split system*. In a low-split system, the upstream passband is from 5MHz to 42MHz, and the downstream passband starts at 54MHz. Most U.S. cable plants are low-split systems. In another popular split, called the *mid-split system*, the upstream passband is from 5MHz to 112MHz; the downstream starts at 120MHz. Both low-split and mid-split plans are shown in Figure 2.1. Other types of split systems are less common. One worth noting, however, is the well-known Time Warner Full-Service Network trial that took place in Orlando, Florida. It used a 1GHz cable system; the upstream passband was placed in the upper part of the spectrum from approximately 800MHz to 1GHz; the downstream passband was everything below 700MHz.

In high-speed data-over-cable systems, having more upstream RF spectrum available upstream is beneficial. Cable has often been called an asymmetric system because of the far greater amount of downstream RF spectrum available, as compared to upstream spectrum. More upstream RF bandwidth means more high-speed data-carrying capacity. More on this in Chapter 3.

In Europe, it is common to find two-way systems operating with an upstream passband from 5MHz to 65MHz, with the downstream passband allocated from approximately 74MHz on up. European systems have a higher potential in the upstream, as compared to U.S. system, for upstream data-carrying capacity. In many European cable systems, the spectral allocation for a video channel is 8MHz.

All-Coaxial Cable Systems

Recall from Chapter 1 that the origin of the cable comes from the need to redistribute television signals to a residential community of subscribers.

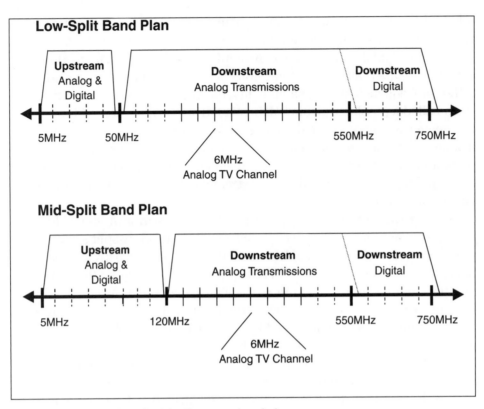

Figure 2.1   Low-split and mid-split system band plans.

As such, all cable systems were designed to optimize the transmission of television from the cable operator to the subscriber.

The layout, or topology, of a cable system follows an optimized deployment of cables and equipment within the serving area. While each deployment of a cable system is completely customized to the individual serving area, a number of components are common to all cable systems:

- *Headend*, the source for all television transmissions from the cable operator.
- *Coaxial trunk cables*, which distribute signals to and from the headend into the cable network.
- *Amplifiers*, which maintain signal quality throughout the cable plant.
- *Feeder coaxial cables*, which connect neighborhoods to the trunk cable.
- *Taps*, which provide for individual subscriber connections to a feeder cable.

- *Drop cables*, which connect a subscriber's home to a tap.

- *Demarcation or grounding block*, which connects the drop cable to the home.

- *In-house cable*, which runs from the block to the set-top box.

- *Set-top box*, or a subscriber's cable-ready TV.

A headend is a building located somewhere within the serving area. Headends take different forms, from small concrete buildings to rooms within large buildings, but typical to all traditional headends are antennas or satellite dishes located next to the building. Television signals are received by these antennas and dishes and brought into the headend. Signals within a headend are typically baseband signals. An RF cable only carries one TV signal, much like an S-video jack on a videocassette recorder or TV. A cable operator assigns different channels for different programs. Each television channel provided on the cable has its own modulator amplifier in the headend. In some cases the modulator may be coupled with a scrambling system, as is the case with premium channels (HBO, etc.) and pay-per-view (PPV) programs. In all cases, the modulator has the capability to modulate a baseband signal of the program to any RF channel and to amplify the signal. (Note: A processor amplifier is similar to a modulator amplifier but its input is RF, not baseband. A processor is used to modulate an RF channel to a new RF channel.)

Exiting the headend are one or more coaxial trunk cables. The number of cables is dependent on the design of the individual cable system. For example, the Palo Alto Cable Co-op in Palo Alto, California, has five trunk cables in its system, supporting an average of 10,000 homes passed per trunk cable.

Trunk amplifiers are located along the trunk cable, at a predefined spacing. The trunk cable itself is a very high-grade coaxial cable. RF signals passing through coaxial cable are attenuated, based on the length of the cable and other factors. Trunk amplifiers as a whole are typically very high-grade, precision equipment; they reamplify the entire downstream RF passband, such that the signal is restored to original power levels at the output of the amplifier. As needed, a bridge amplifier is coupled to a trunk amplifier to provide signals to a branch feeder cable.

Feeder cables provide service to individual neighborhoods. Along the feeder cable, line extender amplifiers are used to maintain signal quality. Feeder cables may branch off other feeder cables to reach all the homes in the neighborhood. Owing to the main trunk and multiple-branch

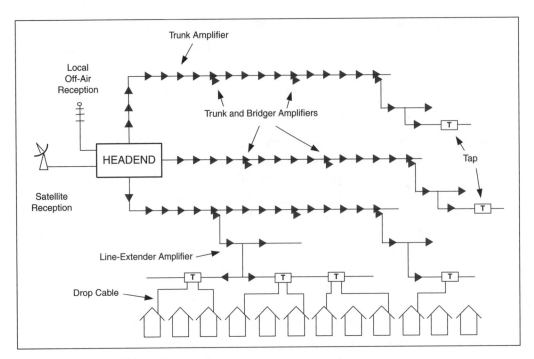

Figure 2.2 Tree and branch network.

topology of the cable network, it has earned the name *tree and branch network* (see Figure 2.2).

The tree and branch network is very well-designed for meeting its objective: that is, to distribute quality cable signals to subscribers. The system makes it possible to have many amplifiers between the headend and the subscriber, sometimes as many as 20 or 30, in "cascade" fashion, depending on the topology of the cable plant. To keep the system running at peak performance, however, these amplifiers must be periodically monitored and adjusted. This is a labor-intensive operation, and scheduling for it is cable operator-dependent.

Located along feeder cables are taps. Taps connect the drop lines from individual subscriber homes to the cable system. Taps are located either high up on telephone poles or wires or in locked cabinets. The connection of a subscriber drop line to a tap is the basic mechanism by which a cable operator controls legitimate access to the cable system (see Figure 2.3).

The drop cable runs from the tap to the subscriber's home or apartment. The cable is owned, installed, and serviced by the cable operator. The subscriber side of the drop cable connects to a *demarcation (demarc) block,*

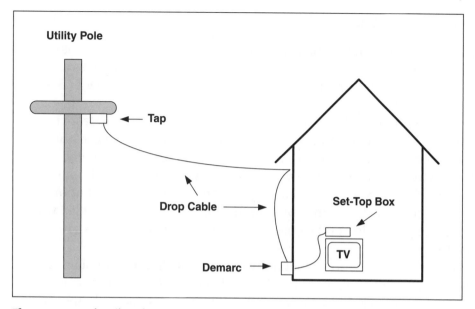

Figure 2.3   Subscriber drop.

also called a *grounding block*. This block is connected to an earth ground to provide lightning protection. A good-quality ground is required.

From the demarcation block, the in-house cable connects to the set-top box and/or television. In the United States, in the past, the cable operator owned and maintained the in-house cable that connected the set-top box. But as regulations changed in America—and elsewhere in the world—the in-house cable has come under the maintenance of the subscriber. More on this in the next chapter.

NOTE To date, cable operators still have access to the in-home cable and to the customer, whereas the telephone companies lost this access in 1968.

Set-top boxes come in many flavors, from many vendors. The cable operator generally selects one or more types, installs it, then rents it to the subscriber for a monthly fee.

A tree and branch network is a lot like the public water system, downstream, in that there is one source of water, feeding many households, which have one or more faucets. To expand the analogy, the interconnection from the water supplier to the home is performed using pipes (cable), pumps (amplifiers), junctions (splitters), water meters, and main valves (taps).

Distribution Hub Architecture

The tree and branch network just described is a very common deployment topology for cable plants. An alternative style of deployment uses a *distribution hub* architecture, in combination with an all-coaxial plant (see Figure 2.4).

A distribution hub is a building that is located downstream from the headend. The building itself can be a variety of sizes, from a prefabricated, small, 10-foot by 10-foot shack to something larger. Usually, distribution hubs have their own power, backup power, and air conditioning systems. The coaxial trunk cables usually terminate in a distribution hub, rather than in the headend. However, the headend is not precluded from terminating a portion of the coax trunk cable or fiber in the system, if needed.

Distribution hubs form a hierarchy in the cable distribution plant. The program point of origin is still in the headend, but the distribution of program information is first sent to the distribution hubs, then into the all-coaxial network. If a cable operator has several distribution hubs, these can be linked to the headend via various networking techniques, including,

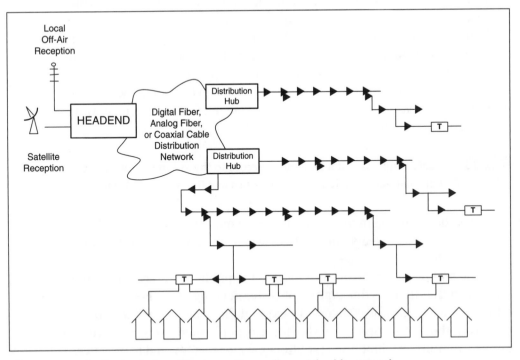

Figure 2.4   Distribution hub architecture with an all-coaxial cable network.

but not limited to, Synchronous Optical Network (SONET) technology, Amplitude Modulated Fiber, and coaxial cable. Generally, the cable operator owns the network that connects the distribution hubs, to avoid paying a fee to another entity.

Downstream Channel Capacity

One of the primary figures of merit of a cable system is the number of downstream NTSC analog television channels it provides. This figure is inherent to the revenue model and business plan of the cable operator. The downstream channel capacity of a cable system is dictated by the age of the technology used in original installation, in conjunction with any limits on capital funding or budgets. If the cable plant is old, coaxial cable and amplifier technologies of the time may have supported only a limited number of channels, as compared with that enabled by more modern technology. For example, certain older plants are 200MHz or 300MHz systems, meaning they can support only 20 to 30 channel systems, whereas newer systems, typically in the 550MHz to 750MHz range, can provide from 80 to hundreds of channels, with migration to 860MHz being deployed in system upgrades. Older system are, however, good candidates for upgrades, a topic we discuss later in this chapter.

Dual Cable Systems

As noted in Chapter 1, government regulations of the 1970s prompted the rewriting of many franchise agreements, and forced cable operators to support 21 to 24 channels. Recall that because the technology of the time couldn't support that capacity on one cable, operators had to install a second cable, creating the dual cable system. This system required double the length of cable, double the number of amplifiers, and double the amount of maintenance when both were active.

Today, thanks to advancements in technology that resulted in the wide downstream passband, the need for dual cable systems has diminished. Cable operators can choose between maintaining the dual cable system or converting over to a single cable system, based on individual objectives and business plans. For example, the TCI/AT&T Broadband cable plant in Mountain View, California, is a dual cable system; however, currently it is using only the primary A cable, for analog TV, digital TV, and two-way high-speed data and telephony services. The B cable remains up on the pole, available for some future use.

One-Way versus Two-Way Cable Systems

Not all cable plants are operated as two-way systems; that is, some cable plants may not support upstream transmissions from the subscriber to reach the headend. This, too, is based on age of technology or budget limits at the time of original installation and the individual business plan. Many all-coaxial cable plants support some amount of upstream transmission, but not necessarily from subscribers.

With respect to subscriber transmissions, coaxial cable systems fall into three different categories: one-way only, partial two-way-enabled, and two-way-enabled.

One-Way Only

A one-way only cable plant is operated to provide television services to its subscribers; it does not plan for future services or remote plant management capabilities, because of several factors, including the maintenance requirements of the system and the business plan of the operator. One-way systems also do not support interactive services such as telephony, though there is a form of cable modem service that can be supported called a *telephone return system*, which is discussed in the next chapter.

NOTE Virtually all cable amplification equipment shipped since the late 1970s is outfitted for two-way operation. The cable operator makes the choice as to whether to invoke two-way service.

Partial Two-Way-Enabled

A partial two-way-capable plant is one turned on for upstream transmissions, but in which two-way services have not been enabled for the subscribers.

A motivation for partially enabling a two-way system may be the result of the cable franchise agreement with the municipality. For example, the agreement may require that city council meetings be televised on the local community television channel. A convenient way for the cable operator to do this is to run a feeder cable by city hall, then enable the upstream only on those amplifiers between city hall and the headend. The TV signal is then modulated and transmitted on the downstream.

Another motivation behind this type of system is that many amplifiers are now remotely manageable and able to transmit status via the upstream plant. This allows monitoring and adjustments to be made from the head-end without having to "roll a truck" and manually inspect the entire system. All amplifiers may be remotely manageable or only a portion, such as the trunk and bridge amplifiers.

Two-Way-Enabled

Two-way-enabled all-coaxial plants are those that support two-way interactive communications between subscribers and the headend. Several services are immediately enabled by this capability:

Interactive set-top boxes that support Impulse Pay-Per-View (IPPV) services. Instead of making a phone call to a specific number for the PPV channel, or hooking up a telephone line to the set-top box, the IPPV set-top box uses interactive communications on the upstream and downstream to enable the purchase of a PPV program.

High-speed data over cable. This enables the immediate deployment of two-way-capable cable modem services. As modems are deployed to subscribers, the upstream transmission capability of the plant can be enabled. For example, if the plant is just turning up cable modem service, there is no need to enable every amplifier for upstream transmissions; thus, only those amplifiers between the subscriber and the headend need be enabled.

Telephone services. Many cable plants today are offering telephone service over the cable plant. That is, rather than receiving service over a twisted copper pair, a special telephone modem is connected to the cable plant. Initially, circuit switch technology is being used for voice over cable, with emphasis on moving to packet voice—for example, voice-over-IP (VoIP), when and where the technology is available.

Plant monitoring and control. The cable operator can make use of remotely manageable amplifiers and taps.

From this description of two-way-enabled cable plants, it might appear that simply converting two-way-capable plants to two-way enabled plants is an easy undertaking. In reality, turning up two-way capability requires a step-up in plant management, for two main reasons: ingress noise management and amplifier management. Ingress noise is discussed in the next section.

In all-coaxial cable plants, there are a small number of trunks exiting the headend, and, potentially, long cascades of amplifiers. The tree and branch topology was optimized for transmissions in the downstream direction, especially for managing power levels. In the upstream direction, cascades of amplifiers feed toward the headend on a trunk-by-trunk basis. Reverse traversing the tree and branch topology requires that amplifiers be consistently monitored and periodically adjusted. This is a straightforward task but one that requires additional personnel, a factor that is addressed in the business and budget plans of the cable operator. Based on available revenue, operator may not be able to enable the entire plant for two-way services at once. They may enable a part of the system, or a subset of subscribers, then add staff as two-way service revenues grow.

An advantage of interactive services running on a cable plant is that each interactive appliance in the subscriber's home is actually a remote sensor. Correlating any upstream transmission errors with the two-way and subscriber location goes a long way toward assisting the cable operator in quickly locating equipment that may need adjustment.

Inside a Two-Way Amplifier

The two-way all-coaxial amplifier is one type of building block in the all-coaxial cable system. There are several types of two-way amplifiers, as mentioned earlier: trunk, bridger, and line extender. All share a common general architecture, but vary in actual design, operating specifications, features, and cost.

A *diplex filter*, as shown in Figure 2.5, is another building block of any cable television network. The diplex filter performs the function of keeping downstream RF transmissions separate from upstream RF transmissions on the same coaxial cable. A diplex filter uses a combination of a high-pass filter and a low-pass filter to route RF signals to the appropriate filter port. These filters are defined as follows:

- A high-pass filter permits RF frequencies higher than a specified frequency (the *cutoff frequency*) to pass through the filter, while greatly attenuating frequencies below the cutoff frequency. For example, a high-pass filter with a cutoff frequency of 54MHz would permit RF signals from 54MHz and higher to pass through the filter, while frequencies lower than 54MHz would be attenuated.

- A low-pass filter permits RF frequencies lower than a specified cutoff frequency to pass through the filter, while greatly attenuating frequencies higher than the cutoff frequency. For example, a low-pass filter with a cutoff frequency of 42MHz would permit RF signals from 42MHz and lower to pass through the filter, while attenuating frequencies above 42MHz.

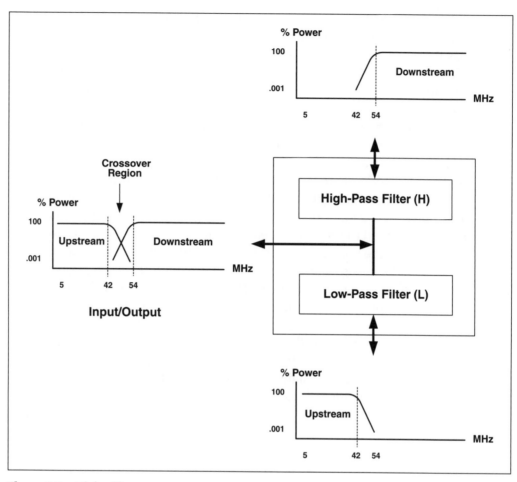

Figure 2.5   Diplex filter.

Note that the cutoff frequency is not a sharp "edge" beyond which attenuated frequencies immediately fall to zero amplitude. Rather, both physics and the specific filter design produce a *rolloff* or *slope region*. In the example of the 54MHz high-pass filter, frequencies below 54MHz are attenuated based on the rolloff characteristics, such that, for example, signals at 46MHz are attenuated 50 to 70 percent, (or more); signals from 40MHz to 42MHz are attenuated almost 100 percent. In the example of the 42MHz low-pass filter, the design of the slope may dictate that signals at 54MHz be attenuated almost to zero.

Some diplex filters are bidirectional They can be used to split a composite RF broadband into separate high and low bands, as well as combine separate high and low bands into a composite RF broadband system.

The example filters described here follow the design of a low-split two-way cable system. The frequencies above the cutoff frequency of the low-pass filter and below the cutoff frequency of the high-pass filter collectively are called the *crossover region,* where the rolloff slopes of the two filters cross over. Cable operators avoid using this region for any services.

The general two-way all-coaxial cable amplifier, shown in Figure 2.6, combines diplex filters with power amplifiers and additional electronics to provide two-way amplification. The input and output ports of the cable amplifier "speak" only to the downstream direction. In practice, however, signals in the upstream RF spectrum flow in the reverse direction on these ports. At the input of the amplifier is a diplex filter. Downstream RF signals are routed to the downstream equalizer; upstream signals are received from the upstream amplifier. From the downstream equalizer, the RF broadband signal passes through a preamplifier stage, a gain control stage, then through the final amplifier stage and into the high-pass port of the output diplex filter. In the upstream direction, signals are received at the amplifier output. The output diplex filter routes the low passband of the upstream RF spectrum to the upstream amplifier. The output of the upstream amplifier is fed to the input diplex filter. From there, amplified upstream signals are passed upstream to the next amplifier toward the headend.

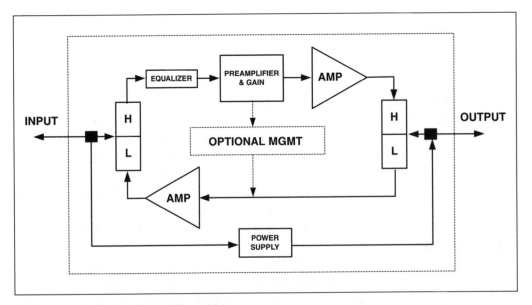

Figure 2.6   Two-way all-coaxial amplifier.

Some cable amplifiers have remote management capability. They have a separate management module that monitors and controls critical aspects of their performance. Communication is two-way, between the amplifier and a monitoring and management station located in the headend. Two-way management communicates by receiving signals from a preconfigured and dedicated frequency in the downstream spectrum and transmitting on a dedicated frequency in the upstream. (The details of the management communication protocol are beyond the scope of this book.)

The cable amplifier is a powered, active, electronic device. Power is usually provided via the input port and passed to the output port. In North America, power is delivered using alternating current (AC) at approximately 60 or 90 volts and a frequency of 60Hz. Power arriving at the input of an amplifier is filtered separately and removed from the RF signal path before the input diplex filter. Power is used by the amplifier and is routed to the output port for use by other downstream amplifiers. (The mechanisms for inserting power into the all-coaxial cable system are beyond the scope of this book.)

NOTE Space limitations preclude more than a simplistic description of the general all-coaxial two-way amplifier. Many other signal processing components than are described here make up this element. The purpose of this discussion is to give the reader a basic understanding of diplex filters and their use with amplifiers to provide two-way amplification of signals using a single RF coaxial cable.

Upstream Ingress Noise Management

The main task associated with enabling the upstream in all-coaxial cable plants is ingress noise management. Looking at the downstream direction for video, voice, or data transmissions, there is one transmitter and many receivers for each channel. In comparison, with interactive services, the upstream direction has many transmitters and one receiver per upstream channel. Noise presents a similar situation. The downstream has only one source of transmission, the headend. In the upstream, however, each subscriber home is a potential source of noise, both from the drop cable from the tap, and from sources within the home. Roughly 70 percent of ingress noise comes from sources inside the home, with another 20 percent from the drop cable. Potential noise sources inside the home include ignition sounds; static electricity discharge; noisy electrical equipment such as hairdryers and microwave ovens; ham or citizen's band radio equipment; and numerous others. Poorer-grade in-house coaxial cable and splitters, such as those commonly available at do-it-yourself home or electronic supply retailers are frequently the leading culprit in picking up noise. Portions of the drop cable are usually run some vertical distance, such as down the side of a house. The vertical portions are more susceptible to other vertically polarized transmissions, such as broadcast radio, business, ham shortwave, and citizen's band radio.

As the cable plant is enabled for upstream, any noise present is transmitted up the branches, and funneled into the headend on the trunk. *Noise funneling* is common to all cable plant topologies, though each cable plant has individual noise characteristics that need to be managed. One attribute of ingress noise relates to the *size* of the noise funnel, that is, the number of HHP that share the same trunk. Since upstream transmissions and noise are funneled equally, if a source of noise is interfering with transmission on an upstream trunk, it could potentially affect all subscribers who are sharing that upstream trunk.

A major benefit to managing upstream ingress noise is a result of the strict FCC requirements regarding emitted radiation. Back in the 1970s, plants were "leakier" with respect to RF radiation than they are allowed to be today. Keeping in mind that a cable plant is one big captive RF antenna with a large number of amplifiers, if RF is emitted from the cable distribution plant—that is, via trunk, feeder, and drop cables—RF signals are propagated over the air as broadcasts, often resulting in Electro-Magnetic Interference (EMI) to some other RF service. Some of those disrupted services could be life-critical, such as police, fire, ambulance, and aviation services, therefore cable operators are strictly required to routinely maintain their plant to keep EMI within FCC specifications. And—this is where the benefit comes in—as with any antenna, if it radiates, it can also pick up signals, so leaky cable plants formerly experienced more ingress noise problems on the upstream. Cleaning up the EMI problems solves most of the ingress noise issues along the trunk and feeder systems. The drop cable and the subscriber home, however, still need to be managed.

NOTE Today, ingress noise management is well under control in many cable plants. In addition, high-speed data services have been engineered to overcome many types of ingress noise issues. Other aspects of the noise issue are addressed in Chapter 3.

Ingress noise management, from an engineering viewpoint, typically involves one or more of the following preventive or curative measures when enabling a subscriber home for two-way services:

- Replacing the old drop cable with a high-quality, well-shielded coaxial drop cable.

- Removing any corrosion on tap connectors or home connectors.

- Ensuring that the demarcation block is well grounded.

- Replacing any in-house cable with a high-quality, well-shielded cable from the demarcation block to the interactive appliance—for example, set-top box or cable modem.

- Using a high-quality splitter in the home, if needed, to connect the cable modem and set-top box.

Ingress noise is often cited by the detractors of high-speed data over cable as the one of the chief reasons that cable data won't succeed. This, simply, is not valid. Over the past half-decade, cable operators have reduced ingress noise issues both on all-coaxial and upgraded cable plants to an occasional—and manageable—nuisance.

Hybrid Fiber-Coaxial Cable Systems

The next step in the evolution of the all-coaxial cable plant is the hybrid fiber-coaxial (HFC) cable plant. Many plants today have already been upgraded to HFC systems. An upgrade to HFC means that a significant portion of the distribution network, specifically the original coaxial trunk cables and portions of the feeder branch cable, has been replaced with optical fiber. At one end of each fiber is the original headend; at the other end is a new device called a *fiber node*. A fiber node is a combination of bidirectional optical-to-electrical conversion electronics, and what amounts to a two-way line- extender amplifier. All fibers nodes are two-way enabled. An upgrade to HFC means an upgrade to two-way enabled plant.

The HFC system is not a digitally modulated system. The technique for modulating information on and off the optical fiber in an HFC plant involves amplitude modulation (AM). The entire broadband downstream passband is modulated onto the fiber and demodulated at the fiber node— essentially, RF to optical and back to RF in a straightforward process. Upstream, the passband is typically 200MHz, and the same RF-to-optical to RF methodology is used as in the downstream.

Figure 2.7 illustrates the general model of an HFC fiber node, whose main function is to bidirectionally convert signals from the remaining all-coaxial plant to optical signals. Two optical fibers connect the fiber node

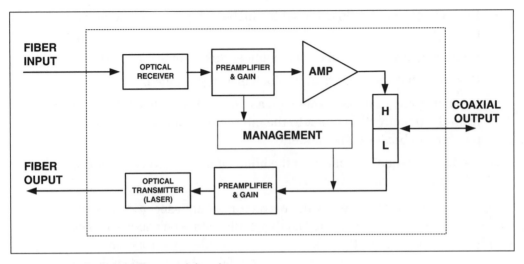

Figure 2.7 The hybrid fiber-coaxial node.

to the headend. One fiber is used for downstream transmissions, the other for upstream transmissions. As compared to the all-coaxial amplifier of Figure 2.6, the fiber node does not use an input diplex filter to separate downstream from upstream signals. The downstream optical cable is connected to an optical receiver, which converts the light signal to the original downstream broadband electrical RF signal. This electrical signal is then passed to the remaining downstream amplifier components that appear very similar to the all-coaxial amplifier. In the upstream direction, the output diplex filter splits out the upstream RF spectrum, and passes the signal to an upstream preamplifier. This preamplifier then sends a signal to an optical transmitter module that converts the upstream RF spectrum to a laser light signal. The laser amplifier connects to the upstream fiber for communications directly to the headend. Fiber nodes are not powered via the fiber, because glass does not transmit AC power. Instead, power is supplied using a separate power cable. Generally, all fiber nodes are capable of remote management.

CAUTION A fiber node is more sensitive to being overdriven by upstream transmissions, as compared to its all-coaxial counterpart. Both the electrical upstream preamplifier and the laser transmitter are subject to being driven into saturation. This may impact the operation of high-speed data transmissions from cable modems. Fortunately, this characteristic has been taken into consideration in the design of modern cable modem systems. More on this in Chapters 3 and 5.

Along with HFC plants, a new metric has emerged, called *node size*, which is the number of households passed by the fiber node. (The traditional HHP value is still used to describe the size of the entire plant.) When upgrading to HFC, cable operators select the average node size for their plant. Dividing that into the total HHP yields the number of fiber nodes that will be required to make the conversion. For example, if the HHP of an all-coaxial plant is 20,000, and the operator picks a node size of 1,000 HHP, the number of fiber nodes needed is 20. When the upgrade is complete, all the trunk cables and trunk amplifiers disappear; in addition, many of the feeder cables may disappear as well as some line-extender amplifiers. What remains are 20 pairs of optical fibers connecting the headend to the 20 new fiber nodes. The fiber nodes are connected to what remains from the feeder coaxial network.

Figure 2.8 illustrates a cable plant that has been converted to HFC. Note that the many long chains of trunk and bridger amplifiers have been removed from the system. Fiber nodes directly connect to the remaining all-coaxial cable plant, which consists of the branches of line-extender amplified coax cable. The specifics of how to connect the remaining all-coaxial network are based on the original plant topology and the planned-for initial node size of the system.

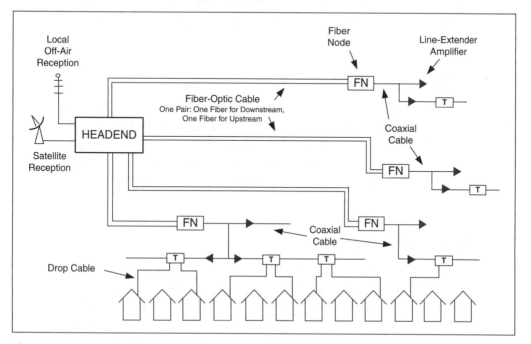

Figure 2.8   Upgraded plant.

An upgrade to HFC has a number of motivators and benefits for the cable plant:

- Removes many coaxial amplifiers, improving signal quality and reducing maintenance overhead.

- Frequently includes the expansion of the downstream bandwidth to 750MHz, creating expanded spectrum for additional analog and digital TV channels and for interactive services.

- Reduces the number of subscribers who are sharing the same "trunk," creating increased RF bandwidth per subscriber.

Furthermore, conversion of an all-coaxial plant to HFC is completely transparent to existing downstream transmissions and upstream transmissions; HFC is a very scalable architecture; and reliability is enhanced

HFC upgrades also serve to reduce ingress noise issues, for two main reasons: First, many of the previously used amplifiers have been removed from the upstream path, making the RF environment cleaner and less likely to suffer from amplifier misadjustment; second, reducing the number of homes sharing the same upstream "trunk" statistically lowers the amount of ingress noise, simply because the size of the noise funnel is reduced. In addition, though there may be some ingress noise causing interference to upstream transmissions, the number of homes impacted will be limited to the node size, which is much smaller than the all-coaxial trunk size.

Distribution Hub Architecture

As demonstrated previously for an all-coaxial tree and branch network, a distribution hub architecture is well suited for use with an HFC network (see Figure 2.9). Within the framework of this architecture, the fiber-optic cables from fiber nodes terminate in a distribution hub, rather than at the headend. And, again, the headend can support fiber nodes directly, if needed.

Fiber Node Splitting

Fiber is expensive to terminate with connectors and active equipment; however, stringing or burying multiple pairs of fiber costs very little more than pulling a single pair. By installing many pairs of fibers, plant expansion is straightforward. For example, suppose a cable operator installs a fiber-optic cable consisting of 24 individual fibers for each initially installed fiber node. Two of the 24 fibers would be used for the fiber node,

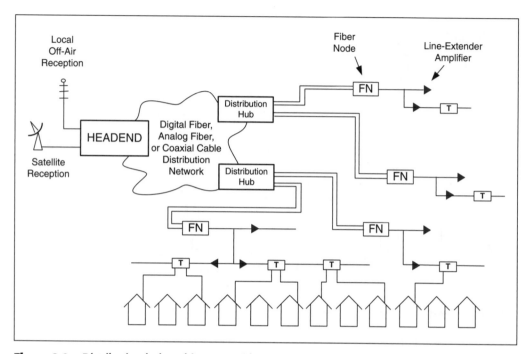

Figure 2.9   Distribution hub architecture with an HFC cable network.

one for downstream transmissions, the other for upstream. That leaves 22 fibers unused. If, at some point in the future, the operator decides to "split" the fiber node from 1,000 HHP to 500 HHP, the procedure is simple: install a second fiber node at the end of the cable and use another two of the 22 fibers. This doubles the amount of available RF bandwidth, both downstream and upstream, to the subscribers who were being served off the original fiber node. Using this technique of laying multiple fibers and node splitting, a cable operator has many iterations of increasing RF bandwidth available to subscribers. Moreover, node splitting only need be done where and when there is a need.

Figure 2.10 illustrates the before and after of a fiber node split. Consider that, on initial installation, the cable operator pulled multiple-strand fiber optic cable. Two of the strands are immediately terminated for use by the fiber node; the rest of the fibers are left unterminated. At some point in time, the cable operator may find that more bandwidth is required to the house served by the original fiber node. The cable operator easily deploys a second fiber node next to the old fiber node, and uses two of the unterminated fibers to communicate with the new node from the headend or distribution hub. The coaxial network is split, and half of the homes served by the old fiber node are moved to the new fiber node.

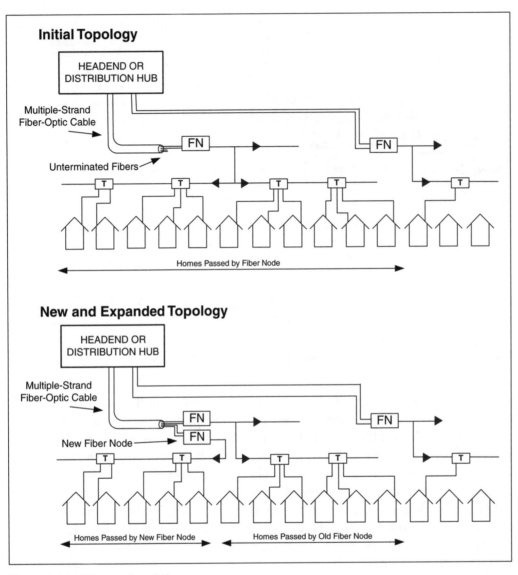

Figure 2.10   Fiber node splitting.

This example demonstrates the doubling of bandwidth to those homes originally serviced by one fiber node. Based on business plans and future planning, the cable operator may choose to split a fiber node into more than two pieces. For example, if the cable operator originally deployed a 500-HHP fiber node performing the node splitting, it may opt to split the node into four pieces—that is, four 125-HHP nodes. In this case, node splitting would quadruple both the downstream and upstream bandwidth

> **EXTRAORDINARILY SCALABLE**
>
> *Fiber node splitting* is a powerful mechanism that enables the cable operator to continually expand bandwidth of the distribution plant for interactive services. Node splitting only need be performed where there is an actual demand for service. This permits the cable operator to tailor both downstream and upstream bandwidth capacity to only those sections of the community where it is required; the entire cable plant does not have to be upgraded.

to the same homes passed by the original fiber node. Stated another way, the use of node splitting enables the cable operator to increase precious upstream bandwidth where needed.

Taken to the limit, and economics permitting, a cable operator has the ability to continue node splitting until there is one pair of fibers for each home. Practically speaking, there have been discussions in the industry to move to a 25-HHP to 50-HHP fiber node. This model is referred to as a *mini-fiber node*, and is discussed in more detail in Chapter 11.

Increased Reliability through Redundancy

Many fiber nodes come with the capability to select downstream light from both a primary fiber and a secondary fiber. The upstream fiber selection follows the downstream selection. If cable operators choose to, they can deploy *path-diverse* fiber to the same fiber node. Path diverse means that two fiber bundles are pulled from the headend to the fiber node, and each follows a different physical path through the community. The node selects the fiber automatically and is able to switch from one fiber to the other in a matter of milliseconds should the primary fiber "go dark" due to a cut fiber, automobile accident, backhoe incident, or other disruption. The notion is that a single incident that breaks one fiber bundle will not affect the other bundle. The fiber node just switches over, thereby offering uninterrupted service for downstream and upstream transmissions.

Combining Return Path in the Headend

Though fiber optic cable has been used in cable systems since the early 1980s, it wasn't until the 1990s that HFC systems became widely deployed.

The technical aspects of fiber optics, cables, lasers, and receivers are beyond the scope of this book, but we do need to mention the type of lasers used in the HFC system. Two basic classes of lasers are used: Fabry-Perot (F-P) and Distributed Feedback (DFB). The DFB is a higher-quality laser than an F-P, and is therefore more costly. DFB lasers are used in the downstream fiber-optic system because that is the more critical transmission direction for the cable operator. The downstream is a single wideband signal composed of many simultaneously operating television and data channels. DFB lasers have lower noise and distortion characteristics than F-P lasers. In the upstream direction, the cable operator has the choice of installing either DFB or F-P lasers, based on cost and other factors. Typically, F-P lasers are selected.

In the headend, the cost associated with an HFC upgrade comes from the replacement of the original trunk cables by multiple sets of fiber node transceiver sets. One set for each active fiber node is deployed, where a set consists of a downstream electrical-to-optical converter and an upstream optical-to-electrical converter. Diplex filters are not needed if the cable operator chooses to run downstream and upstream signals on physically separate coax cables. Refer back to Figure 2.9 to see the fiber termination portion of a headend.

An optical HFC receiver is required in the headend for each fiber node deployed. Cable operators can optimize costs by combining several of the upstream reverse RF-path coaxial cables (one from each fiber node transceiver) into one. This joining is done electrically by use of a simple combiner. When F-P lasers are used in the upstream, cable operators typically link the upstream returns from fiber nodes using a 4:1 combiner. When DFB lasers are used, a 10:1 combination is possible. The chief limitation of combining upstream fiber node returns is based on the thermal noise characteristics of F-P versus DFB lasers. The maximum 4:1 or 10:1 combining has direct impact on the design of high-speed data systems.

Summary

This chapter illustrated the basics of cable plant topology by describing a number of the basic building blocks available to cable operators. These building blocks, though general in nature, are useful for conveying the underlying RF broadband transmission environment of the physical cable plant necessary for supporting high-speed data services. Key points presented in this chapter included:

- Cable operators can choose which building blocks they will use and how they will "build out" their cable plants.

- The cable plant is essentially a high-capacity antenna, which carries RF broadband signals. In North America, the downstream signals are typically divided into 6MHz channel allocations following a band plan.

- All-coaxial cable plants are capable of two-way operation, dependent on the business plans and budget limitations of the individual cable operator.

- Ingress noise in all-coaxial plants is manageable, and industrywide, can be considered under control.

- Upgrading to hybrid fiber-coax is a straightforward process, one that offers numerous improvements and benefits.

- Through the technique of node splitting, an HFC plant becomes highly scalable, allowing cable operators to push more bandwidth toward the customer, where needed.

For Further Information

For a more in-depth discussion on cable television, the technology, and more, read *Modern Cable Television Technology*, by Walter Ciciora, James Farmer, and David Large, San Francisco, CA: Morgan Kaufmann Publishers, 1999.

An excellent review of cable plant renewal and HFC upgrade strategies is presented in the paper *On Plant Renewal Strategies* by Dan Pike and Tony E. Werner. This paper was presented at the NCTA Annual Convention, 1998.

Additional information can be obtained at the following Web sites:

CableLabs, www.cablelabs.com

The National Cable Television Association, www.ncta.com

The Electronic Industries Alliance, www.eia.org

Elements of Cable Modem Style

An understanding of high-speed data over cable requires knowledge of the underlying cable plant topology, the underlying RF environment, and the components that make up a cable modem. This chapter builds on the information presented in Chapter 2, which covered cable plant topology and the RF band. This chapter presents a detailed overview of the basic functional building blocks of a cable modem system.

At a high level, cable modems have a simple set of requirements:

- The cable modem system must be able to move Internet Protocol (IP) packets to and from a subscriber's home via the broadband cable network.

- The cable modem system must be Ethernet-friendly in the home and headend.

- A cable modem should be subscriber-installable.

- A cable modem system must maintain acceptable performance, as viewed by the subscriber, for packet data and packet voice communications.

- A cable modem system must provide sufficient benefit such that cable operators and multiple systems operators (MSOs) can run a viable business; that is, offer a manageable and reliable service and low-cost subscriber equipment.

- A cable modem operation must be friendly to other services operating on the same cable plant: for example, video, other data services, management and monitoring services, pay-per-view services, and others.

Modulation and Demodulation Overview

The word modem is an acronym for MOdulator/DEModulator. The process of turning data packets into a form suitable for transmission on a physical wire medium is called *modulation*. After receiving a transmission, the process of turning the information back into data packets is called *demodulation*. Two-way RF cable modems are similar to their analog telephony dial-up modem counterparts; however, in addition to performing modulation and demodulation, they must convert signals on and off the broadband RF cable, rather than narrowband signals from twisted pair wires. Another difference is that with standard telephone dial-up systems there is a single modem at each end of the phone call, or the copper pair. In contrast, in a cable modem system, in the downstream direction, there is one modulator and many demodulators; and in the upstream, there are many modulators and one demodulator.

The process of modulation and demodulation is part of the physical layer of the Open Systems Interconnection (OSI) model's seven-layer stack. The industry usually refers to this layer as the PHY layer (pronounced "Fie"). In a cable modem system, many cable modems share the same RF spectrum. This introduces the need for a Media Access Control (MAC) protocol to arbitrate access to the RF spectrum. A MAC protocol is a data-link layer process in the OSI's seven-layer stack. The industry typically refers to this layer as the MAC ("Mack") layer. Standards for cable modems, such as those presented in Chapter 5, always document both MAC and PHY layer specifications.

Early two-way cable modem systems implemented a straightforward and simple approach for arbitrating the exchange of packets between cable modems. This approach was quite successful for over a decade, but became inadequate in the face of today's large-scale deployment of mixed-packet data and packet voice systems. We will examine the elements of these systems later in this chapter because that information is useful for understanding the design choices made in modern systems. Some operators have deployed cable modem systems on one-way cable plants. But because the cable modem cannot transmit upstream to the headend directly, a form of cable modem system called a *hybrid telephone return system* was envisioned in the earlier 1980s, with deployment taking place throughout the 1990's. This system combines the benefit of the higher-speed downstream performance of a cable plant with a telephone modem to return IP packets to the headend.

Modern two-way cable modem systems share a consistent architectural approach, which supports large-scale deployments while maintaining strict control over QoS, cable operator management, and subscriber privacy. In addition, these modern systems are more flexible, allowing a cable operator to tailor the deployment of data-carrying capacity to meet subscriber demand, as well as matching capacity for different plant topology schemes. These systems employ modern RF modulation and error-recovery techniques.

Fundamental to almost all two-way cable modem systems past and present is the notion of using Ethernet as an underlying MAC transport for IP packets. Due to the distributed nature of cable modem systems, Ethernet frame processing at the headend and at each cable modem has evolved from an Ethernet repeater system to a fully functional distributed Ethernet switch with sophisticated packet filtering.

Technology advances are ongoing in the area of physical layer modulation and demodulation techniques. Modern cable modems systems can take advantage of these new PHY protocols as they emerge and as they are socialized, but there are some caveats to incorporating new technology and to the support of existing deployments.

RF Modulation and Demodulation

The exchange of digital data over an RF channel is based on the transmission of modulated information from the sender to the receiver. All cable modem design, of any generation, features one demodulator and one modulator. That is, a cable modem has a single receiver that demodulates digital information received in the downstream direction and a single transmitter that modulates digital data in the upstream direction, toward the headend. The headend controller, however, has one modulator and transmitter that sends information to all cable modems. In an upstream data channel, the headend controller has one receiver that is shared among all cable modems.

Table 3.1 Bits Per Symbol

MODULATION TECHNIQUE	BITS PER SYMBOL
QPSK	2
16 QAM	4
64 QAM	6
256 QAM	8

Modulators exchange information with demodulators using symbols. A symbol is a slice of transmission information that encodes one or more bits of digital information. There are many different types of modulation techniques, and each encodes a different number of bits per transmission symbol. Four commonly used modulation techniques for data over cable networks are: Quadrature Phase Shift Keying (QPSK), 16 Quadrature Amplitude Modulation (16 QAM), 64 QAM, and 256 QAM (see Table 3.1). QPSK is typically used in the upstream, 64 QAM and 256 QAM in the downstream. There are uses for 16 QAM in both the downstream and upstream.

Symbols are sent from the transmitter to the receiver at a given rate measured in *modulation symbols per second*. Once the symbol rate and modulation type have been identified, it is often called a channel. The fundamental, or raw, digital data capacity of a channel is calculated as the bits per second rate times the symbol rate:

$$\text{Raw channel rate} = \text{bits/symbol} \times \text{symbols/sec} = \text{bits/sec}$$

Two examples:

- If the modulation technique is QPSK (2 bits/symbol) and the symbol rate is 1.28 million symbols per second, the raw channel rate would be 2.56 million bits per second (Mbps).

- If the modulation technique is 64 QAM (6 bits/symbol) and the symbol rate is 5.0 million symbols per second, the raw channel rate would be 30.0Mbps.

RF Channel Size

RF channels in a cable system occupy a certain amount of continuous RF spectrum. For example, in North America, NTSC video channels are 6MHz wide. The width refers to channel spacing, or how close RF carriers can be placed next to one another in frequency, without causing interference to each other. Evolution in technology has dictated that, in North America, NTSC television channels can be placed no closer than 6MHz, carrier-to-carrier distance, and that NTSC channels are 6MHz wide, regardless of spacing. Because of this restriction for analog video signals, in the new world of digital transmission, digital channels must be able to occupy the 6MHz space between two NTSC analog video channels without causing any interference to adjacent channels.

NOTE Digital modulation and encoding improves downstream transmission efficiency. In the more modern digital world, several digitally encoded 6MHz NTSC channels may be carried in the same 6MHz RF spectrum that previously only carried one analog NTCS channel.

The amount of RF spectrum occupied by a digital channel is based on the symbol rate and a design parameter called *Alpha*, which defines the channel's signal power rolloff such that the signal from the channel is sufficiently attenuated so that it doesn't cause interference with adjacent channels. Figure 3.1 illustrates a digital channel between two adjacent analog channels. Note that the value of Alpha defines the slope of the rolloff of the digital channel on either side, which is a parameter that digital RF engineers use when building conforming transmission equipment. Alpha is usually expressed in terms of a fraction that is less than 1.0.

The total RF spectrum occupied by a digital transmission channel is calculated as the symbol rate times 1 plus the Alpha design specification. That is:

$$\text{RF spectrum size} = \text{symbol rate} \times (1 + \text{Alpha})$$

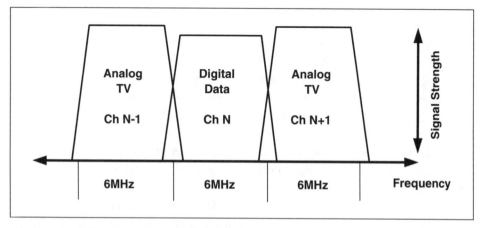

Figure 3.1   Adjacent analog and digital channels.

Two examples:

- A raw data channel rate of 1.28 million symbols per second with an Alpha design specification of 0.25 would produce an RF spectrum of 1.28 times 1.25, equaling 1.60MHz.

- A symbol rate of 5.0 million symbols per second with an Alpha of 0.18 would produce an RF spectrum size of $5.0 \times 1.18 = 5.90$MHz.

Continuous versus Burst Modulation

Two fundamental types of modulation modes are used in cable television networks: *burst modulation* and *continuous modulation*. A receiver listening on a channel must be able to derive the same symbol clock used by the transmitter. When the receiver's clock is aligned, it can properly decode symbol boundaries and, therefore, correctly demodulate the signal, turning the symbols into bits of data.

Burst Modulation

In this mode, the transmitter produces a burst of information. Bursts come in many sizes, but usually contain a packet of digital information being sent from the transmitter to the receiver. An aspect of burst systems is that the transmitter clock and the receiver clock are not locked precisely to one another. The receiver of a burst cannot properly demodulate a burst unless it can accurately lock to the symbol rate of the transmission. Thus, burst modulation is also referred to as *asynchronous modulation*, meaning the symbol clocks of the transmitter and the receiver are not strictly in synchronization.

Figure 3.2 illustrates a typical burst profile. A leading piece of transmission modulation is called a *preamble*, whose purpose is to synchronize the receiver's clock, so that it can decode the data. The transmitter and receiver both know the format of the preamble in advance. The length of the preamble is variable; the longer the guard time, the better synchronization is achieved; however, this comes at the expensive of increased overhead to the packet and reduced efficiency of the channel. Shorter guard times can work, but may lead to clock synchronization errors and packet loss if the preamble is too short. Adjusting the length of the preamble is dependent on the type of modulation being used, as well as the noise conditions in the plant.

Burst modulation systems are typically found where many transmitters are sharing the same channel. For example, the receiver at the headend

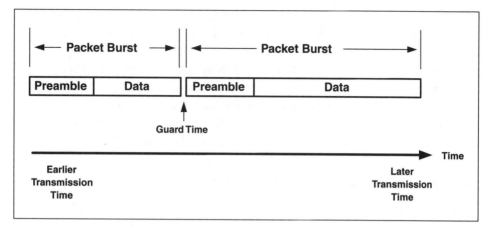

Figure 3.2   Burst modulation.

will be receiving individual transmission bursts from any cable modem in the network on an upstream RF channel. The preamble is needed because different cable modems will have slightly skewed transmission clocks, and the preamble assures decoding accuracy. Furthermore, the physical amplifier in a cable modem takes a little time to ramp up in power level, and a little more time to turn off; burst RF transmitters do not turn on and off instantly. Consequently, a *guard time* is inserted between the end of one burst and the beginning of another burst. This guard time allows the transmitter from one cable modem to ramp down while the transmitter from another cable modem is ramping up. Note that the guard time may be either a distinct part of the burst or just a longer preamble. Between adjacent bursts, the recently sending cable modem is ramping down and the next scheduled cable modem is ramping up. Between nonadjacent bursts, the channel is quiet; no cable modems are transmitting.

Continuous Modulation

In this mode, the transmitter is continuously producing modulation symbols for reception by receivers. This technique is used almost exclusively in downstream transmissions of analog and digital video and with high-speed digital channels for cable modems. One aspect of a demodulator is that it needs to synchronize its own symbol reception clock with the clock used by the transmitter. A continuous stream of symbols in the downstream allows a digital receiver to synchronize its clock easily, then stay locked and stabilized as long as symbols are transmitted. This type of transmission and reception method is called a *synchronous modulation system.* Two features of synchronous transmission are, one, it provides for more efficient use of the channel as preambles, and, two, guard times are not needed.

Continuous modulation systems are present only where there is one transmitter of multiple transmitters on the same channel are not permitted. In the case of cable networks, the RF transmitter is located at the headend, and it is broadcasting on a specific channel; there are many receivers located on the cable system tuned to that same channel.

Synchronous Upstream Burst Modulation

There is a form of upstream burst modulation that uses a mechanism that tightly synchronizes the upstream modulator and demodulator to the same clock. This is a more complex system than asynchronous burst modulation, but has the advantage of reducing preamble and guard time size, allowing the channel to be more efficiently operated. Synchronous burst systems fall under the category of advanced physical layer modulations, and are briefly discussed in Chapter 5.

Forward Error Correction

A key performance metric of an RF transmission channel is its error performance, or predicted bit error rate. This is a value expressed either in terms of bits errored per total bits sent or as a fraction of errored bits. For example, an error rate can be expressed as "1 bit error in 1 million bits" or a bit error rate of 1×10^{-6}.

In everyday Internet traffic, using the Transmission Control Protocol over IP (TCP/IP), reliability is increased using a technique known as *retransmission.* It works this way: If a packet is received with errors, the receiver can ask the transmitter to resend the same packet. In cable systems, there is no capability to retransmit information for one-way services, such as digital video. Because of this, and to achieve the highest-quality television picture as possible, a technique called Forward Error Correction (FEC) is employed.

FEC is a technique whereby extra information is transmitted along with the real data. The extra information, or FEC *overhead,* contains sufficient redundant information to allow a receiver to correct one or more bit errors in the real data. The FEC includes not only error detection, but also error correction capability. FEC can be provided in a variety of different amounts, to permit more bits to be corrected. However, the larger the number of bits to correct, the more FEC overhead is sent with the real data. This has the effect of reducing channel real-data carrying efficiency in exchange for better bit error rates.

FEC and Noise

FEC is fundamental to the operation of high-speed digital services. Often, a transmission channel's bit error rate can be improved by several orders of magnitude through the use of FEC. In the downstream direction, the bit error rate of a 6MHz channel is usually quite low—that is, extremely good. In the upstream, as mentioned in Chapter 2, ingress noise is present; therefore, the presence of FEC greatly helps to overcome bit errors introduced by noise-related interference.

The modulation order (bits per symbol) of a channel also demands varying amounts of FEC. For example, QPSK is the least susceptible to ingress noise-related bit errors, as compared to 256 QAM, which is the most susceptible. Therefore, QPSK requires less FEC than 256 QAM; put another way, QPSK achieves better error rate with the same FEC. In general, the higher the order of modulation, the more FEC is needed to maintain the same bit error rate in the same RF spectrum conditions.

The 64 QAM and 256 QAM downstream digital modulation techniques, including FEC, are specified in a worldwide standard called ITU J.83. ITU J.83 has several annexes: Annex B defines 64/256 QAM for use in North America. Annex A and C define 64/256 QAM for use in Europe and internationally. The FEC of Annex B is not compatible with Annex A or C systems, and vice versa. Therefore, a cable modem built to operate to the U.S. downstream modulation standard will not work on systems outside of North America unless the vendor has also provided Annex A and C support.

With all these systems, the raw channel data rate includes combined real data and FEC data overhead. A common term for the real data capacity is called the *information rate*. The ITU J.83 specification includes the information rate calculation. More detail on the actual information rate provided by the North American standard will be presented in Chapter 5.

Mapping RF Data Channels to Cable Plant Topology

Key to understanding cable modem systems is learning how cable modems make use of RF channels and how the RF is then distributed on cable plants. Figure 3.3 shows which spectrum has been allocated for a single

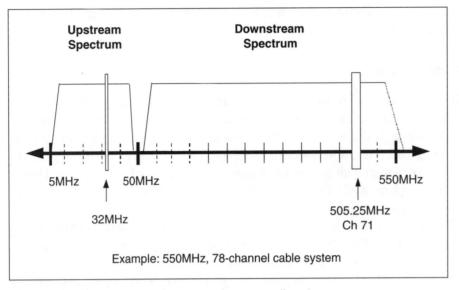

Figure 3.3 Downstream and upstream frequency allocation.

6MHz downstream high-speed data channel and for a single upstream channel. In this example, the downstream channel is positioned at Channel 71 at 505.25MHz in the standard frequency plan. The upstream has been placed at 32MHz.

Figure 3.4 illustrates the distribution of that signal over the downstream cable plant and the upstream cable plant. For this example, an all-coaxial tree and branch network is illustrated, but this applies equally well to an HFC plant.

Key points in the distribution of RF digital data channels over cable plant:

- Downstream RF data signals follow the physical plant topology. Once a signal leaves the headend via a coaxial trunk or fiber, it is distributed to all homes passed by that trunk and its attached branches.

- Upstream RF data signals follow the same physical path in reverse to the headend—that is, back up the branches and the trunk.

- A single downstream transmitter on a channel on a trunk is received by all downstream receivers tuned to that same channel, which are fed by that trunk.

- A single upstream transmitter on a channel is received only by the headend; that is, the signal is not sent back down the branch or trunk to reach other receivers.

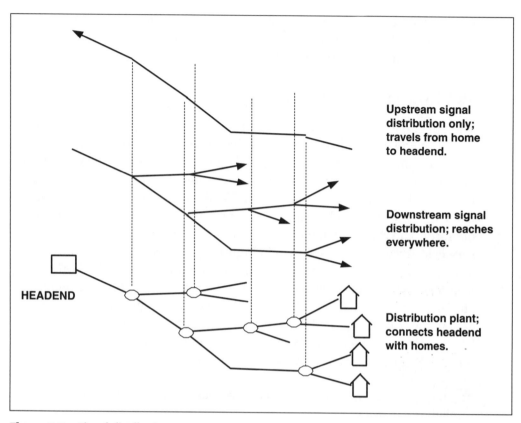

Figure 3.4 Signal distribution.

The upstream transmission signal from one home might be faintly received by a nearby neighbor; however, there is a great deal of isolation due to significant signal attenuation between homes in the upstream direction of the cable plant. As soon as the signal is received by the first line extender, only the headend receives the signal at proper amplitude to be received properly.

The downstream direction of a cable plant is a one-to-many configuration, in that one transmitter in the headend can transmit simultaneously to many receivers in the downstream. In the reverse direction, the cable plant is a many-to-one configuration, whereby many transmitters in homes on the same data channel send information to one receiver in the headend. The signals are funneled toward the headend by the amplifiers, following the topology of the tree and branch network.

Within the headend, cable operators can configure their RF cables in any fashion they choose. In a multiple trunk or fiber headend, the cable operators choose on a per trunk and fiber basis which channels to allocate for downstream and upstream data transmissions. The mapping of data RF channels to physical plant topology can change at any time, based on the needs and plans of the cable operator.

The Downstream Rolloff Region

The upper end of the usable RF spectrum in any cable plant is called the *rolloff region*. It's a subscriber-subjective portion of the downstream upper RF spectrum, where analog TV signals start to become too noisy due to RF propagation characteristics of analog video signals. The TV picture quality begins to denigrate, developing "snow." While not good for TV viewing, from an economic and business standpoint, this is good news for the cable operator. The rolloff region can be mined for additional revenue-bearing services. For example, as shown in Figure 3.5, digital high-speed downstream data channels can be placed in the previously unused rolloff region, which is clearly preferable to replacing existing revenue-bearing television channels. Specifically, ITU J.83-based downstream digital systems work well in the roll off region. For example, in a 550MHz plant, channel 78 at 547.25MHz might be the last analog TV channel usable. Channels 79 through 81 may be used for high-speed digital data channels.

NOTE Any modern digital channel can be tuned to operate in the downstream rolloff region of a cable plant.

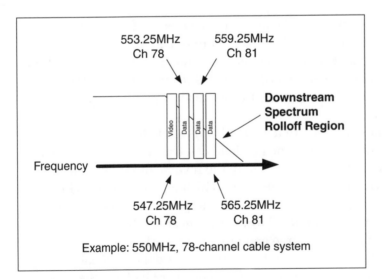

Figure 3.5   Rolloff region.

Digital data modulation does, however, have limits. For one, downstream channels cannot operate too far in frequency above the analog signal rolloff limit. For another, generally, two to three digital channels may be operated, though this still allows a cable operator to provide 12MHz to 18MHz of digital downstream modulation. As will be shown later in this chapter, that amounts to 60Mbps to 90Mbps of raw high-speed digital data capacity.

Early Two-Way Cable Modem Systems

Given the building blocks already established—cable plant topologies, in Chapter 2 and RF channels and modulation, earlier here—how is it possible to get two cable modems talking to one another? This was the challenge faced by researchers and vendors working on high-speed data-over-cable in the late 1970s. Eventually, they settled on a technique used in satellite data communications, which had been developed in the late 1960s, called the ALOHA protocol.

In these systems, the goal was to make a transmitted packet burst from one modem be receivable by all the other modems. Figure 3.6 illustrates the general architecture, whose key points are:

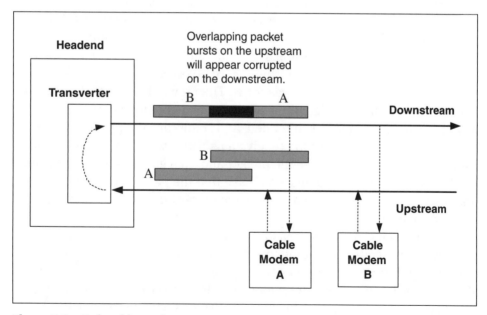

Figure 3.6   Early cable modem systems.

- A data channel is allocated in the downstream RF spectrum.

- A data channel is allocated in the upstream RF spectrum.

- A transverter or up converter device is installed at the headend. The headend receiver is tuned to the upstream channel frequency; the headend transmitter is tuned to the downstream frequency.

- Both the downstream and upstream channels use the same modulation and symbol rates; the channels have to be identical.

- The system uses packet burst transmissions on the upstream, and, therefore, packet burst transmissions on the downstream.

- A cable modem has a single transmitter and a single receiver. It can be listening on the downstream while transmitting on the upstream.

The purpose of the transverter is to receive PHY signals from the upstream channel, convert the frequency of the PHY signal to the transmit frequency, and transmit downstream exactly what was received from the upstream. With this style of communication, if cable modem A wanted to send a packet to cable modem B, A would encode its address as the source address in the header of the packet, and B's address as the destination address. Modem A would also compute a cyclic redundancy check (CRC) for the packet. Modem A would then transmit the packet, but keep the packet in memory. Modem A's transmission would be upconverted at the headend and broadcast on the downstream to all cable modems.

Cable modem B would examine the packet and compute the CRC; if there were no errors, and it saw itself as the destination, it would accept the packet for further processing. Cable modem A would also examine the packet and compute the CRC; if there were no errors, it would look at the destination address and see it was for B. Then it would look at the source address and see it was originally from itself, and conclude that B must have received the packet, as intended, and so discard the packet. If there were a CRC error, or if A didn't receive a packet after a timeout, it would assume that B did not receive the packet and then go into a retransmission mode. All other cable modems would see that the packet was not for them and discard the packet. All cable modems discard the packet when there are any errors.

The retransmission mode is also called *contention resolution mode*. If there were two stations sending upstream transmissions, and if any part of their packet bursts overlapped—that is, collided—the CRC check would show errors. If the packets overlapped significantly, the RF signal might come across as noise on the downstream. That is why there are CRC checks and timers.

ETHERNET CONTENTION RESOLUTION

Ethernet uses a form of contention resolution similar to ALOHA. The Ethernet algorithm is called *truncated binary exponential backoff*. Stations compute a random-number selection over the range of 0 to 2^k. Each time a station collides, it increments the value of k, thereby doubling the range, and statistically lowering the probability that it will transmit sooner rather than later. The algorithm says that k can only grow from 1 to a maximum value of 15. Ethernet, like ALOHA, is inherently unfair to "older" colliding stations, because newly colliding stations enter the algorithm with k equal to 1. The range exponent k is not shared among all colliding stations.

Part of the ALOHA protocol standard dictates that if a station is in contention-resolution mode, it waits a random amount of time before attempting retransmission. However, if a collision does take place again, the station doubles (following a power of 2 exponential increase) the length of time before attempting retransmission. The theory is that two colliding stations will wait different random times; statistically, they are not likely to collide again. If they do, the window of time during which they wait is doubled. For example, if A and B both collide, each will go into its contention-resolution algorithm, and continue to compute a random selection of time to wait over an incrementally larger time window for each subsequent collision. If a new station, say C, collides with A or B while they are running, station C enters its contention-resolution algorithm. However, since this is the first time C has collided, it has a shorter time window, making it more probable that it will attempt a retransmission before A or B. Thus this form of contention-resolution algorithm, in the process of sorting out the stations, is inherently preferential to new stations.

The preceding is necessarily a simplified description of the ALOHA protocol. ALOHA was originally developed to permit ground stations in Hawaii to communicate within one another using a geosynchronous satellite, which merely echoed everything it heard on the upstream back on the downstream. The protocol left it up to the ground stations to figure out whether transmissions were received correctly, and how to work out collisions and dropped packets. The satellite transverter and the cable transverter never demodulate packet bursts; they operate on PHY signals only, hence they are considered "dumb" devices in many respects.

Numerical calculations based on the statistics of queuing theory demonstrate that an ALOHA data channel with multiple stations is operating at 18 percent efficiency. That is to say, for a channel of given size x, only 18 percent of that x is real data, or what is also called *good put*. Total throughput is higher, but as channel loading goes up, more and more stations go into contention. For a cable operator, it means that if you allocated a 10Mbps channel in 6MHz of RF spectrum, only 1.8Mbps would actually be available for subscribers. It also says that, effectively, only 1.28MHz is being used at capacity. Because cable operators place value on the dollar return for a 6MHz downstream spectrum allocation, clearly, an ALOHA-based protocol is not suitable for the long term.

Slotted ALOHA

The 18-percent efficiency of ALOHA can be improved to 36 percent through use of a concept called *time slots*. In an ALOHA satellite system, one of the ground stations (or the satellite itself) sends a periodic time signal. The new rule in Slotted ALOHA is that a ground station has to hold off transmission until it receives the periodic signal. This effectively aligns the transmission times so that simultaneous bursts from different stations nearly align themselves.

Figure 3.7 demonstrates the Slotted ALOHA concept in a cable system when the transmitters of two cable modems are aligned in time. This system will have an efficiency, or good put, of 36 percent. Though this allows cable operators to get a better revenue stream for their allotted RF spectrum, it still wastes 64 percent of the RF spectrum.

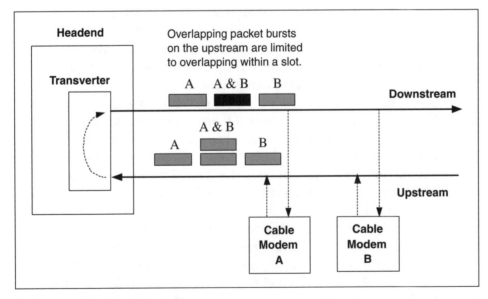

Figure 3.7   Slotted ALOHA system.

It is important to note that in a cable plant using either ALOHA or Slotted ALOHA, cable modems can be located anywhere along the cable path, that is; from 0 microseconds of delay up to the maximum of 400-plus microseconds. Without any controls for timing and fairness, cable modems closer to the headend, in time, gain more preferential treatment than those further away because their response time to and from the headend is much faster, hence they can react more quickly.

Some of the early cable modem systems could be adjusted to set the delay of the modem in an attempt to produce a reasonable grouping of modems so as to achieve better efficiency and fairness. This chapter will not delve into the actual mechanisms used, except to say that adjustments had to be performed at the modem by the cable operator before the modem could be deployed.

Signal Propagation Delay

RF signals in coaxial cable or light signals in fiber, travel at speeds lower than the speed of light. Cable systems sometimes have wire distances of up to 50 miles in length; that is, following the path of the coaxial or HFC plant, there is physically 50 miles of coaxial cable or fiber-optic cable and coaxial cable between the headend and the subscriber for any given trunk or fiber leaving the headend. The typical one-way delay value used for a 50-mile cable plant is 400 microseconds, or 0.0004 seconds. Cable modems can be located anywhere along the cable plant.

An example of the effect of propagation delay in an ALOHA-based cable modem system, where two cable modems A and B are located approximately 50 miles away from the headend, is as follows: If A were to start transmitting a burst, it would be 800 microseconds before B would receive the start of A's burst. In a 10Mbps channel, similar to Ethernet speeds, 800 microseconds amounts to approximately 8,000 bit times. The minimum length of an Ethernet packet is 64 bytes or 512 bits. Assume for example, that the preamble for the packet burst is 8 bytes, or 64 bits. The total burst length would be 576 bits—which, in a 10Mbps channel, takes exactly 576 microseconds, or 0.000576 seconds, to transmit. The difference between this and 800 microseconds is 224 microseconds, or the time that A has to wait until it receives the start of the same packet to check for errors.

The impact of this with an ALOHA protocol is that A has to wait 800 microseconds before the end of the burst arrives. Consequently, if it had another packet queued for transmission, A could not send the second packet until the first packet was verified correct. Waiting the 800 microseconds throttles the amount of packets that can be sent in one second—that is, the packet rate—to 1,250 packets per second, which is calculated as 1/0.0008 = 1250. This is the theoretical maximum, assuming packet verification happens instantly and there are no collisions or packet transmission errors. Transmitting smallest-size packets has the most overhead, in terms of the ratio of the preamble size to the Ethernet frame size. The minimum Ethernet frame size is 512 bits, so 512 bits/packet × 1250 packets/second = 640,000 bits/second maximum. If there are any other stations transmitting during the same interval, actual "good put" is significantly reduced due to the presence of collisions and the time spent in contention resolution.

Why Not Ethernet on the Cable?

Ethernet is a more efficient protocol than ALOHA, so why not use it instead? Ethernet gains its efficiency for LAN use by being in a class of protocols called Carrier Sense, Multiple Access, with Collision Detection, or CSMA/CD for short, defined as follows:

- *Carrier Sense* means that a station is able to listen to the media before attempting to transmit a packet. If another carrier is sensed on the media, the station waits until the media is clear before transmitting. In cable systems, a cable modem in a home does not have a receiver tuned to the same frequency as the transmitters in other cable modems or its own. Recall that the upstream transmissions are on a different frequency than the downstream.

- *Multiple Access* means that multiple stations are participating in a media access control protocol.

- *Collision Detection* means that, within the first 512 bits while transmitting a frame, a station can listen to the media and detect whether its transmission has collided with that of another station. If so, the station transmits a jabber signal, then moves into contention resolution. In the previous example, under propagation delay, any given station that transmits the minimum size Ethernet frame (512 bits) has already transmitted the packet before it can detect anything. Ethernet was designed for the LAN environment, where the collision-detection delay limits the size of the Ethernet to 1,500 meters of cable length.

Therefore, for reasons of lack of carrier sense and collision detection, Ethernet is not a suitable MAC protocol for use on the cable.

Ethernet Packets

Ethernet framing is, however, very suitable for use on the cable. Figure 3.8 illustrates an Ethernet frame, also called a packet, composed of a preamble, a source address, a destination address, and a type field (also called EtherType), user data, and a frame checksum (FCS). The type field identifies the type of protocol contained in the user data; that is, there is a type value that indicates the user data is an IP packet. The user data is of variable length, from 46 bytes to approximately 1,500 bytes. The FCS is a cyclic redundancy check (CRC), 32-bit value, which is computed by the transmitter over the entire packet and verified by the receiver. Note that the preamble shown in Figure 3.8 is used when transmitting an Ethernet packet over a traditional media link, such as twisted-pair or LAN coaxial cable. The Ethernet preamble is not used in cable networks, and therefore is not present. When talking about Ethernet over cable, an Ethernet frame or Ethernet packet refers to everything presented in Figure 3.8 except the preamble.

The source address and destination addresses are each 48-bit unique addresses. Blocks of addresses are issued to vendors by the Institute of Electrical and Electronic Engineers (IEEE) (www.ieee.org). The Ethernet vendor assigns a unique 48-bit hardware address for the interface, which is variably called the IEEE 48-bit MAC address, a MAC address, or a universal address.

An Ethernet 48-bit MAC address is usually represented by six pairs of hexadecimal values, representing the 48-bit address, for example, 00-A0-73-00-00-2A. The letters may be uppercase or lowercase; in other words, it

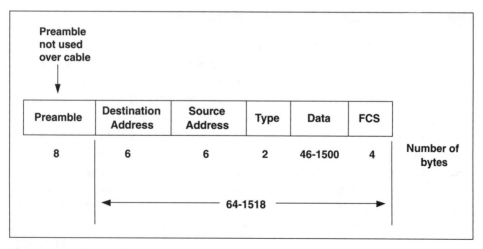

Figure 3.8   Ethernet frame format.

ETHERNET VENDOR ASSIGNMENTS ARE PUBLIC

The formal term for an IEEE vendor block assignment is called an *IEEE Organizationally Unique Identifier (OUI)*. Most vendors make their assignment publicly known. Assignments can be viewed at the IEEE at http://standards.ieee .org/regauth/oui/index.shtml. The details of converting from hex representation to binary transmission form are also available at the same URL.

---

is case-insensitive. The leftmost six hexadecimal pairs (24 bits) identify the vendor and are assigned by the IEEE. The rightmost six hexadecimal pairs (24 bits) are assigned by the vendor. The hex representation makes human interpretation of a MAC address easier; however, there is a specific binary transmission order that is different from the hex representation.

A detailed examination of the actual algorithm is beyond the scope of this chapter; but it is important to note here that the first bit transmission represents a value of 0 for *individual address* or 1 for *group address*. An individual address is the unique hardware address assigned by the vendor. A group address is a multicast address. The remainder of the 47 bits represents a multicast group identifier value. In Ethernet, a station may belong to one or more multicast groups, and a group may have zero or more members. If a transmitter sends a frame to a multicast group, all members of that group process the frame as if it were sent to their unique address. A special multicast value of FF-FF-FF-FF-FF-FF (all ones) represents a broadcast address, and all stations on the LAN process broadcast packets.

Upstream Transmit Power Control

A critical aspect of a successfully deployed cable modem system is the control of the transmitter power of each cable modem. Power levels in the individual upstream amplifiers are adjusted according to the noise management plan set out by the individual cable operator. If a cable modem's upstream signal is too weak, it will not reach the headend within acceptable power limits to be properly demodulated or distinguished from the noise. If the power level is too strong, the signal from that individual modem can overdrive an amplification stage somewhere along the return path to the headend, potentially distorting the signal beyond the limits to properly demodulate it. Moreover, power levels too strong in the upstream can saturate amplifiers such that the entire upstream RF spectrum is distorted. If any other services are running on different upstream frequencies, such as voice or amplifier management communications or impulse pay-per-view (IPPV) communications from set-top boxes, all these signals can be corrupted by a single transmitter that has too much power.

NOTE Hybrid fiber-coaxial upstream laser receivers and modulators are more sensitive to being overpowered than the all-coaxial amplifiers they replaced.

Upstream power management is very critical. Early cable modem systems may or may not have had power management control. When they did, it was usually in the form of setting some power level switches on the cable modem before deploying it, or using external RF attenuators called "pads" to drop the signal level to where the cable operator wanted it. Needless to say, once deployed, fine-tuning power levels in cable modems required sending a technician out to the home.

An excessive power level from one cable modem has been identified as sufficient to impair upstream communications if its power level is too strong. Recall that the ALOHA- and Slotted ALOHA-based systems discussed previously relied solely on the use of contention. Collisions and contention resolution mean that more than one cable modem can be transmitting at a time. But, if too many modems are transmitting at the same time, the combined power can oversaturate the upstream system. Statistically speaking, the greater the number of cable modems that are active and under load, the more often this problem will happen. ALOHA and Slotted ALOHA systems have no other means to control access to the upstream channel other than through contention.

NOTE Early cable modem systems are not suitable for dense deployments on cable systems because contention is their only means to arbitrate access to the upstream channel. At some point of deployment, they will frequently saturate one or more amplifiers or lasers in the upstream return path.

Upstream Noise Impairments

The simple (and dumb) transverter in the headend does not make a distinction as to what it receives on the upstream channel. Since it operates at an RF signal processing level and does not demodulate or modulate packets for transmission, it electrically repeats anything it receives on the downstream channel. This is true for any noise impairments received and any signal distortions. All impairments received on the upstream channel are simply echoed back on the downstream channel.

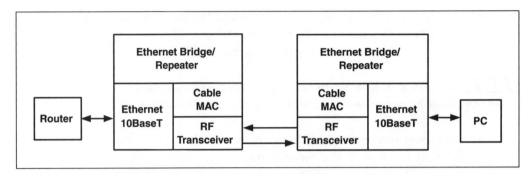

Figure 3.9 Ethernet and RF stack.

Ethernet Processing

Generally, the early cable modem systems were constructed to move Ethernet packets from place to place. Figure 3.9 illustrates a simple Ethernet repeater or Ethernet bridge cable modem system used with a transverter-based system. Each cable modem's protocol stack is essentially the same, consisting of an RF transceiver, a cable media access control (MAC) function for moving packets on and off the cable, a repeater or bridge function, and an Ethernet interface. This example shows that a PC connected off one cable modem would access the Internet via a router located off another cable modem.

In these early systems, the goal of a cable modem was to receive an Ethernet packet from the subscriber's PC or LAN, then place the Ethernet packet into an RF burst packet by adding some extra header information and a preamble, then transmit the burst upstream, based upon the MAC protocol used by the particular vendor. Bursts received on the downstream were demodulated and checked for errors. The Ethernet frame was extracted from the packet and transmitted on the Ethernet interface to the subscriber's PC or LAN. Ethernet processing in the cable modem was originally a repeater process; it evolved into a bridge process.

Ethernet Repeaters

Early cable modem systems usually provided an Ethernet repeater service for the subscribers. The early design goals were geared to providing campus and residential LAN services. The Ethernet LAN model was used in the design for several generations of early modems, and has persisted even in modern cable modem design.

An Ethernet repeater is a device that has two or more Ethernet ports. Today, we can purchase small, 4- to 16-port Ethernet repeaters, also called *hubs*, off the shelf for under $50. A repeater merely echoes the electrical signals received on one port to all the other ports, thereby allowing all connection devices to communicate using the Ethernet LAN protocol. Repeaters can be linked to form larger networks.

One important aspect of Ethernet hubs and repeaters is that any traffic received on one port is echoed, or repeated, to all the other ports on the device. If hubs are linked, signals are repeated further along. Due to the propagation delay nature of the cable plant, it is not possible for a cable modem system to operate as a small Ethernet hub. However, a type of repeater solution called a *buffered repeater* receives an entire Ethernet frame from a port, and stores it in a buffer. The frame is then transmitted across a link to another buffer repeater, and the packet is transmitted on the port(s) of the linked repeater. Originally, a system of half-repeaters was used to link two distant LAN segments using a high-speed serial line.

The Ethernet port on a cable modem can be connected to a single PC or to a LAN. When connected to a LAN, an abundance of communication goes back and forth between other devices on the LAN that do not need to be sent on to the cable plant. Clearly, blindly repeating every packet received by the cable modem from a LAN on the upstream and downstream of the cable plant wastes precious bandwidth.

Early cable modem systems were essentially the same as a large buffered half-repeater system. LAN communications were supplied to an entire campus or city. Because of the shared media nature of the downstream and upstream data channels on a cable system, many cable modems can simultaneously participate in a large buffered repeater network.

NOTE A large buffered repeater network based on cable modems will repeat any Ethernet packet received.

Ethernet Bridges

Another type of Ethernet processing is called *bridging*, specifically a style of bridging called a *learning bridge*. An Ethernet learning bridge examines the source and destination addresses of frames as they are processed through the bridge. The bridge remembers the source address for each MAC address it hears on the subscriber's Ethernet port. There are several styles of learning bridge algorithms; this example presents one such style, for which we will assume that an early cable modem performs this algorithm.

On the upstream:

1. Check the FCS for correctness.

2. If the source address is not in the bridge table, cache the address in the table.

3. Determine whether the destination address is a group address. If it is, forward the frame upstream.

4. Determine whether the destination address is in the bridge table. If it is, discard the packet.

5. If the destination address is not in the bridge table, forward the Ethernet frame upstream.

On the downstream:

1. Check the FCS for correctness.

2. Determine whether the source address is in the bridge table. If it is, discard the packet.

3. If the source address is not in the bridge table, forward it to the subscriber Ethernet interface.

The sample demonstrates a simple learning bridge algorithm that has the following properties:

- Multicasts and broadcasts are allowed to pass through the bridge.

- Individual addresses are examined.

- Ethernet frames whose source addresses were heard on the subscriber's Ethernet interface are not forwarded upstream.

CABLE MODEM ETHERNET BRIDGES

Using a bridge-based system is very important for keeping unwanted subscriber LAN-to-LAN traffic off the upstream channel. It does not, however, stop subscribers from being able to communicate with every computer connected to an early cable modem system that employs a learning bridge system. Bridging only limits nonessential use of the upstream channel. All computer-to-computer address-discovery protocols use either broadcast- or multicast-addressed packets, which are not impeded by bridging. Once discovered, any computer can exchange Ethernet frames with any other computer using individually addressed packets.

This has the effect of keeping subscriber LAN to LAN traffic off the upstream channel.

In practice, bridging algorithms are more complicated than the sample implies. Two areas of importance are size of the learning table and dating learned addresses. Bridge table sizes in cable modems can range from eight to many hundreds of entries, depending on the amount of table memory used by the vendor. Dating entries is important, as it makes periodic cleaning of the table easier. Algorithms vary from vendor to vendor, and in regard to standard specifications.

Quality of Service

The goal of quality of service (QoS) support in cable modem systems is to assign preferential bandwidth access to communication services that require it. For example, packet voice communication needs a higher-priority access to bandwidth than simple Web browsing, so voice packets get from source to destination on time. The cable modem system must be able to regulate access to the system individually for different communication systems.

Extant early cable modem systems have no mechanisms to provide differentiated services over the cable plant. They simply implement one QoS level called "best-effort" services. Best effort means that the system does its best to get a packet across the network in time.

NOTE Best effort service is also referred to as *elastic* or *delay insensitive* services, meaning, the applications have to be able to tolerate varying amounts of delay on a packet-by-packet basis. The entire Internet today is a large best-effort service.

In addition to its best-effort policy, there are no provisions in an early system to adequately control cable modems (or subscriber's PCs) that attempt to abuse the system by trying to use more than their fair share of bandwidth (called *bandwidth hogs*). In such a system, all cable modems have equal access, so hogs try to access more bandwidth by trying to send huge amounts of bandwidth across the network.

Like an Ethernet LAN at work, performance for all cable modems suffers when the total load on the system goes up, regardless whether the load is from a hog or because every cable modem trying to access. A best-effort system with no central controller has no means to maintain minimum or maximum bandwidth allocations for cable modems.

Communications Privacy

Early cable modem systems used a shared downstream RF channel. Every cable modem could decode all packets transmitted downstream on the channel. This meant that one cable modem could decode the traffic sent to another cable modem. This is a fundamental attribute of the way a so-called dumb transverter-based cable modem MAC protocol operates.

Cryptographic techniques could be used to encrypt individually addressed packets sent from one cable modem to another, but the expense of doing this at the time was prohibitive.

There is a difference between maintaining privacy versus maintaining LAN security of the home computer. Privacy issues focus around preventing other parties from observing the private communications of another. On a cable modem system, the intent is to prohibit other subscribers from observing communications, from "snooping" on other subscribers.

LAN security involves protecting against unauthorized access to home computers and other devices in the subscriber's home. While cryptographic techniques can solve the snooping problem, the Ethernet bridging service employed by the cable modem system *actually* facilitates unauthorized access to a subscriber's PC or other LAN equipment. This is just a simple fact of these systems. Therefore, subscribers should be instructed to educate themselves and, if necessary, purchase home firewall protection in the form of PC software (which protects only the individual PC) or home firewall appliances (which protect the entire home network).

Summary of Early Cable Modem Systems

The following list summarizes the many aspects of early cable modems systems presented in this section. In such systems:

- ALOHA- and Slotted ALOHA-based cable modem systems work, and can provide viable high-speed Internet service.
- Upstream and downstream data channels are the same size and modulation type, thereby creating a symmetric bandwidth system.
- Low channel efficiency, sufficient for entry to the high-speed data business; it has no long-term prospects.
- Best-effort service is quality policy; there is no real QoS control.
- There is no central control for bandwidth allocation; therefore it is very difficult to enforce fairness for all cable modems. Available

THE LANCITY UNILINK SYSTEM

The notable exception to the general ALOHA system is the cable modem system developed by the LANCity Corporation in the late 1980s and early 1990s. The designers of this system took steps to overcome some of the deficiencies of the ALOHA system. Specifically, they created a protocol called UNILINK that had the following attributes:

- It was a simple transverter-based system.

- It featured MAC encapsulation for Ethernet on the downstream and upstream.

- A "pacer" station was elected out the population of cable modems, which established a notion of timing to all cable modems for establishing framing on the upstream channel. The pacer controlled the timing and size of the upstream framing through the use of a special MAP frame, which was transmitted to all cable modems.

- Upstream channel frames were divided into station management, contention, and guaranteed regions.

- Special MAC packages for station management and station-to-station communications were included.

- Stations were able to *range* themselves and adjust for their individual propagation delay from the headend. This allowed stations to be in much tighter synchronization time-wise with the upstream framing structure.

- A community LAN system based on Ethernet bridging was provided.

LANCity modems gained much success and market share in North America from the early 1990s through 1998. The success of the product allowed the LANCity system to be selected in the fall of 1996 as the basis for the North American cable industry's DOCSIS specification. DOCSIS is detailed in Chapter 5.

bandwidth is shared among the number of other active users; as the total load increases, individual bandwidth goes down.

- Simple transverters echo all transmissions errors received on the upstream right back on the downstream.

- Contention is part of the basic operation of the protocol and may lead to overpowering upstream amplification equipment.

- Modems have parameters that must be manually set before being deployed in the home.

- Ethernet interfaces are a universally accepted means of connecting a subscriber's equipment to the cable modem. An Ethernet repeater model places excess traffic on the upstream channel; therefore, an Ethernet learning bridge model is the best approach.

- Packets are sent in the clear, making snooping easy, and, therefore, privacy uninsurable.

- A community LAN model for Ethernet services requires subscriber education and protection measures to avoid unauthorized access problems.

Despite their shortcomings, the early cable modem systems paved the way for the future. They opened the door for cable operators to start offering high-speed Internet services and to generate a revenue stream. These early systems also created an experience base that was used to design the next-generation systems.

Modern Two-Way Cable Modem Systems

Through late 1994 until December 1995, North American cable operators communicated their collective vision of high-speed data-over-cable services via a series of Request for Proposals (RFPs), which were then issued from CableLabs to the vendor community. So many responses to those RFPs were returned that reporting on their would likely fill an entire book; therefore, because of space limitations, we can offer only a short summary of the key requirements from those responses to describe the vision of industry insiders for this technology at that time. They determined that:

- Cable modems had to share a single high-speed 6MHz-wide downstream channel. The speed of the channel had to be as high as possible, up to and including 64 QAM (~30Mbps) and 256 QAM (~40Mbps). Frequency agility had to be in the range from 54MHz to 860MHz. The channel had to be able to run adjacent to downstream analog NTSC video, without causing interference.

- There must be one or more shared upstream data channels; QPSK or 16 QAM modulation. Frequency agility had to be in the range from 5MHz to 42MHz.

- An Ethernet interface in the cable modem was necessary to connect to the subscriber's PC.

- An Ethernet interface at the headend was necessary to support connection to the backend network.

- Focus was to be directed on IP over Ethernet, with support for unicast, multicast, and broadcast addressing.

- The protection and privacy of individual subscriber information in a shared channel had to be ensured.

- Future support had to include voice telephony or other services that required QoS.

- The system had to be highly manageable.

- Solutions had to be found, leading to customer-installable, low-cost cable modems.

Vendors at the time were faced with overhauling the early cable modem architecture in favor of a new architecture that emerged over a two-year time frame (1995 through 1996), as seen in the products of several vendors (namely, Com21, Motorola, Hybrid, IBM, and Hewlett-Packard) and in the standards development of the IEEE 802.14 Cable TV Working Group, the ATM Forum (www.atmforum.com), and in the European-based DAVIC (www.davic.org) industrial consortium. The major change to the architecture was in the headend, where the dumb transverter was abandoned in favor of the *intelligent controller*.

The Intelligent Controller

In the architecture that evolved, the upstream transmissions from cable modems were no longer retransmitted on the downstream, thanks to the Cable Modem Termination System (CMTS). (CMTS, originally used in CableLabs' Data over Cable Service Interface Specification, was quickly adopted as the general-use term for the headend controller.) This intelligent controller, located at the headend, actively terminates (demodulates) transmissions from cable modems, processes these communications, performs switching and/or routing functions, and modulates transmissions on the downstream channel. As a result of the architectural shift, the responsibility and control of the downstream and upstream data capacity (resources) comes under control of the CMTS. Today, the cable modem (CM) is essentially a remote servant of the CMTS. This shift has also meant it is less expensive to build CMs.

Figure 3.10 illustrates the major components of the intelligent controller. It consists of a MAC processor, a transmitter (TX), one or more receivers (RX), a scheduler, a system manager, and a WAN interface. The transmitter is responsible for converting digital MAC packets into RF modulation and transmitting the information on the downstream channel. Information

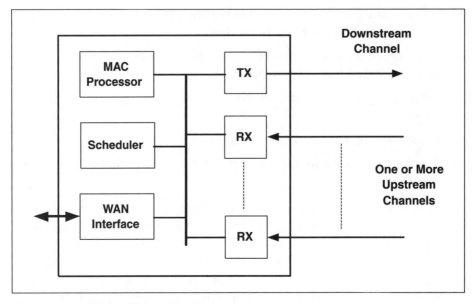

Figure 3.10   The intelligent controller.

transmitted is received by all cable modems listening to that downstream channel. In North America, a CMTS supports a very high-speed downstream data rate channel based on ITU J.83 Annex B digital video transmission specifications. The raw data rate for this 6MHz wide channel for 64 QAM and 256 QAM is presented in Table 3.2. After the FEC is processed, the remaining data rate is called the *information rate*; it reflects the maximum MAC packet rate. (The DOCSIS specification presented in Chapter 5 contains standardized downstream transmission channels.)

The receiver is responsible for converting RF modulation bursts that have been received on the upstream channel into packets. The packets are then sent to the WAN interface, the scheduler, or the MAC processor. Upstream channels can vary in bandwidth and modulation type. Table 3.3 lists the various combinations of typical symbol rates and modulation type. Recall that QPSK is a 2-bit per symbol modulation, and that 16 QAM is a 4-bit per symbol modulation. The RF channel with is based on an alpha of 0.25. Upstream channel rates supported are based on the vendor's capabilities, the cable operator's deployment methods, and the ingress noise environment on the upstream cable plant. In comparison to 16 QAM, QPSK with a good FEC is much more tolerant of ingress noise environments. As seen in the table, the minimum data rate is 320Kbps with the maximum of 20.4Mbps. The amount of FEC used for upstream packet bursts is vendor-

Table 3.2   Downstream Raw Channel Rates and Information Rates

	64 QAM (MBPS)	256 QAM (MBPS)
Raw Data Rate (approx.)	30	43
Information Rate (approx.)	27	39

dependent. (The DOCSIS specification presented in Chapter 5 lists standardized upstream transmission channels.)

The MAC processor is responsible for overseeing all aspects of the cable modem system protocol and management of individual stations.

In close coordination with the MAC processor, is the scheduler, which is responsible for managing the upstream channel resources allocated to cable modems. Cable modems are assigned upstream bandwidth based on a number of factors calculated on individual need, available resources, and priority of communications, including QoS. (The details of how a cable modem communicates its bandwidth needs are presented later in this chapter in the subsection titled "Requests and Grants" starting on page 78.)

The system manager is responsible for supporting remote system management of the CMTS via a standard network management protocol, such as the Simple Network Management Protocol (SNMP). The system manager is closely coupled with the WAN interface and all management elements within the intelligent controller.

The WAN processor is responsible for communicating with the backend network of the cable operator. The WAN processor may be implemented as an Ethernet switch or as an IP router, depending on the CMTS vendor.

Table 3.3   Upstream Data Rates and RF Channel Sizes

SYMBOL RATE (1000 SYMBOLS/SEC)	QPSK (KBPS)	16 QAM (KBPS)	RF CHANNEL WIDTH (MHZ)
160	320	640	0.180
320	640	1,280	0.400
640	1,280	2,560	0.800
1,280	2,560	5,120	1.600
2,560	5,120	10,240	3.200
5,120	10,240	20,480	6.400

MAC Packets

A universal change resulting from the implementation of an intelligent controller is the use of cable modem station identifiers, which are part of the MAC protocol, not the Ethernet frame. Station identifiers allow packets and MAC messages to be handled in a much cleaner manner.

Downstream and upstream MAC packets are very similar in structure; in fact, depending on the cable modem protocol, they may have identical structures. Each packet contains the following fields:

MAC header. Contains the cable modem identifier, MAC-specific flags, and some indication regarding the contents of the data. A MAC header has its own CRC so that a receiver can detect errors in the header portion of the packet. A MAC header may be extensible (variable in length) or fixed in size. The cable modem identifier is assigned by the CMTS's MAC process when the cable modem comes "online" in the system.

Data. Consists of either MAC management data or user data. MAC management messages may be of variable length, may have a minimum size limit, or may be null, depending on the specific MAC protocol. If the data were user data, it might be of fixed size or variable length. For example, if the user data is an ATM cell, it would likely be a fixed size; but if the user data contained an Ethernet packet, the entire MAC packet, including data, would be variable in length. The end of the data portion may or may not contain a CRC.

The difference between user data and MAC management messages is that user data is intended to be communicated from the cable modem's Ethernet interface to the WAN interface, and vice versa. MAC management messages are private to the CMTS and the collection of CMs it is controlling. Subscribers never see MAC management messages; the messages stay within the cable modem.

Sharing the Downstream and Upstream Channels

The intelligent controller is an asymmetric system, in that it supports one high-speed downstream data channel and multiple lower-rate upstream data channels, one per receiver. A cable modem's receiver is always tuned to the downstream channel. A cable modem's transmitter is told which upstream channel to use. If there are many upstream channels, the CMTS will direct a cable modem to the appropriate channel.

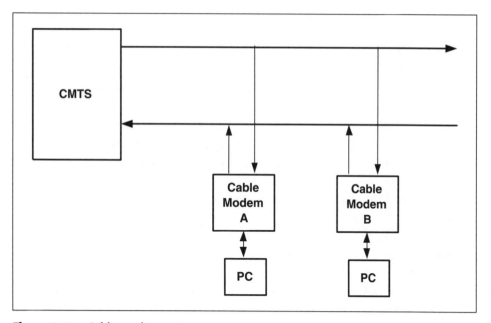

Figure 3.11   Cable modem system.

Figure 3.11 illustrates a CMTS with two cable modems, both of which are connected to the downstream channel and receive and decode MAC management messages and MAC messages containing user data. In this example, both cable modems are sharing the same upstream channel. A PC is connected to each cable modem.

With intelligent controllers, cable modems do not transmit without permission from the headend. That permission may be explicit, directing a single cable modem to transmit, or implicit, permitting members in a group to transmit.

Slotting the Upstream Channel

Upstream channels are slotted to permit optimal sharing of the capacity. A slot (also called minislots) is a measure of time that has been selected to synchronize with the raw bit rate of the channel; it is set by the CMTS to align the start of a slot with the start of a byte of data. Slotting systems come in two basic flavors: in one, the slot size is the same as that of an upstream packet burst, which is fixed in size (e.g., ATM cell plus overhead); in the second, the slot size is smaller than any MAC packet burst, and multiple slots are used to allocate time for the packet burst. A single slot or a multiple of minislots much be sufficiently lengthy to hold an upstream packet burst, including any preamble, FEC, and guard time overhead.

If a slotted system is to function properly, two fundamental adjustments must be made after the slot size has been determined by the CMTS. First, a cable modem must be *ranged*; second, all modems must share the same temporal notion of *slot numbering*.

The CMTS accomplishes ranging by establishing a time reference in the downstream channel, such as a time stamp or a symbol clock. The CMTS then adjusts a timer in each cable modem to synchronize it with the slot timing. The receiver of each channel at the CMTS is responsible for synchronizing and time stamping the arrival of packet bursts with that of a master clock used within the CMTS. MAC management messages are used to communicate between the cable modem and the CMTS. The CMTS can precisely adjust a cable modem's timing.

After the slot adjustment is made, the CMTS synchronizes each cable modem with a slot numbering scheme. A slot number is an integer that increments with every slot/minislot. At some point, the CMTS resets the number back to a value of 0.

Ranging cable modems in a slotted system results in the following: If the CMTS instructs any two aligned cable modems to each transmit a packet burst in the same slot number, n, then regardless of how far away either cable modem is on the cable plant, the first symbol of their bursts will arrive at the CMTS receiver at the same time at the start of slot n. Said differently, if any cable modem is told to transmit in slot n and any other modem is told to transmit in slot $n+1$, the headend receiver will note that the two bursts arrived at the headend, did not overlap, and had minimal separation in time.

During the process of initial ranging, the CMTS receiver also can measure received RF power. The MAC management process will make adjustments to the power output of the cable modem to ensure that it is within proper thresholds.

Requests and Grants

In the intelligent controller system, cable modems send bandwidth requests to the CMTS. These requests are in the form of a distinct MAC management message or are included as part of a packet burst. The request itself announces the arrival at the CM of one or packets of information that needs to be transmitted upstream (actually, the request specifies the amount of data that needs to be sent upstream). Upon receipt, requests are sent to the CMTS's scheduler process. The scheduler

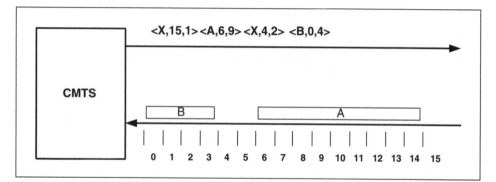

Figure 3.12   Request and grants.

processes the requests of all cable modems, and sends messages, called *grants*, on the downstream.

Grants come in three basic forms: direct, contention, and management:

- A *direct grant* gives permission for a single cable modem to transmit on the upstream. The direct grant includes a cable modem identifier, a starting slot number, and the number of slots to use.

- A *contention grant* gives permission for multiple cable modems to attempt to send bandwidth requests in the same slot(s).

- A *management grant* reserves a portion of the upstream slots for MAC management use, typically for ranging new stations.

Figure 3.12 illustrates a CMTS with a minislot system issuing two direct grants that give cable modems A and B permission to use the upstream channel. B is assigned slot 0 for a length of 4 slots, and A is assigned a length of 8 slots beginning at 6. The CMTS has also assigned slots 4 through 5, and 15 as contention slots. These provide the opportunity for any cable modem to send a bandwidth request, if needed. The result is that B sends up one packet in slots 0 through 3, and A sends a larger packet in slots 8 through 15. No station made any bandwidth requests in this example.

Contention Algorithm and Avoiding Collisions

Modern cable modem systems make use of contention for optimizing response time for packet transmissions from cable modems. Contention is used only so that a cable modem can, essentially, wave a hand as if to say, "I've got something to send," and have this signal noticed by the CMTS.

Here are the basic rules of using contention with an intelligent controller:

- Only bandwidth request messages are put into contention. User data is held in a queue waiting for transmission.

- The CMTS will acknowledge the receipt of a bandwidth request with either a direct grant or an acknowledgment. Until receipt of either, the cable modem enters a contention algorithm.

- While in contention, the cable modem will roll a random integer x over the range $0 <= x <= 2^k$, where the value of k is set by the CMTS. This is called *directed exponential backoff*, and means the CMTS periodically directs the value of k based upon its knowledge of the load presented by all cable modems in the system. The significant change over previous truncated exponential backoff systems is that newly contending cable modems do not have an unfair advantage.

The CMTS has the capability to adjust both the value of k and the number of contention slots available based on the number of cable modems in contention. Therefore, it can adjust both k and the contention slot rate to keep the number of simultaneous cable modem transmissions below the upstream amplifier RF power overdrive threshold. This alleviates the transmission power problems experienced by older systems. This shift in controlling contention from each cable modem to the CMTS is another significant advantage of an intelligent controller.

Scheduling, Queues, and Quality of Service

The request and grant mechanism suits a number of scheduling algorithms from strict polling, if contention is turned completely off, through a very advanced, weighted, fair-queuing virtual clock algorithm. Cable modem standard specifications do not detail the implementation process of the scheduler in the CMTS; the capabilities are left to the vendors to develop. There are, however, some general scheduling responsibilities that can be discussed.

Reactive, or Best-Effort, Scheduling

Figure 3.13 depicts the general two-way request and grant flow between a CMTS and a cable modem. In the cable modem, there is a small scheduler that is aware of the upstream channel slot and numbering structure, a

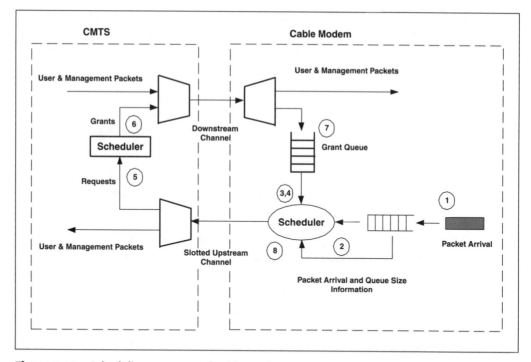

Figure 3.13   Scheduling process and cable modem queues.

grant queue, and one or more distinct data queues that hold user data
packets that have arrived from the subscriber's PC over the cable modem's
Ethernet interface. Here is a walkthrough of the general process of transmitting a packet on the upstream channel:

1. A user data packet (e.g., an Ethernet frame) arrives in an upstream
   data queue in the cable modem.

2. The cable modem scheduler calculates the number of minislots
   needed to transmit the packet on the upstream and to prepare a
   bandwidth request message.

3. The cable modem waits for a contention opportunity, then transmits
   the bandwidth request to the CMTS.

4. The cable modem enters contention mode and calculates when it will
   try to send another bandwidth request.

5. The CMTS receives the bandwidth request from the cable modem,
   and calculates when it is able to schedule upstream bandwidth for
   the particular cable modem.

6. If the CMTS can schedule immediately, it issues a direct grant to the cable modem, then transmits it on the downstream. If delayed, it makes note when in the future it will schedule a grant, and sends an acknowledgment to the cable modem.

7. The cable modem receives either the direct grant or the acknowledgment. Receipt of either one forces the cable modem out of contention. If it is an acknowledgment, it waits for a direct grant.

8. On receiving a direct grant, the cable modem prepares the packet for transmission. When the current slot number increments to the starting slot number contained in the direct grant, the cable modem transmits the packet.

This is the basic transmission algorithm for scheduling bandwidth for cable modems based on the arrival of a packet in the cable modem's upstream queue. A number of steps have been glossed over to more distinctly communicate the basic request grant mechanism. The actual mechanisms used by the standards will be presented in Chapter 5.

The scheduling mechanism just presented is termed reactive scheduling or best-effort scheduling because resources are assigned only after the cable modem reacts to the receipt of a packet in an upstream queue. As explained previously, the Internet at large uses a concept of scheduling called best effort, whereby the scheduler in the CMTS is constantly accepting bandwidth requests from cable modem and assigning bandwidth; as long as the bandwidth is assigned fairly, eventually every cable modem will get an opportunity to transmit on the upstream channel. In best-effort scheduling, every cable modem is at equal priority, and the scheduler does its best to provide bandwidth fairly. From the individual subscriber's point of view, however, best effort is actually worst effort.

EMBEDDED BANDWIDTH REQUEST

Another form of bandwidth request is transmitted in the MAC header of an upstream packet burst containing user data. We will call it an *embedded bandwidth request*. Here's how it works: While the cable modem is waiting to transmit one packet, it may receive additional packets in the upstream queues. Before transmitting the packet (in step 8 in the preceding sequence), the cable modem can include or update the bandwidth request message in the MAC header. Using this, the CMTS will receive an updated bandwidth request without the cable modem having to use contention. This feature also helps to reduce the use of contention in modern cable modem systems.

Delay-Sensitive Scheduling

Delay-sensitive scheduling (also referred to as QoS scheduling) is a mechanism whereby a scheduler performs best-effort scheduling as a default, but is aware that one or more cable modems require priority allocation of upstream bandwidth. For example, packet voice services require that packets be transmitted upstream with a guaranteed limit on delay as too much delay will cause the human ear to notice problems (the human hearing mechanism is very sensitive to variable sounds delays). A best-effort scheduler cannot guarantee delays as every cable modem is treated equally. Too many users and delay sensitive traffic will be impinged. A scheduler which understands the QoS requirements of each cable modem will prioritize access to upstream bandwidth when needed for delay sensitive traffic.

Implementing QoS scheduling in an intelligent controller systems is very straightforward, provided QoS is designed in from the start. As shown in Figure 3.14, the cable modem is augmented to have several data queues. User data is classified into these queues based on the priority of the application or service. For example, a packet containing voice will be

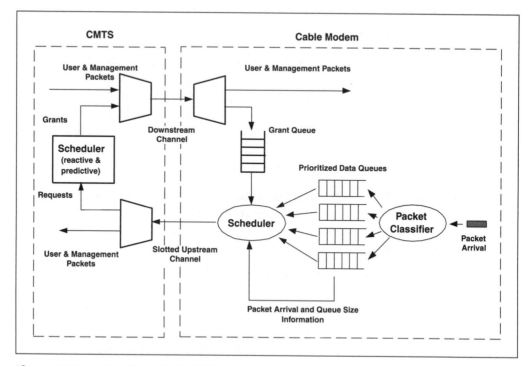

Figure 3.14 QoS enhanced scheduling.

placed in a queue that has a higher transmission priority than a packet containing electronic mail. (The details of how the packet is placed in the queue are covered in Chapter 5.) The cable modem scheduler and the CMTS are already aware of the different priority queues in the cable modem. This is communicated between the CM and the CMTS as part of system startup.

Generally, higher-priority QoS traffic will fall into one of two categories: *constant bit rate* (CBR) or high-priority *variable bit rate* (VBR). Both categories are delay-sensitive services, with CBR being more sensitive than VBR. For CBR traffic, scheduling in the CMTS is very straightforward predictive scheduling. The CMTS only need issue grants that satisfy the cable modem's needs to transmit CBR packets at the constant rate. The cable modem does not have to make bandwidth requests for CBR packets; that is, CBR traffic does not use contention. For VBR, the CM and the CMTS understand that when a VBR packet arrives in the cable modem, the bandwidth request is treated with a much higher scheduling priority, based on the needs of the application service using VBR. In all cases, for QoS, assigning queues and scheduling priorities is performed either by MAC management messages or signaling protocol messages. (Certain of these messages are discussed in Chapter 5.)

Round-Trip Timing

The discussion thus far has presented two-way communications between the CM and the CMTS to imply that they cross the cable plant in zero time. In practice, a significant round-trip time in a cable plant must be compensated for in the CMTS scheduler and in the design of the MAC protocol. Packet delays in the system fall into two categories, *fixed delay* and *variable delay*.

Fixed delays are composed of the following:

Propagation delay for transmission in combinations of coaxial and fiber cable. The maximum value for one-way is approximately 400 microseconds. For two-way, the maximum fixed delay is 800 microseconds.

Modulation and demodulation in the downstream channel. This is dependent on which mode of the ITU J.83 Annex B standard is used. The minimum is approximately 1 millisecond to a maximum of several milliseconds.

Modulation and demodulation in the upstream channel. This is fixed, based on the configuration of the upstream channel set at deployment time. For this discussion, the amount of delay will be 1 millisecond.

Grant-processing time in the cable modem. Here, we assume this happens very fast—in less than 200 microseconds.

Variable delays are composed of the following:

CMTS scheduler processing delay. This is the time between when a scheduler receives a bandwidth request from a cable modem and that either a direct grant or acknowledgment is placed onto the downstream transmission channel. This could be on the order of 1 to several milliseconds.

User data access delay. This is the delay experienced by a packet arriving in the upstream queue of a cable modem until it starts to transmit on the upstream channel. The minimum for this is the round-trip time, which is the sum of the fixed delays plus the CMTS scheduler delay. In this discussion, for a cable modem at the maximum cable distance, the round-trip delay would be a minimum of 4.0 milliseconds.

A subtlety in the system is that the CMTS scheduler must ensure that a cable modem receives a direct grant before the opportunity passes on the upstream channel. Another subtlety in the system is that the CMTS has a long round-trip time reaction time. That is, the CMTS is limited by the upstream access time and transmission propagation delay to noting the change in state of a cable modem queue (time for a cable modem to successfully transmit a request upstream) and is further limited to reacting to the change in state, i.e., by scheduling a grant, by the time to calculate when to schedule a grant, and the downstream transmission propagation delay of sending the grant. Both of these nuances require that the scheduler process be somewhat sophisticated about scheduling upstream resources.

Multicast Services

One of the key differentiating factors of high-speed data over cable systems is the inherent capability to easily implement multicast services. In the downstream direction, there is one transmitter at the headend and a receiver in each cable modem. It is possible to send downstream packets to a subset of cable modems such that they all receive and process the packets. Layering IP multicast packets onto Ethernet frames with multicast group addresses onto a cable modem MAC identifier is very straightforward.

Until now, cable modem identifiers were defined to be unique per cable modem. An extension of this concept is to have one unique identifier for the cable modem that would be used in the MAC packets for sending all MAC messages and individually addressed Ethernet frames. If the cable modem had a table of additional identifiers, assigned by the CMTS, then the same identifier value could be assigned to more than one cable modem. This would allow the CMTS to send one packet and have it received by those cable modems.

Figure 3.15 illustrates the concept. Suppose there are four cable modems, each with its own unique identifier: 1, 2, 3, and 4. Suppose, too, that the CMTS assigns additional identifiers, as follows: 1 (100, 101, 255), 2 (100, 101, 255), 3 (101, 255), and 4 (255). Cable modem 1 is a member of multicast groups 100, 101, 255, and so forth. If the CMTS sends a MAC packet to cable modem address 100, then modems 1 and 2 will decode the address, check in their table, and process the packet. The other modems will decode the address, see that it is not for them, and discard the packet. Similarly, identifier 101 would be received by 1, 2, and 3, and processed. The value 255 is special in this example, in that it is a broadcast identifier. If the CMTS sends a MAC packet to cable modem identifier 255, all stations will process the packet. In this manner, an Ethernet broadcast frame can be sent in a MAC packet to cable modem identifier 255.

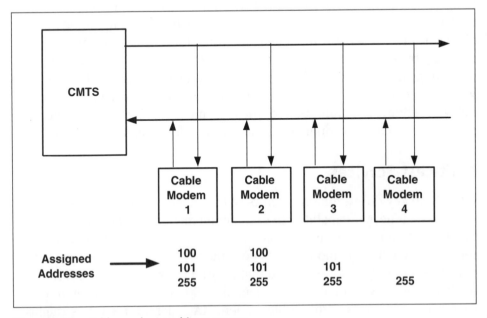

Figure 3.15 Cable modem multicast groups.

This relatively straightforward scheme can be expanded to support thousands of cable modems. The simple rules are:

- When a cable modem comes online, it is assigned a unique identifier value by the CMTS. Both the CMTS and the CM understand it is the unique identifier. The CMTS does not assign this value to any other active modem. The unique identifier is used for all MAC management message communications and all individually addressed user data communications.

- The cable modem system has an identifier value that is used as an all-stations broadcast address.

- The CMTS may assign additional cable modem identifier values to more than one cable modem, to form a group address. The CMTS may add or remove cable modems from the group at any time. The CMTS manages which group identifiers it has assigned. Using this system, there may be many active multicast groups. The main intention of this group address facility is to directly map an IP multicast group to a MAC multicast group.

- Multicast addresses are used only in the downstream, to leverage the power of the cable transmission system: one copy of a packet reaches all members of a group. In the upstream direction, the CMTS is always the receiver of packets; hence, MAC group addresses are not supported in the upstream direction.

Privacy

In modern cable modem systems, the downstream and upstream communication of user data is encrypted. This is done to make it computationally difficult for another subscriber or anyone else to invade an individual's privacy by snooping on the contents of user data. Encryption is performed in both the downstream and upstream channels.

Typically, when a cable modem first begins to operate with a CMTS, a public key encryption system is used to exchange security system messages between the CM and the CMTS. These messages include a set of secret DES keys, which are used to perform the actual encryption of MAC packet data. The keys are linked to the cable modem identifiers assigned by the CMTS. A field within the MAC header identifies which key it is to use. That information, along with the cable modem identifier, determines which key is to be used. Keys may be changed at any time by the CMTS in such a way as to allow continuous, unimpeded communication.

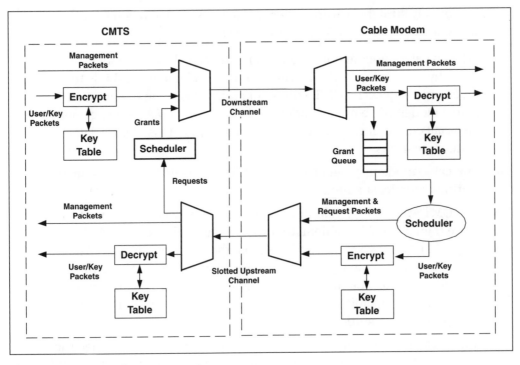

Figure 3.16   Encryption components.

Figure 3.16 illustrates the placement of the encryption components in the CMTS and CM. The CMTS must keep a master table of cable modem identifiers, the secret keys it has given out, as well as public key information for any future public key conversations. The cable modem must maintain a smaller table and a set of secret keys for each cable modem identifier that it has been assigned. Note: Only the user data portion of a MAC packet is encrypted. The MAC header is always sent "in the clear."

For example, in the downstream direction, the CMTS could encrypt a packet for cable modem 1 using key number 1. Both the CMTS and the CM have the same secret key for key number 1. The CMTS encrypts the data portion of the MAC packet, and indicates in the MAC header that it used key 1 to encrypt the data. The CM would receive the packet, process the MAC header, see that that packet was sent to it, and that it was encrypted with key 1, then select the proper key and decrypt the user data. If the wrong key were selected for encryption or decryption, the cable modem's decryption would produce an Ethernet frame that would fail the FCS check, and the user data would be discarded.

The power of this generic mechanism is that multicast group members can share the same secret keys and decode multicast group messages.

Only bona fide members of the group would be able to decode the message properly. Any snoopers on the downstream would not be able to decipher the multicast messages.

> **NOTE** MAC messages sent to the MAC broadcast identifier generally are not encrypted, as everyone has to process the message anyway.

In the upstream direction, the CM would encrypt the packet and note which key was used for encryption. The CMTS would then know to select the appropriate key for decrypting.

The privacy mechanism described here is often referred to as *link privacy protection*. The use of encryption for packets being transmitted over the cable system is completely transparent to Ethernet or IP.

Plug-and-Play Cable Modems

For a cable modem to be defined as customer-installable, the customer must be able to remove it from the shipping box, connect it to the coaxial cable in his or her home, and go on-line without the need for any local configuration adjustments (either by the customer of the cable operator).

Most modern cable modems, whether proprietary or built to a standard, are designed to be hands-off plug-and-play installable. Here is an example of the process of bringing a cable modem online with the CMTS:

1. Customer takes modem out of the box, and hooks it up to RF coaxial cable, power cable, and Ethernet R48 jack.

2. Cable modem begins searching the downstream frequencies for an active, digitally modulated, RF carrier.

3. When it finds one, it waits to see if there are any MAC messages present on the downstream. If not, it goes back to step 2 and continues hunting for a channel.

4. The CMTS periodically issues MAC messages specifically for "new" cable modems. These messages contain information that designates which upstream frequency, modulation type, symbol rate, and initial transmit power new modems should use to begin talking to the headend on the upstream channel.

5. After configuring the transmitter for the upstream channel, the modem then looks for MAC scheduler grant messages that tell when the slot counter number rolls over, followed by which upcoming slots offer the next management opportunities. The scheduler gives

the cable modem a round-trip time window in which to attempt first contact.

6. Seizing such an opportunity, the cable modem transmits a special MAC management message that basically says, "Hello, I'm new; here is my unique Ethernet MAC address." (Each cable modem is assigned a unique MAC address at manufacturing time by the vendor.)

7. The cable modem continues transmitting in management slots using a backoff mechanism until the CMTS responds.

8. The CMTS responds with a special MAC message in which the Ethernet address is used by the cable modem to decide whether the message is meant for it the modem. (This is required when multiple cable modems are attempting to come online at the same time.) The message contains an initial ranging offset adjustment, a temporary identifier, and a transmit power adjustment.

9. Once it has a temporary identifier value, the cable modem begins to listen for direct grants for itself. Once heard, the cable modem transmits another MAC message to the CMTS. The CMTS and CM can continue to talk privately now, and the CMTS can make fine-tuning adjustments for ranging and power. When complete, the CMTS issues a cable modem identifier.

10. At this point, the CM and CMTS begin to exchange information that includes CM software version numbers, manufacturer or model number, and so on. Optionally, the CMTS may force the CM to do a software download to update its firmware.

11. After any updates, the CM and CMTS begin a public key encrypted conversation. The CMTS assigns to the CM its secret keys for use with the cable modem unique identifier.

12. The CMTS assigns the CM to zero or more multicast groups, and supplies needed secret keys for each group.

13. The CMTS tells the CM to begin operation.

14. The CM allows user data to be passed on the upstream, and begins participating in the MAC protocol to request bandwidth, and so on.

15. Periodically, while the CM is powered up, the CMTS may adjust parameters for ranging, transmit power, secret keys, or others.

This step-by-step description is meant to convey a plausible scenario for bringing a new cable modem online. The specifics of starting up a DOCSIS cable modem will be presented in Chapter 5.

Telephone Return Cable Modem

All-coaxial cable plants, as discussed in Chapter 2, may be run either as a one-way plant or a partial two-way plant. That is, the cable operator has decided not to offer two-way cable services to its subscribers. Deploying high-speed data services on one-way plant is possible using a telephony return modem system. Telephone return cable modems are deployed in many cable operator systems in North America.

Figure 3.17 illustrates a one-way telephone return cable modem system. The downstream cable plant is used to provide a high-speed data path from the headend to the subscriber's cable modem. The return path, however, uses a standard dial-up telephone modem, instead of the upstream cable plant. The dial-up connection terminates in a remote access server (RAS), which is operated by the cable operator's ISP. In the downstream direction, the packets are transmitted using an IP over Ethernet protocol, similar to the normal two-way cable operation. In the upstream direction, packets are transmitted over the telephone as IP over Point-to-Point Protocol (PPP). IP over PPP is widely used for everyday ISP dial-up services. The cable modem acts as a three-port router in the telephone return model. IP over Ethernet is received over the downstream high-speed cable RF port. IP over Ethernet packets are exchanged between the cable modem and the PC over the Ethernet port. The cable modem converts IP

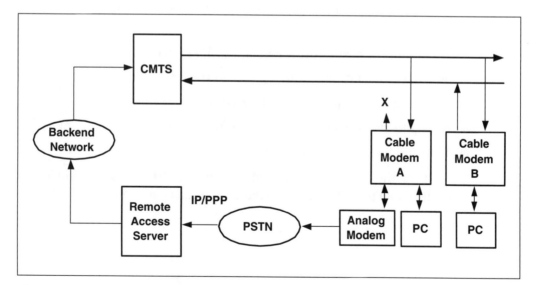

Figure 3.17   Telephone return cable modem.

over Ethernet packets received from the PC into IP over PPP packets, and transmits them over the telephone link.

Because the telephone return model is IP over PPP, an Ethernet switching model does not apply. Instead, in the upstream direction, it is more of a standard IP routing model, where the cable modem forwards IP packets to the default upstream router, which is usually the RAS. The cable operator and ISP have set up their routers to manage packet flow such that IP packets returned to the PC are routed down the high-speed cable plant, rather than back to the RAS.

Summary

This chapter presented the basic elements of cable modem systems, both the early systems and the modern systems. The early systems had a number of shortcomings which prevented the technology and architecture from being more widely deployed as the pervasive solution. Modern cable modem system development was able to make use of the experience gathered with these early systems. Modern cable modem systems share a number of common elements in design which include the following:

- Intelligent headend controller providing high-speed downstream and upstream data channels
- Bandwidth allocation and QoS support through sophisticated scheduling and a request and grant protocol architecture which provide for:
  - Support of best-effort, CBR, and VBR services
  - High-efficiency use of RF spectrum resources
- Link privacy for individual cable modems
- Straightforward use of multicast addressing in the downstream
- Plug-and-play cable modem operation

In addition, the use of an intelligent headend controller can be applied to one-way cable plant by using a telephone return cable modem system.

Internet Services over Cable

A cable modem system is actually a portion of the entire system that a cable operator must deploy in order to start supplying Internet access services to subscribers. The cable modem system—that is, the CMTS and all the cable modems—provide only the *last-mile* (also sometimes called the *first-mile)* access over the cable operator's network. The rest of the system lies in the cable operator's and service provider's network, behind the headend.

The remaining elements of entire system are composed of the cable operator's backend network, the service provider's backend network, a variety of servers, and the connection to the rest of the Internet. Some cable operator's provide their own Internet service; others work with an Internet service provider (ISP) partner. The partner's network may or may not be co-located in the cable operator's backend network. The servers in the network provide traditional Internet services, such as email and Web access; but there are also specialized servers for cable modem management and, perhaps, for streaming media services.

A new subscriber is added to the cable modem network via a customer service system that provisions elements of the entire network to accept the new cable modem and to allocate resources to the subscriber. Two of these resources are Internet addresses and bandwidth allocation. To the new subscriber, the path to obtaining service may be rocky and problematic; however, the system has been designed to accommodate future customer installations and auto configuration. Parts of these refinements are in operation in today's systems.

Once installed, the subscriber is provided with an *always on* service. This offers the advantage of rapid response time from power-up on the home computer, as it avoids the delays with dial-up modems. In addition, cable modem services frees up the phone line that was previously used for Internet access.

Managing the cable modem Internet access system requires the ISP and the cable operator to proactively plan deployments and upgrades to support the growing number of subscribers and their subsequent bandwidth needs.

The environment and technology for cable networks continues to improve. Many multiple systems operators (MSOs) have taken advantage of digital optical networking technology to improve the interconnections of headends and to create a better backend distribution network for video, voice, and data.

Service Provider System

Figure 4.1 shows the basic architecture of the Internet services network for a cable operator and ISP. This example shows that the ISP and the cable operator run distinct networks.

Several network elements make up the entire system, from the cable operator's headend through the ISP to the Internet:

- One or more CMTS systems
- Cable operator backend network
- Headend link router
- ISP link router
- ISP backend network
- Internet address and configuration server
- Web server
- Email server
- Web cache server

- ISP Internet router, plus provisioning and authentication system
- Network management system

The actual number and placement of these elements will vary from deployment to deployment, based on the needs of the cable operator and the ISP; thus, the entries in the preceding list should be considered a set of generic building blocks for the system.

It is possible to operate more than one CMTS at a headend. The number of CMTSs deployed is based on the cable topology within the operator's network, as well as the number of subscribers who are being supported. Obviously, the more subscribers, the more data capacity is needed.

The Internet uses routing to get IP packets from place to place. A link router is required within the cable operator's headend. This router connects the headend facility with the ISP's facility. In many cases, the CMTS will itself serve as a router, which means the connection to the ISP may be provided directly by the CMTS. However, if more than one CMTS is

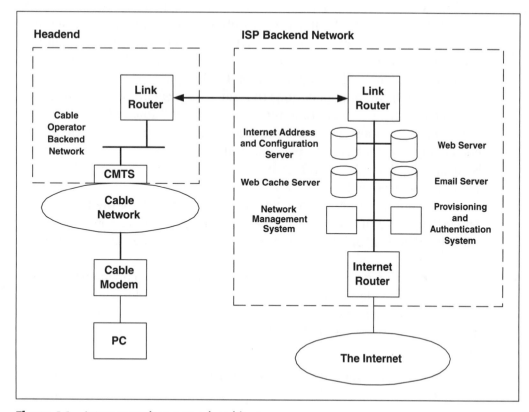

Figure 4.1   Internet services network architecture.

installed at the headend, there will be a local cable operator backend network, which interconnects each CMTS with the router. Typically, this is a 100Mbps Ethernet network.

At the ISP, a link router is used to support that side of the interconnection between the ISP's and the cable operator's facility. The actual physical device used may be a port from a multiple-port router. The ISP link router connects to the ISP's backend network.

Within the ISP's network, several servers are required to support the cable subscribers. First is an Internet address and configuration server. It uses the Dynamic Host Configuration Protocol (DHCP) as well as the Trivial File Transfer Protocol (TFTP) to assign IP addresses and provide configuration information to cable modems, as well as to provide IP addresses to subscribers' personal computers. DHCP and TFTP are two widely used standardized protocols for the autoconfiguration of Internet devices.

ISPs provide a customer Web environment to support their cable users. The servers are typically located in the ISP's facilities. Email servers follow the same deployment as Web servers and are also located at the ISP.

A Web cache server provides a mechanism by which Web pages are temporarily stored locally. A subscriber's Web browser is directed to use the cache server as a *proxy* server. This is important because any frequently accessed but unchanging Web pages are provided locally by the cache server rather than by the original server. Caching Web pages is a technique employed by browser applications to reduce the need to pull Web pages over the Internet connection. In this model, the additional ISP's network Web cache server also helps to reduce load on the connection to the Internet, an important advantage, because, today, the major subscriber activity is surfing the World Wide Web. A Web cache server can be located at the ISP or at the headend.

The ISP Internet router connects the ISP with the rest of the Internet. The ISP typically runs more than one of these routers to connect to different ISP peers. This builds in some redundancy as a safeguard in case of link failure.

The provisioning and authentication system is used to manage the other elements to provide services to subscribers. For example, when new subscribers set up their service with the cable operator's customer service department, the provisioning system may perform a number of operations, including:

- Configure the Internet address server to recognize the new cable modem.

- Configure the Internet address server to provide one or more IP addresses for use by the subscribers for their personal computers.

- Assign a bandwidth allocation configuration to the server, which is used by both the CMTS and the cable modem to regulate data capacity allocation for the subscriber.

- Configure a new email address on the email server.

- Configure a custom Web page on the Web server.

- Test the connection to the subscribers' new cable modem (if connected and turned on).

Provisioning and authentication is a fairly detailed task, and is very dependent on the ISP and the cable operator. In some cases, the provisioning system may be linked back to a cable operator data management system, which keeps billing information along with other subscriber information. The details of an individual cable operator's system are beyond the scope of this chapter, but the general procedures just listed are illustrative of those that must be taken to bring a new subscriber online.

The management system is responsible for monitoring the health of each network element, from the ISP Internet link router down to each and every cable modem. If any problems arise, the management system can identify where and what the problem is, and alert network operations personnel. In addition, the management system may be able to issue *trouble tickets* as a means of tracking fixes. Moreover, every active cable modem on the network is itself a remote sensor; this enables the cable operator to determine the health of the cable network's plant. By observing statistics that are kept in each cable modem and CMTS, the operator can spot certain problems before subscribers experience any service degradation.

PROACTIVE NETWORK MANAGEMENT For the cable operator, every cable modem is a remote sensor that can be used to identify problems in the cable network before they become problems for subscribers.

Subscriber Provisioning

A cable operator can't provide high-speed data service to a customer unless the following three pieces are in place:

- Cable modem services are available on the plant which directly passes the subscriber. That is, a CMTS must be installed at the headend, and the plant capable of two-way communications between the headend and subscriber's home. In some cases, the cable operator may only be able to provide two-way services to a portion of the plant. Subscribers not in the activated portion will have to wait until the operator enables more plant.

- There must be an active drop line to the subscriber's home.
- The subscriber must have a personal computer that can support both the hardware and software applications for the service.

The goal of cable modem efforts in North America is to allow a subscriber to purchase a cable modem off the shelf or via the Web, self-install the modem at home, request service, and start operation almost immediately. Unfortunately, the cable networks and provisioning systems currently cannot yet meet that goal, although they are continuing to advance. At this time, most provisioning is performed manually.

Manual Provisioning

Manually provisioning a new subscriber follows these basic steps:

1. The subscriber calls up the cable operator or cable ISP and requests new service. In some cases, the subscriber can initiate this by filling out a form on the cable ISP's Web site.

2. The subscriber talks to a customer service representative (CSR) over the phone. The CSR collects and verifies the following information:

   a. *Account information.* The subscriber may already have cable TV service; if not, he or she is considered a new subscriber.

   b. *That cable service can be provided to the subscriber's home.* This step validates that the downstream and upstream channels used by a CMTS are already present, or can be accessed easily, on the cable that is passing the new subscriber's home address.

   c. *That the subscriber's personal computer has the necessary hardware and software features to support the connection to the service.* The personal computer can be a generic PC running Microsoft Windows, a Macintosh system, a Linux system, or any other system that can support an Ethernet or Universal Serial Bus (USB) interface and a TCP/IP protocol stack. Generally, the personal computer will need to have an Ethernet network interface card (NIC) installed; if one is not present, the CPU must be of sufficient power, and there must be enough disk space to hold the ISP's applications.

d. *That new subscriber can receive service, and his or her personal computer is capable of supporting the service.* If so, the CSR schedules an appointment for the subscriber with a cable technician for the installation. (In some cases, a subscriber may not know the capability or configuration of his or her personal computer, in which case a technician is sent out, essentially hoping for the best.) Billing information is confirmed at this time. The CSR may also set up a login name and password or email account name and password at this time.

3. The CSR uses the provisioning system to update the necessary servers with the information for the new subscriber. This includes any login or email names and passwords, IP address assignments, and bandwidth allocation parameters.

4. The technician arrives at the subscriber's home and verifies the quality of the drop cable. This is done by visually inspecting the drop cable for wear, age, and part number. The connectors at either end are inspected for corrosion and proper fit. (End connectors are easily replaced.) Finally, the ground block is inspected, and replaced if needed. Inside, some wiring changes may be needed to accommodate the connection of the new cable modem. For example, a new splitter may be installed and a new cable extended to, say, the den.

5. The technician installs the cable modem and verifies that it correctly operates by checking the status indicators. (The technician brings the cable modem, meaning the serial number and other information were already entered into the provisioning database.)

6. The technician prepares the customer's personal computer. This may including installing the Ethernet NIC and any necessary software. Newer cable modems may provide a USB interface, in which case, the Ethernet NIC is not required.

7. Two modes of IP address assignment are possible for the personal computers. One is to manually enter the necessary information; the other is to configure the personal computer to use DHCP. After assigning the IP address, the PC is rebooted. The system will then have the following four pieces of IP network information configured: IP address assigned to the personal computer; IP subnetwork mask, also called the netmask value; IP address for the default gateway; IP address for one or more domain name servers (DNS).

At this point, barring no unforeseen problems, the subscriber's personal computer is now operational on the high-speed cable modem network.

Automatic Provisioning

An advantage of automatic provisioning is that it requires fewer visits by cable technicians to subscriber homes, and is, therefore, more economical for the cable operator.

Typically, today, a new cable modem subscriber will already have access to the Internet over a dial-up modem service and can surf to the cable ISP's Web site to complete this process; otherwise, phone registration with a CSR will be necessary. Assuming the former, the process of automatically provisioning a new subscriber follows these basic steps:

1. The subscriber surfs to the cable ISP's Web page and follows the procedures for establishing new cable modem service. This includes filling out forms with the information necessary to meet the three basic requirements (cable access, drop line, and capable personal computer) so that the Web registration system can proceed. In addition, and if known, the subscriber selects the bandwidth allocation level he or she wants.

2. If the Web registration process goes smoothly, the customer is given the option to purchase an approved cable modem from a local store or have one shipped to him or her. Billing information is also confirmed in this step. The customer reads and accepts the service agreement.

3. The subscriber follows the directions to self-install the cable modem, then verifies correct operation.

4. The subscriber installs an Ethernet NIC, if required, and configures it for DHCP operation, then connects it to the cable modem's Ethernet port.

5. The customer reboots the PC, launches a browser application, and starts to surf.

6. The cable ISP, recognizing that this is a newly attached cable modem and personal computer, intercepts the Web page access and directs it to a validation page. Here, the subscriber is required to enter information that validates the new service subscription. The Web page may require the subscriber to download cable ISP application software and reboot the computer again.

7. The subscriber now has full high-speed access to cable ISP services, as well as access to the Internet.

The preceding is a generic example of automatic provisioning. Each cable operator and cable ISP will have its own methods.

IP Protocol Stack Configuration on the Subscriber's Computer

The majority of subscribers who use cable modem service do not need, nor want, to know the details of the configuration of their PC; they just want to be assured that it is configured properly and that it works. Two methods are widely used to perform the actual initial IP network configuration of the computer:

- The cable technician configures the network settings.

- The subscriber is given the necessary information, and he or she performs the configuration process.

Likewise, there are two methods by which a computer's IP network can be configured: manually and automatically. Manual operation requires that the following four pieces of IP network information be entered by hand, by the person performing the configuration: the station's assigned IP address, the IP subnetwork mask, the IP address of the default gateway, and one or more DNS server IP addresses. Automatic means that computer must already be configured to accept these four pieces of IP network information using DHCP.

Here is a brief overview of how DHCP works on local area networks (LANs):

1. When a computer reboots, it reaches a point where it needs to initialize the IP network interface (if one is installed in the computer).

2. If the configuration information for the interface is set to access addresses automatically using DHCP, the IP stack initialization routine transmits a broadcast packet, called a DHCP_Request packet, on the Ethernet interface. Inside the DHCP_Request packet is the 48-bit IEEE MAC address of the Ethernet interface. As a broadcast packet, the Ethernet packet is received by all Ethernet stations on the LAN, including one or more stations that are performing the role of a DHCP server. All nonserver stations just drop the packet.

3. When a DHCP server receives a DHCP_Request packet, it consults its configuration database. (An administrator of the DHCP server must have previously set up the database.) DHCP can allocate IP network information using one of two methods: *static* or *pooled assignment*. For static operation, the administrator must have previously entered the 48-bit MAC address into the database and configured it with a specific IP address. For pooled assignment, the administrator must have allocated one or more IP addresses, which may be given out on

a first-come first-served basis. When receiving a DHCP_Request packet, the server examines the static configuration first, then the pooled information. Whether static or pooled, the server constructs a DHCP_Reply packet that is transmitted back to the request station's unique 48-bit MAC address on the Ethernet. The reply contains the four pieces of IP network information: the station's assigned IP address, the IP subnetwork mask, the IP address of the default gateway, and one or more DNS server IP addresses. (DHCP has additional information that may be included in the reply, which is used for other functions. More on this in Chapter 5.)

4.   The station receives the DHCP_Reply packet, extracts the IP information, and configures the IP protocol stack (as if the information were manually entered), and continues bringing up the computer.

DHCP has two other features that make it a very robust service: *address lease time* and *DHCP relaying*. When DHCP assigns addresses in the DHCP_Reply packet, it also specifies the length of time for which the addresses are valid, called the *lease time*. According to the DHCP protocol, it is the responsibility of the DHCP client (the home computer) to refresh its lease within that time; this is done automatically, and requires no subscriber knowledge and/or intervention. If this doesn't happen, the server can reallocate the address to another computer. Sometimes, the cable operator or ISP will need to renumber its IP subnetwork, that is, change from one IP address block to another. This may be necessary when reconfiguring CMTS or cable plant topologies for alterations or to grow the network. The use of the lease enables each computer to periodically be reset (often, when next turned on) to new addresses.

The DHCP relay function enables a large network, composed of many LANs, to use a single DHCP server. In this mode, the router that connects the LAN to the rest of the network is configured with a DHCP helper address. Once configured, if the router receives a DHCP_Request packet, it modifies one field in the DHCP_Request packet and forwards it on behalf of the requesting station to a specific server. The server notes the information in the packet and sends the reply back to the router; the router then forwards the DHCP_Reply to the request station. This relay operation is performed transparently to the requesting station.

With pooling assignment, there is no guarantee that the next time a computer reboots, it will receive the same IP address. This is problematic for cable networks, as it is more efficient in terms of support and management if the subscriber's cable modem and personal computer retain the same IP addresses from reboot to reboot. For this reason, some cable operators and ISPs use static allocation for the subscriber's computer. This method offers the advantage of allocating the same IP address to the computer yet maintaining address assignment flexibility when the computer is configured to use DHCP.

Manual IP Network Information Configuration

Most personal computers used by subscribers are one of three types: a PC running Microsoft Windows, an Apple Macintosh, or a PC running Linux. Each must be configured differently for cable, as explained here:

Windows 98. To configure the TCP/IP network information for an Ethernet interface, the subscriber must open the Network control panel located under Start Menu -> Settings -> Control Panel. The Network Control Panel displays various interfaces, from which the subscriber must open Properties for TCP/IP configuration for the Ethernet interface that is installed on the computer. Under Properties are various tabs that allow the user to manually enter the IP network configuration; alternatively a DHCP button is provided. Windows 98 (and 95) computers must be rebooted after the network information has been changed. This is the only way for any new configuration to take effect.

Windows 2000. The subscriber must open the Network and Dial-up Connections panel located under Start Menu -> Settings. From there, double click on the Local Area Connection item and select Properties. From there, double click on the Internet Protocol component. Select the "Obtain an IP address automatically" and "Obtain DNS server address automatically" buttons if the cable operator uses DHCP. Otherwise, select the "Use the following IP address" button as well as the "Use the following DNS server addresses" button and manually enter the address information that was provided by the cable operator.

MAC OS 9. Every new Apple Macintosh computer shipped today is cable modem-ready. Every Mac has a built-in Ethernet interface. Configuration is straightforward. The subscriber opens the TCP/IP Control Panel. The interface is set to Ethernet. The user chooses between manual configuration or DHCP. For manual, all the information is on the same page. After closing the panel and saving the configuration, the new settings take effect immediately; no reboot is necessary.

Linux. The Linux operating system is a little more complicated than either Windows or Mac. There are many different Linux OS distributions (e.g., Debian, Red Hat, Caldera, etc.), and each has a different style of installation. However, if the system is already running, and the user is running an X Windows interface, usually an administration tool is available to the *root user*. Consult the administration manual that came with the specific Linux distribution release for more information.

Sizing the System

It is very important for the cable operator and cable ISP to proactively scale their services and interconnects so that subscribers never experience degradation in service below acceptable levels. What is "acceptable" is, of course, subjective, but broadly used relates directly to the subscriber's view of the quality of the cable modem experience. Occasionally, news reports tell of conflicts that emerge because of the difference between the subscriber's view of performance versus that of the cable operator. Most such conflicts can be explained easily. To that end, this section overviews how the cable operator and ISP scale the bandwidth capacity of their networks.

Transmission Control Protocol Characteristics

Understanding the operational characteristics of the Transmission Control Protocol (TCP) is fundamental to sizing the cable modem system. TCP is a reliable transport protocol and, as such, has the capability to recover from packet loss errors that occur during retransmissions. Though the precise operation of the protocol is complex, a much simplified description of the operation between a sender and receiver will suit our purposes here:

1. The sender transmits a TCP data packet to the receiver. The packet contains a sequence number, which is a byte counter that indicates where in a stream of bytes the beginning of the packet is.

2. The receiver accepts data packets, and notes the sequence number.

3. The receiver sends an acknowledgment packet (ACK) to the sender, which specifies the number of bytes received correctly at this point. If there is a packet "hole," that is, a lost packet between two good ones, the receiver acknowledges packets only up to the hole; neither the hole nor packets beyond are noted.

4. The sender receives the ACK, and knowing what it has sent, examines what the receiver has gotten, then decides if one or more packets need to be retransmitted. The sender also uses time delays, and will resend a packet if an ACK from the receiver gets lost.

TCP also employs a variety of sophisticated flow and congestion control algorithms that are beyond the scope of this simplified description.

Note that a receiver can be a sender, and vice versa. In the case of a subscriber surfing the Web from his or her personal computer, most of the packets from Web servers to the subscriber's Web browser are TCP data packets, while packets from the Web browser back to the server are mostly TCP ACK packets. The size of the ACK packets is always less than the size of the data packets. This means that, from the sender to the receiver, the TCP packet flow is always asymmetric; that is, more bytes per second flow downstream to the subscriber in the form of data packets than flow upstream in the form of ACK packets.

In a normally operating system with no congestion or packet loss, the ratio of the downstream data rate for a World Wide Web TCP connection is approximately 8 to 10 times that of the upstream ACK rate. This means that, for proper sizing in the cable plant, the downstream data channel capacity should be sized at least better than 8 to 10 times the upstream channel capacity.

The flow control nature of TCP has one observable attribute with respect to arrival of ACK packets at the sender. If the rate of ACK packets slows down, the rate of data packets also slows down. In a cable modem system with a predominance of Web-surfing traffic, the downstream TCP data rate is approximately 8 to 10 times the upstream TCP ACK data rate, while information is being transferred from the Web server to the subscriber's computer.

TCP ASYMMETRY In a cable modem system where most traffic is from Web surfing, the downstream TCP data rate is approximately 8 to 10 times the upstream TCP ACK data rate.

Today, much of the traffic on a cable modem system is from the TCP protocol. Other future services and applications will use TCP or other transport protocols. Web-browsing TCP traffic is asymmetric, as are streaming video and audio. In contrast, interactive voice and video is much more symmetric—that is, the data rate flow in each direction (i.e., in the downstream and the upstream) will be approximately the same for the service. But because these symmetric services will be mixed with normal TCP Web-browsing traffic, traffic as a whole will be less asymmetric than pure TCP Web browsing.

An emerging type of public service promotes file sharing among consenting users of the Internet. Such systems rely on a subscriber's personal computer running an application that offers files to the service. For example, one, from Napster (www.napster.com) provides a central Web-based directory of files offered by people with the app loaded. When a user wants to download a file, the service contacts the app on the computer of the person providing the file to transfer the file. If this type of public file-sharing service becomes more widely deployed and used, it will shift the balance between downstream and upstream traffic in a cable modem system, because more traffic will be leaving the subscriber's home than arriving. Therefore, in consideration of this service and emerging services, understanding how to predict, then balance, between asymmetric and symmetric data loads on the cable system is essential.

SYSTEM SIZING Understanding the aggregate packet load, in terms of symmetry, on the cable modem system is important for future sizing of the system.

Sizing a cable modem system is directly tied to understanding the efficiencies of high-speed data channels, with respect to allocated RF bandwidth, as well as the capital dollars spent per homes passed.

Symmetric versus Asymmetric Cable Modem Systems

Recall from Chapter 2 that, initially, cable modem systems were symmetric in nature—they had one downstream data channel and one upstream data channel. These channels were identical in their data-carrying capacity size, and usually provided about 10Mbps of service.

These early systems were operated as LANs; they are distinguished from the modern cable modem system by their use of a "dumb" transverter architecture. This meant that the Internet connection to the cable ISP was located off one of the cable modems in the system. Consequently, traffic from a Web server sender also used the upstream channel to reach a cable modem receiver. This had the effect of blending the traffic load, as just described, so that it was more symmetrical.

The major deficit of these systems was that a 10Mbps downstream channel could not operate at peak efficiency versus a modern 30Mbps downstream channel. Thus, the system could not support as many modems as the modern system; and that 20Mbps of potential downstream data-carrying capacity was wasted. Therefore, these early systems were limited by the symmetrical—one down, one up channel—nature of the system.

Even modern versions of symmetric cable modem systems, which have an "intelligent" headend controller are wasteful. In these systems, traffic from Internet server senders do not consume upstream bandwidth, only downstream bandwidth. Nevertheless, in this architecture, downstream and upstream capacity and RF bandwidth are wasted for these reasons:

- Downstream capacity of 10Mbps or 3Mbps is much less than modern system capacity of 30Mbps. This means that the cable operator loses access to, potentially 20 to 27Mbps for every symmetric channel deployed.

- Based on the asymmetric nature of TCP, the maximum upstream data rate will be approximately 8 to 10 times less than the downstream data rate. This means that approximately 8Mbps of the upstream channel would remain unused by TCP traffic. This suggests that approximately 75 percent of the upstream RF bandwidth is wasted.

MODERN SYMMETRIC SYSTEMS ARE INEFFICIENT Modern, so-called intelligent, headend systems that use one downstream channel and one upstream channel of the same data-carrying capacity waste both downstream and upstream RF bandwidth due to the characteristics of TCP traffic flow.

Modern asymmetric systems, such as those based on the specifications developed for North America, are more efficient than their symmetric predecessors. The reason can be traced to early recognition during standards development that using the highest data rate downstream channel as possible and supporting multiple upstream channels comprise the best approach for efficient RF bandwidth allocation and growth capability to meet subscriber needs. Today, as noted earlier, in the absence of interactive voice and video services, the predominant traffic comes from World Wide Web browsing. This means that until the traffic ratios change, a CMTS only needs an upstream channel that is approximately one-eighth to one-tenth the data-carrying size of the downstream channel. And because modern systems support multiple upstream channels, channels can be added to suit changing the traffic mix or until the downstream channel becomes fully loaded.

The ability to tailor upstream bandwidth to suit the subscriber base means that the cable operator can efficiently allocate RF bandwidth as needed in the plant, on a per-CMTS basis. This scaling model best matches capital dollars to a given subscriber population.

Eventually, the data channels may become full, requiring the cable operator to deploy another CMTS in the same plant or to subdivide the plant with HFC node splitting.

Adding Another CMTS and Node Splitting

In service, a CMTS cable modem system is much like an Ethernet switch in a business office. If the capacity of the switch is too heavily loaded, users get degraded performance. One remedy is to buy another switch, interconnect it with a high-speed link, and distribute the load. The same is true with cable modem systems. Eventually, the RF data channels will become loaded to the point at which performance degrades. At this time, the cable operator has at least two choices:

- To allocate additional downstream and upstream RF channels, and install another CMTS.

- If not enough RF spectrum is available, to split the fiber node(s), leave the old CMTS connected to the old nodes, and connect the new CMTS to the new nodes.

Both of these methods effectively double the amount of data-carrying capacity in the downstream and upstream. Choosing which method to use will be based on the cable operator's business plan and budget. The power of node splitting is far-reaching, and can evolve over time, following traffic demands placed on the system; for example, a cable operator may only split the nodes where the data traffic requirements are high, and leave the others alone until capacity is reached. This incremental method allows cable operators to spend capital to follow revenues received from the targeted area of the cable plant.

It is important to note, however, that node splitting may affect subscriber IP address assignments. When a node is split to upgrade capacity, a new CMTS may be placed on the new fiber node, depending on the plans of the cable operator. If this new placement requires that the old IP subnetwork be renumbered or resubnetted, or if a new IP subnet is installed, then certain current subscribers will be directly affected. If they are using DHCP, these subscribers may need to reboot their computers and cable modems to obtain the new addresses to continue operation. Personal computers that have been manually configured will need to be manually reconfigured (as discussed previously in this chapter), then rebooted. The cable operator should send advance notice of this event, followed by directions to the affected subscribers.

MINI-FIBER NODES When node splitting leaves an HHP of a 50 to 100 homes or less, it will be possible to move the future mini-CMTS out of the headend to be coresident with the fiber node.

Ultimately, node splitting can continue until the HHP for the node is fewer than 100 homes. This is called a *mini-fiber node*. Technologically speaking, it is possible to construct lower-cost CMTS systems and move the CMTS into the network to be located at the mini-fiber node.

Clearly, a cable operator today has a great deal of scaling capacity in modern cable modem systems and HFC plants. However, other areas, aside from scaling cable network data-carrying capacity affect cable modem performance.

Cable Modem Performance: Separating Fact from Fiction

Simply put, subscribers of high-speed broadband services are paying for shorter delays when accessing the Internet. If dial-up modems met that demand, subscribers probably would stick with those. But as we know, the World Wide Web is quickly evolving toward more capacity-hungry applications and services, and dial-up modems world just can't cut it. Users want quick access, and they are willing to pay for it.

Initially, subscribers were very pleased by the performance enabled by cable modems . But all too soon, from time to time, performance degraded beyond acceptable limits. Subscribers and cable ISPs pointed the finger of blame at cable modem technology. As usual, however, where to place the blame was less clear-cut in fact. As mentioned at the beginning of this chapter, the cable modem system is just one facet of the larger system that brings the Internet into the home. As such, there are many places in the system where things can go awry. Some of these places are discussed in this section.

Plant RF Noise

We explained earlier in the book that ingress noise in the upstream channel has been an issue for cable operators. Though the advent of HFC upgrades and better plant management reduced ingress noise dramatically, the first cable modems were deployed over all-coaxial systems, which were symmetric systems that did not use forward error correction (FEC). Some of these systems are still in place today and they are significantly less robust in the presence of noise than are modern systems that employ FEC and better channel RF modulation and demodulation systems.

The good news is that all cable operators are quickly moving to deploy these modern cable modem systems and to upgrade their plants to HFC. In the future, RF noise problems affecting cable modem performance will continue to be less of a problem. That is not to say that ingress noise cannot creep into a system; it can, but now it can be quickly found and remedied. Furthermore, management and monitoring equipment for modern cable modem systems make it possible to remotely monitor RF plant health by observing CMTS and cable modem statistics such as packet error rates, FEC performance, and excessive modem registrations. This last point means that if a cable modem senses that it is disconnected from the CMTS either through timeouts or packet error problems, it will reboot and reregister. If this is happening too often, it is a sign of a plant RF problem. Likewise, degraded packet error performance can be correlated to regions of the cable plant, and this correlation will help operators to more quickly locate any problems.

Capacity Allocation

Recall from Chapter 3 that early deployed, so-called dumb, cable modem systems could not adequately control the allocation of upstream and downstream data capacity resources; nor could some of the first deployed modern systems. They delivered bandwidth in a best-effort manner, as does the Internet. In contrast, take an early subscriber and move him or her from a dial-up modem to a lightly loaded cable modem system, and he or she will be rewarded with high-speed Internet access.

Complicating the issue was that early service agreements didn't really address delivered bandwidth rates. Not surprisingly, as the number of active simultaneous subscribers increased on these systems, the available shared bandwidth decreased and users experienced degraded service. Several remedies are available to cable operators for avoiding these problems:

1. Be clear with subscribers up front about what they will experience with service over time.

2. Deploy a cable modem system that has adequate capacity allocation controls built into it.

3. Allocate one or more tiers of bandwidth allocation, and charge subscribers appropriately. Tailor capacity to cap subscribers' use of upstream data capacity to agreed-to limits.

4. Scale the system to ensure acceptable performance for subscribers.

Today, more systems are being deployed with sufficient controls. The technology is, however, only as good as the policies and practices of the cable operator and cable ISP that enable those controls.

Oversubscription

Every shared network, network link, and server in consumer use (e.g., ISP, telephone, and email services) are always oversubscribed. Service providers continue to take on more subscribers than their base capacity permits, because statistics indicate that, typically, all those subscribers will not use the network at the same time. Oversubscription in general is a good thing. However, too much can lead to performance problems that affect every subscriber. The trick is for the operator and ISP to balance oversubscription with performance, especially when the system is growing.

If, on the other hand, the cable modem system itself is undersubscribed, and there are no RF or "cockpit" errors with the cable modem system, yet the subscribers are complaining of degraded performance, the problem is elsewhere in the network. Nevertheless, whenever users have problems with cable networks, they tend to blame the cable modem.

In fact, any one of the following noncable modem-related problems can cause degraded performance:

- The cable operator backend network is overloaded.
- The link between the operator and the ISP is undersized.
- The cable ISP's backend network is overloaded.
- The cable ISP servers are overloaded.
- The cable ISP's link to the Internet is undersized.

The most typical problem is that the backend network or the link to the Internet is undersized. Why? As often is the case, it's cost-related. It costs money to increase capacity, and the subscriber population might be growing faster than the operator's or ISP's planned upgrades. There may also be cockpit and operator errors at any point in the network.

NOTE It doesn't matter whether it is a cable system or a DSL system. If the operator's or ISP's server or backend network elements (links and routers) are too oversubscribed, all users will experience unacceptable delays to the Internet. However, they will always point at the broadband modem system as being the culprit when in fact the problem is located elsewhere.

SONET in the Backend Network

The cable industry is undergoing a backend network evolution. MSOs can take advantage of linking headends using Synchronous Optical Network

(SONET) technology, a multimedia interconnection technology. When deploying SONET in the backend network, cable operators can use the same fiber and switching system for all their needs, including analog video distribution, as well as for digital distribution, including video, telephony, and Internet. This means that, as operators update their own backend networks to SONET, they are laying down a network technology that can support many future telecommunications services.

Developed by CableLabs in the early 1990s, SONET has three tiers: the bottom is the original headend, the next level is the regional hub, and top is the super-headend, as illustrated in Figure 4.2.

The first step in the evolution of this architecture was to interconnect headends to a regional hub with highly reliable, self-healing SONET technology, then to move all nonlocal program origination from the headends to the regional hub. For example, this means moving the satellite dishes

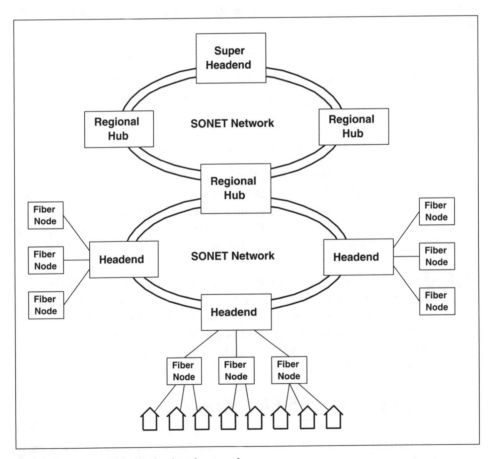

Figure 4.2   SONET in the backend network.

which receive nonlocal programming, e.g., Home Box Office, from the headend to the regional hub.

The second step was to interconnect the regional hubs with a superhub, using highly reliable, self-healing SONET technology, then move all nonlocal program origination to the superhub.

Summary

This chapter presented an overview of providing Internet services to subscribers through a cable operator network. There are a number of challenges that a cable operator and Internet service provider must overcome in order to provide consistent service to all new and old subscribers. These challenges include:

- Provisioning new subscribers with cable modem service. This may be accomplished via manual or automatic means.

- Providing servers and services which meet the needs of the subscribers. For example, electronic mail servers, Web servers, etc.

- Resizing the data carrying capacity of the system to meet the needs of subscribers. For example, this includes installing higher capacity links to the Internet, installing additional CMTS facilities in a headend, or fiber node splitting if the subscriber demand exceeds the capacity of the current data channel capacities.

- Locating and fixing RF plant noise problems promptly that interfere with high-speed data communications.

In addition, many cable operators are following the CableLabs' plan of converting backend networks to SONET technology. This permits the backend network to grow quickly in capacity as well as increase the reliability of the entire system.

For Further Information

There are two major nationwide cable ISPs: Excite@Home and Road Runner. More information about them and their services can be found at their Web sites:

Excite@Home: www.home.net

Road Runner: www.rr.com

CHAPTER

5

The DOCSIS Project

As touched on in the chronology in Chapter 1, the North American cable industry established a process in early 1996 with the objective of creating a suite of specifications for high-speed data-over-cable services. The process was initiated under the auspices of the Multimedia Cable Network System (MCNS) Partners Limited, and later transferred to CableLabs. Under the CableLabs auspices, it became known as the Data Over Cable Service Interface Specification (DOCSIS) project. The intent of DOCSIS was to rapidly develop a suite of specifications that would lead to multiple-vendor interoperability and availability of retail off-the-shelf cable modems. The DOCSIS specifications cover:

- Cable Modem (CM) and Cable Modem Termination System (CMTS)
- Radio Frequency Interface (RFI)
- CMTS network side interface
- CM customer premises interface
- A suite of management system interfaces, which include:
  - Cable service Management Information Base (MIB)
  - RF interface MIB

- Baseline Privacy MIB
- Baseline Privacy Interface (BPI)
- Telephone Return Interface
- Acceptance Test Plan

The RFI specification is the fundamental specification that defines the physical layer (PHY) and media access control (MAC) layers of the DOCSIS system. Consequently, by itself, RFI is frequently referred to as DOCSIS, because all other specifications build upon it. But it is important to keep in mind that DOCSIS is more than just the RFI specification.

As the fundamental specification, the RFI was the first of the set created. The first draft appeared as DOCSIS Version 1.0 in December 1996. It has since been updated five times as Interim Releases between March 21, 1997, through November 5, 1999. Cable modems and CMTSs built between 1998 through 2000 follow the DOCSIS V1.0 specification. A major revision to DOCSIS V1.0 first appeared on March 11, 1999, and was given the label of DOCSIS V1.1. The fourth interim revision to DOCSIS V1.1 was published on April 7, 2000. DOCSIS V1.1 added support for quality of service (QoS).

NOTE For more information on DOCSIS, surf to the public entry section on the CableLabs Web site, www.cablemodem.com.

This chapter focuses mainly on the RF interfaces as defined in the public DOCSIS specification document SP-RFIv1.1-I04-000407 and on the operation of the protocol. We will not attempt to cover the numerous details of this DOCSIS RFI specification in this chapter; rather we will explain the DOCSIS protocol operation at a high level. Specifically, we will omit, as much as possible, definitions of such terms as bits, bytes, timers, and certain parameters. We will, instead, focus on:

- DOCSIS architecture
- CM and CMTS protocol stacks
- Downstream and upstream channels
- Ranging and minislots
- Packet sizes
- CM bandwidth requests and allocation
- Quality of service
- Management messages exchanged between the CMTS and CM

- Baseline privacy
- Cable modem registration
- Simple Network Management Protocol (SNMP)
- Multicast support

Reference Architecture

The DOCSIS system has a data-over-cable reference architecture, which is shown in Figure 5.1. The purpose of the architecture is to itemize the functional pieces of the system (e.g., cable modem, CMTS, etc.) and the interfaces between these pieces. The DOCSIS specification details the operation of protocols and services over these interfaces, which include:

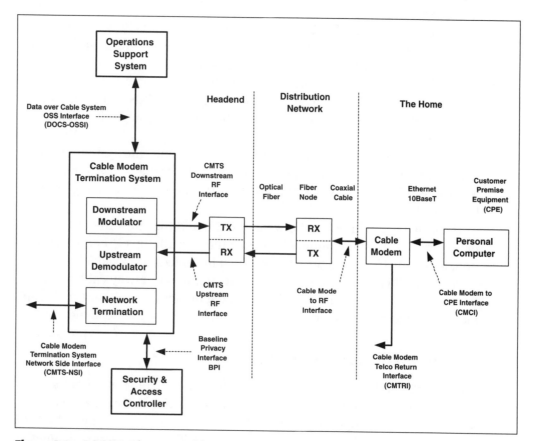

Figure 5.1   DOCSIS reference architecture.

- Cable Modem Termination System Downstream RF Interface
- Cable Modem Termination System Upstream RF Interface
- Cable Modem Termination System Network Side Interface (CMTS-NSI)
- Baseline Privacy Interface (BPI)
- Data over Cable Systems Operations Support System (OSS) Interface (DOCS-OSSI)
- Cable Modem to Customer Premises Equipment (CPE) Interface (CMCI)
- Cable Modem Telephone Return Interface (CMTRI)

The CMTS downstream and upstream interfaces define the over-the-RF cable protocol, which connects the CMTS to every cable modem. The interface is implemented via a coaxial cable RF transmitter and multiple receivers in the downstream and multiple transmitters and one receiver in the upstream.

The function of the CMTS NSI is to exchange packets between the CMTS and the backend network of the cable operator. This is most often implemented as a 100Mbps Ethernet connection.

The BPI provides for link security over the RF shared media. The management of the BPI is a logical function within the CMTS and each CM. The purpose of the system is to protect the privacy of subscriber communications.

The OSS interface is the management interface into the system. It is a logical function, which may operate via the NSI interface. It is implemented as a Simple Network Management Protocol agent running on the CMTS and each CM.

The CMCI is the interface between the CM and the subscriber's premises. It is most commonly implemented as a 10Mbps Ethernet connection, although, Universal Serial Bus (USB) interfaces are available.

The CMTRI is an interface in a CM that supports one-way cable operation. The CMTRI is an interface to an analog modem, which uses a dial-up modem connection to send packets back upstream to the headend.

Shared Media HFC Architecture

The DOCSIS systems implements an intelligent controller architecture whereby the CMTS controls resources on shared downstream and shared upstream channels operating on a hybrid fiber-coaxial cable plant. A CMTS may support more than one upstream channel. This architecture is illustrated in Figure 5.2.

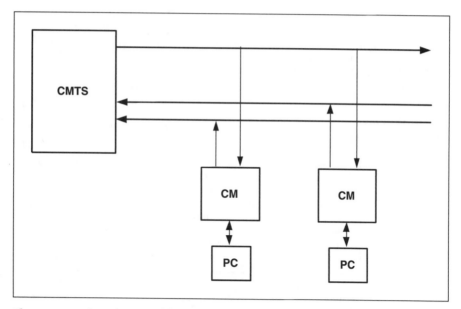

Figure 5.2   Shared HFC architecture.

WORKS ON ALL COAXIAL PLANTS Even though the DOCSIS specification calls for HFC operation, the protocol runs equally well over all-coaxial plants.

In the shared media architecture shown in Figure 5.2, the CMTS typically offers one downstream channel and multiple upstream channels. The result is that all CMs listen on the shared downstream. During the course of registration, the CMTS will assign each CM to an appropriate upstream channel; a CMTS may assign a CM to another upstream channel for load-sharing reasons, that is, to balance the load on all upstream channels.

CM and CMTS Protocol Stacks and Data Forwarding

The DOCSIS CM and CMTS share the same protocol stack architecture which is illustrated in Figure 5.3. CM and CMTS are each IP hosts which make use of the DOCSIS MAC and PHY as well as Ethernet. Each host is identified by a 48-bit IEEE MAC address. The Ethernet interface must operate with DEC-Intel-Xerox (DIX) original Ethernet or IEEE 802.3 LLC framing. IP, Internet Control Message Protocol (ICMP), and Address Resolution Protocol (ARP) are supported at the network layer. Each CM and

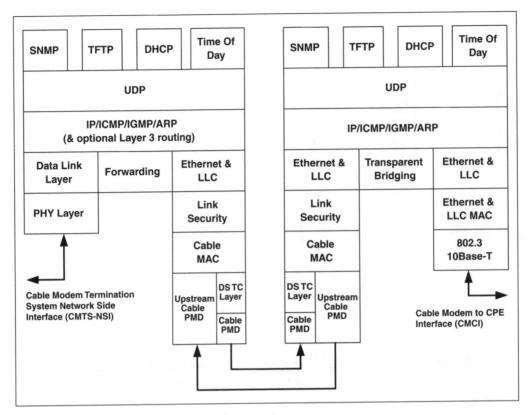

Figure 5.3   CM and CMTS protocol stacks.

CMTS has User Defined Protocol (UDP) transport support, as well as the application services of Simple Network Management Protocol (SNMP), Trivial File Transfer Protocol (TFTP), Distributed Host Configuration Protocol (DHCP), and Time of Day protocol.

The downstream PHY layer is composed of a transport convergence (TC) sublayer, which takes DOCSIS MAC packets in and out of Moving Picture Evaluation Group Version 2 (MPEG2) Transport Stream (TS) frames, in addition to the physical media-dependent (PMD) support (transmitter and receiver) for the downstream cable plant. The upstream PMD is composed of a DOCSIS-specified upstream channel, which is organized as packet bursts. A PMD is used in standards as the bottom layer of the physical layer that connects to the transmission media. It is that segment of the architecture that directly attaches to, therefore is very dependent on, the type of media to which it is attached.

The functions of the CMTS protocol stack may include IP routing or transparent Ethernet bridging. The CM is a transparent Ethernet bridge;

the bridge function supports IP over Ethernet, and may support the bridging of other protocols, for example, EtherTalk and the like.

The CM and CMTS may optionally support the IEEE 802.1d spanning protocol. This protocol eliminates Layer 2 bridging loops when the same Ethernet segment is connected to two or more CMs. If a CM is to be placed in commercial, as opposed to residential, service, the CM and CMTS must support the spanning tree protocol standard.

The CMTS is a three-port bridge or router. The three interfaces are the NSI, the downstream channel, and the upstream channel. When operating as a bridge, the CMTS acts as an Ethernet switch. When acting as a router, the CMTS must follow the Internet Engineering Task Force (IETF) Router Requirements, as defined in IETF document RFC-1812. In general, these specify:

- IP packets or Ethernet frames are not duplicated.

- IP packets or Ethernet frames that sit in queues too long are discarded.

- IP packets or Ethernet frames within a given service flow (defined later in this chapter) are not delivered out of order to the CM.

In addition, when the CMTS is operating as a router, connectivity between cable modems is accomplished via IP forwarding, not through Ethernet bridging.

Before forwarding a unicast packet on the downstream channel, the CMTS must associate the packet with the destination CM. During normal operation, the CMTS observes MAC registration messages as well as normal Ethernet frames to build a large learning bridge table, which associates CM and CPE devices (e.g., personal computer) with a service flow used to send packets to and from the CM.

The operation of the MAC bridge or IP forwarder may differ from a standard implementation, if required to enforce local policy decisions. For example, an upstream Ethernet frame received from an upstream channel may be restricted to be forwarded only to the NSI, as opposed to the NSI and the downstream channel, as would happen with a normal bridge.

CM-Specific Forwarding Rules

The CM implements a learning bridge algorithm both to discover and to remember the IEEE 48-bit MAC address of computers that are connected to the CMCI port. In addition, DOCSIS implements a set of extensions to more precisely control the learning table.

- The CM learns of 48-bit MAC addresses by observing the address information within Ethernet frames; or the addresses may be administratively provisioned by the cable operator. Provisioned addresses take precedence over learned addresses.

- The CM has a physical maximum number of addresses it can learn; this value is cable modem (vendor)-dependent. When the learning table is full, the CM is restricted from replacing or aging any previously learned addresses.

- The CM is restricted from using nonvolatile memory for retaining addresses over a soft reset or power cycle.

Downstream Channel Specifications

The DOCSIS specification calls out two different downstream channel configurations, as shown in Table 5.1. Each configuration is based on the ITU J.83 Annex B standard for digital broadcast channels. Two modulations types are used: 64 Quadrature Amplitude Modulation (64 QAM) and 256 QAM. The ITU J.83 specification documents the forward error correction (FEC) details for each modulation type. As FEC adds overhead for its operations, the remaining data rate available to be used is called the *information rate*. This is the data capacity available for use by DOCSIS for moving MAC packets downstream.

The downstream channel is frequency tunable from 91MHz to 857MHz ±30kHz. A CM supports both 64 QAM and 256 QAM downstream channel operation.

Downstream Transmission Convergence Sublayer

DOCSIS requires that MAC packets be transferred downstream, encapsulated within the MPEG2 Transport Stream (MPEG-TS) frame structure, as

Table 5.1 Downstream Channel Details

PARAMETER	64 QAM	256 QAM
Bits/Symbol	6	8
Symbol Rate (symbols/second)	5056941	5360537
Channel Width (MHz)	6	6
Raw Bit Rate (Pre-FEC, Mbps)	30.34	42.88
Information Rate (Mbps)	26.97	38.81

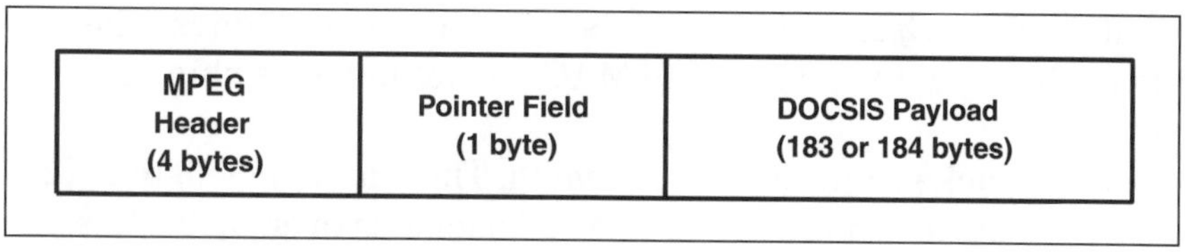

Figure 5.4   MPEG packet format.

shown in Figures 5.4 and 5.5, following the specifications in the ITU-T H.222.0 standard.

Essentially, an MPEG-TS frame is 188 bytes long with the first 4 bytes comprising a header, leaving 184 bytes for payload data. Within the header is a 13-bit field called the Program Identifier (PID), which identifies the type of material within the payload. DOCSIS has reserved a well-known value of 0×1FFE (in hex) to indicate that the payload contains DOCSIS information. Digital video frames use a different PID value, allowing, for example, the intermixing of digital video frames with DOCSIS frames. Each DOCSIS receiver in a CM only selects frames with the DOCSIS PID value.

Another value in the MPEG-TS header, called the Payload Unit Start Indicator (PUSI), if set, indicates that the first byte following the header is interpreted as the Pointer Field. The presence of the Pointer Field indicates that within this payload is the start of a DOCSIS MAC packet. The value of the Pointer Field represents the number of bytes to skip over to locate the beginning of the MAC packet. The DOCSIS downstream channel in the CMTS has the option of filling gaps between MAC

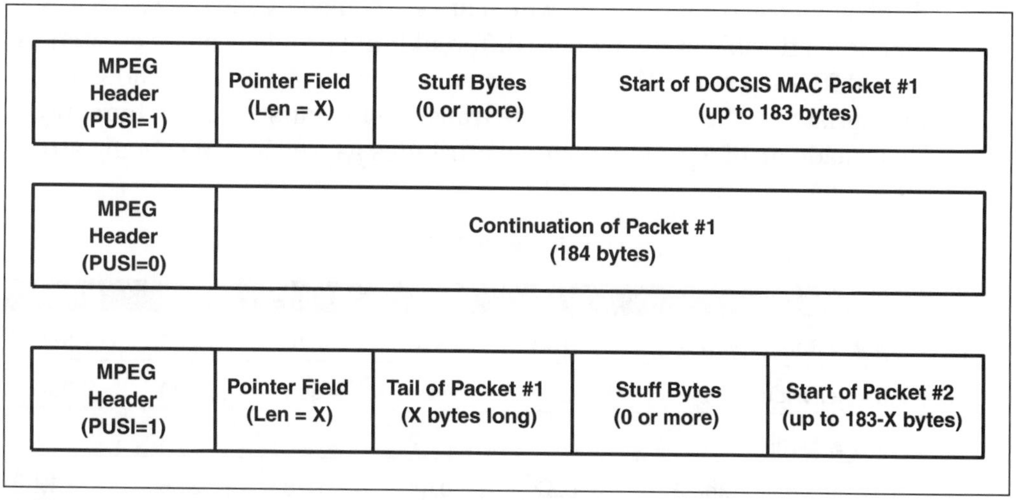

Figure 5.5   DOCSIS MAC packets in MPEG frames.

packets with a *Stuff Byte* whose value is 0×FF (hex) or all ones. The algorithm for locating the start of the MAC packet includes skipping over Stuff Bytes.

DOCSIS MAC packets are variable in length. The minimum length is 72 bytes; the maximum size of the DOCSIS MAC packet is over 1500 bytes. Clearly, then, at most, two DOCSIS MAC packets can fit within the 183-or 184-byte payload of the MPEG-TS frame. Likewise, it takes several frames to transfer a large DOCSIS MAC packet. The use of the PUSI and the Pointer Field facilitates locating the beginning of a MAC packet anywhere within the MPEG-TS payload.

Upstream Channel Specifications

DOCSIS specifies a number of choices for upstream channel data rates that must be implemented by the CM. Essentially, there are two modulation options: Quadrature Phase Shift Keying (QPSK) or 16 QAM. There are five choices for symbol rates, ranging from 160 ksymbols/second to 2.56 Msymbols/second. Tables 5.2 and 5.3 summarize the upstream channel.

The upstream channel is frequency agile over the range of 5MHz to 42MHz. A CM supports all upstream channel symbol rates, QPSK, and 16 QAM

Upstream Burst Specifications

A CMTS can support multiple upstream channels. Transmissions on a single channel use packet bursts, which are scheduled by the CMTS. DOCSIS supports a flexible system where different burst profiles can be created by the CMTS for use by CMs on an upstream channel. A CM will follow the appropriate profile to construct the transmission burst. A given burst profile is made up of a general channel attributes as well as CM specific attrib-

Table 5.2   Upstream Channel Details for QPSK

PARAMETER	QPSK	QPSK	QPSK	QPSK	QPSK
Symbol Rate (ksym/sec)	160	320	640	1,280	2,560
Channel Width (kHz)	200	400	800	1,600	3,200
Bits per Symbol	2	2	2	2	2
Raw Data Rate (Mbps)	0.32	0.64	1.28	2.56	5.12

Table 5.3 Upstream Channel Details for 16 QAM

PARAMETER	16 QAM	16 QAM	16 QAM	16 QAM	16 QAM
Symbol Rate (ksym/sec)	160	320	640	1,280	2,560
Channel Width (kHz)	200	400	800	1,600	3,200
Bits per Symbol	4	4	4	4	4
Raw Data Rate (Mbps)	0.640	1.28	2.56	5.12	10.24

utes called the Unique Burst Profile. Tables 5.4 and 5.5 show the general and unique attributes.

NOTE The DOCSIS systems provides broad flexibility to tune upstream channel attributes to the actual cable network at deployment time.

Certain attributes of these burst profiles have operational details that are beyond the technical scope of this chapter. They have been listed here in Tables 5.4 and 5.5 to illustrate the broad capability of the DOCSIS specification for controlling upstream packet bursts on a per-channel and per-CM basis. Attributes that contribute to packet bursts length are detailed in the following:

Table 5.4 Burst Profile Attributes

CHANNEL ATTRIBUTES	CONFIGURATION SETTINGS
Modulation	QPSK or 16 QAM
Differential Encoding	On or Off
Preamble Length	0–1024 bits
Preamble Value Offset	0–1022
FEC Error Correction	0 to 10 (0 means no FEC)
FEC Codeword Information Bytes	Fixed: 16 to 253
	Shortened: 16 to 253
Scrambler Seed	15 bits
Maximum Burst Length (minislots)	0 to 255
Guard Time	5 to 255 symbols
Last Codeword Length	Fixed or Shortened
Scrambler	On or Off

Table 5.5 Unique Burst Profile

UNIQUE ATTRIBUTES	CONFIGURATION SETTINGS
Power Level	+8 to +55 dBmV (16 QAM)
	+8 to +58 dBmV (QPSK) in 1dB steps
Offset Frequency	Range = ±32 kHz; increment 1Hz
	Implemented to ±10 Hz of accuracy in the CM
Ranging Offset	0 to 216 − 1 increments of 6.25 μseconds/64
Burst Length	1 to 255 minislots
Transmit Equalizer	Up to 64 coefficients; 4 bytes per, 2 real 2 complex

Modulation. Capability to set the modulation for this packet burst profile to be QPSK or 16 QAM.

Preamble Length. Sets the length of the preamble for the burst. For QPSK, the preamble length uses only the power of two lengths, starting with the sequence 0, 2, 4, ... up to 1024 bits. For 16 QAM, the preamble length uses only power of two lengths, starting with the sequence 0, 4, 8, ... up to 1024 bits.

Forward Error Correction. Sets the value of error protection used by the Reed-Solomon FEC algorithm. The higher the value the more bits can be detected and corrected in burst packets received by the CMTS. The higher the value, the more FEC overhead bytes are added to the burst length, hence reducing channel efficiency in favor of reducing errors. In general, the FEC value is set at deployment time and tuned by the cable operator. The number of additional bytes added to the burst is two times the value per FEC *codeword*. An FEC value of 0 means there is no FEC included in the packet burst. Details on the FEC codeword and impact on packet burst length is discussed later in this chapter in the section titled "Upstream Packet Burst Construction" on page 128.

FEC Codeword Information Bytes. Specifies the length of the codeword to be used by the Reed-Solomon FEC algorithm. This also is discussed later in the "Upstream Packet Burst Construction" section.

Maximum Burst Length. Specifies the maximum length of the burst, expressed as the number of minislots that the CM may allocate for the burst. If the value is 0, the burst length is variable for this burst type, and the length is controlled by the CMTS on a per-upstream burst allocation. Minislots and ranging are discussed in the next section.

Guard Time. Specifies the length of the burst guard time length in modulation symbols.

Last Codeword Length. Specifies fixed or shortened. When fixed, the CM must transmit the entirety of the last codeword, even if it contains no MAC packet data. When shortened, the CM is allowed to truncate the length of the last codeword to contain just a MAC packet, thereby making the channel slightly more efficient. This is especially useful for burst profiles that have longer FEC codeword information bytes.

Burst Length. The CMTS will fix the size of the packet burst for each CM, up to the maximum. If the maximum length is variable, this value is set on a burst-by-burst basis by the CMTS.

Ranging and Minislot Length

Ranging CMs in the DOCSIS system happens initially just after each CM is powered up and begins to interact with the CMTS. (The details of the protocol for bringing a CM online are discussed in the section "MAC-Specific Messages" later in this chapter.)

DOCSIS uses a *time offset* for ranging that is in increments of 6.25 microseconds (µsec) divided by 64, yielding a length of time of 0.09765625 µsec. This length was chosen to be one-quarter the time to transmit a modulation symbol at the highest symbol rate of 2.56Msym/sec. The 6.25 µsec value, called the *Timebase Tick*, is key for DOCSIS. Not only is it used as the basis for obtaining the ranging increment, it is also used as the basis for calculating the length of a minislot. Specifically, a minislot is a power of two multiple of Timebase Ticks (variable T), selected from the sequence of 2, 4, 8, 16, 32, 64, or 128. This results in the following µsec time length options for a minislot: 12.5, 25, 50, 100, 200, 400, and 800.

The symbol rates selected for the upstream channel are directly related to the Timebase Tick. The data-carrying capacity of a minislot is based on the modulation symbol rate and the modulation type: QPSK or 16 QAM. Table 5.6 lists the permutations of minislots sizes based on symbol rate, modulation type, and T.

This table illustrates that DOCSIS has flexibility in deciding what size minislot to use for an upstream channel. The specific sizing has been left up to vendor discretion in the implementation of the scheduling algorithms within the CMTS. In DOCSIS, the CMTS allocates upstream data capacity resources in multiples of minislots on a CM-by-CM basis. That said, recall from Table 5.4, that the maximum burst size allowable in DOCSIS is 255 times the minislot size. Clearly, the minislot size should not be so big that the end of a packet burst leaves too much unused space. Likewise, it

Table 5.6 Bytes per Minislot Values

SYMBOLS RATE SYM/SEC	160000	320000	640000	1280000	2560000
Symbol Period (μsec)	6.25	3.125	1.5625	0.78125	0.390625
Symbols/Timebase Tick	1	2	4	8	16
QPSK bits/symbol	2	2	2	2	2
QPSK bits/timetick	2	4	8	16	32
MiniSlotSize T=2 (bytes)	N/A	1	2	4	8
MiniSlotSize T=4	1	2	4	8	16
MiniSlotSize T=8	2	4	8	16	32
MiniSlotSize T=16	4	8	16	32	64
MiniSlotSize T=32	8	16	32	64	128
MiniSlotSize T=64	16	32	64	128	256
MiniSlotSize T=128	32	64	128	256	512
16 QAM bits/symbol	4	4	4	4	4
16 QAM bits/timetick	4	8	16	32	64
MiniSlotSize T=2 (bytes)	1	2	4	8	16
MiniSlotSize T=4	2	4	8	16	32
MiniSlotSize T=8	4	8	16	32	64
MiniSlotSize T=16	8	16	32	64	128
MiniSlotSize T=32	16	32	64	128	256
MiniSlotSize T=64	32	64	128	256	512
MiniSlotSize T=128	64	128	256	512	1024

should not be so small that is does not support the maximum Ethernet packet size of 1500 bytes, plus DOCSIS MAC and packet burst overhead. Since 1500 bytes/255 is 5.9 bytes, the next larger minislot size is 8 bytes. This suggests that, in actual deployment, the minimum size minislot will be no less than 8 bytes in length.

Upstream Packet Burst Construction

Figure 5.6 shows four examples of the construction of a DOCSIS upstream packet burst. The Reed-Solomon FEC algorithm provides error detection

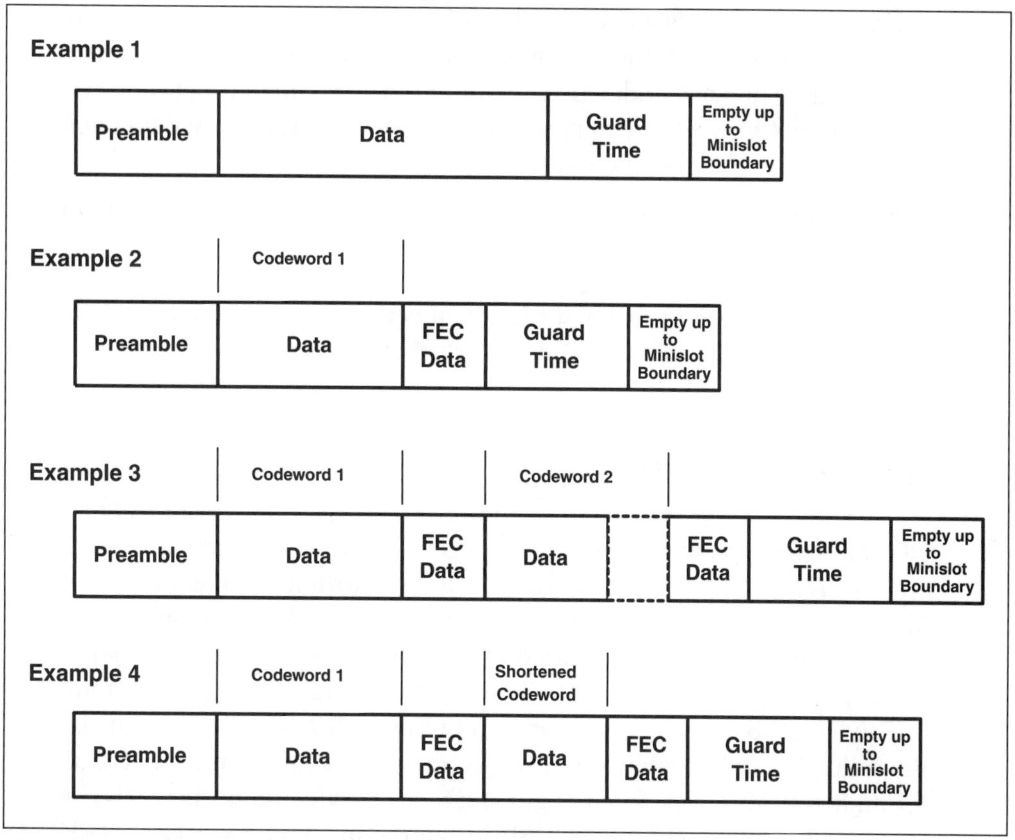

Figure 5.6 DOCSIS packet burst structure.

and correction for a specific block of data called a codeword. In DOCSIS, codewords can vary from a minimum of 16 bytes to a maximum of 253 bytes. The codeword size is set on a burst profile-by-burst profile basis, including being turned off. The redundant information that the FEC algorithm adds when turned on is called *FEC parity bytes*. The number of bytes used is also specified on a burst profile-by-burst profile basis. Reed-Solomon is a well-known and accepted method to provide forward error correction over blocks of data.

Specifically, in this figure note the following:

Example 1. Shows a packet burst consisting of the preamble, data, and guard time. In this example, FEC is turned off. In addition, any remaining time from the end of the guard time to beginning of the next minislot boundary is left unused, that is, empty.

Example 2. Shows a packet burst with FEC turned on, where the length of the codeword exactly matches the length of the data.

Example 3. Shows a packet burst where the length of the data is longer than the length of the codeword size, resulting in the use of two codewords. The Last Codeword attribute of the channel is set to Fixed, resulting in wasted empty space between the end of the data packet and the end of the codeword.

Example 4. Shows the benefits of the Last Codeword attribute being set to Shortened.

NOTE In all these examples, the length of both the preamble and guard time is adjustable and is set by the CMTS in actual operation.

MAC Packet Format

DOCSIS uses the same MAC packet format for the upstream and downstream. The only difference between the two formats is that some DOCSIS MAC-specific management messages are used only in the upstream and downstream. These are discussed in detail in the section "MAC-Specific Messages" on page 141. The MAC packet has header and data sections.

The DOCSIS MAC header is shown in Figure 5.7. The header consists of the following fields, which are always present: Frame Control (FC), MAC Parameters (MAC_PARM), Length (LEN) or Service Identifier (SID), and Header Check Sum (HCS). DOCSIS supports an Extended Header (EHDR) format, which is optional. The fields have the following meanings:

FC. Identifies the type of MAC header.

MAC_PARM. Added parameters based on the type of Mac header.

LEN/SID. Length of the MAC package as calculated from the length of the Extended Header (if present) and the number of bytes following the HCS field. If the MAC packet is a Request Packet (see "MAC-Specific Messages"), this field contains a SID value. The SID is a unique value assigned to the CM during the initialization and registration process.

EHDR. Contains supplemental information pertinent to the handling of the MAC packet.

HCS. Contains the Cyclic Redundancy Check (CRC), to protect the preceding fields, and is used to indicate one or more bit errors in the MAC header.

The minimum size of the MAC header is 6 bytes, plus the size of the EHDR field, if present.

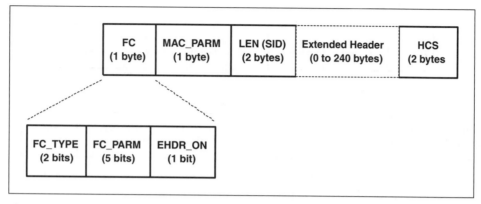

Figure 5.7   MAC header format.

The FC field is encoded as three fields: FC_TYPE field, FC_PARM field, and EHDR_ON field, as shown in Table 5.7.

FC_TYPE field. Indicates how the entire packet should be treated. There are two major uses in DOCSIS: a packet containing an Ethernet packet, and a packet containing a MAC-specific header. (Note: DOCSIS was designed to carry an ATM cell in a MAC packet, but this has not been put to use.)

   In the downstream direction, recall that the Stuff Byte contains a value of 0×FF (hex) or 0b1111111 (binary). This reserved value means that the values of the FC field can never be all ones, or 0×FF (hex).

FC_PARM field. Interpreted based on the FC_TYPE value.

EHDR_ON field. Indicates that the EHDR field is present in the MAC header. This is used for functional extensibility beyond the basic MAC header.

Table 5.7   FC Field Encoding

FC FIELD	SIZE	USAGE
FC_TYPE	2 bits	MAC Frame Control Type Field:
	00	Data PDU packet
	01	ATM PDU packet
	10	Reserved MAC Header
	11	MAC-Specific Header
FC_PARM	5 bits	Parameter bits; use depends on FC_TYPE value
EHDR_ON	1 bit	When 1, indicates presence of EHDR

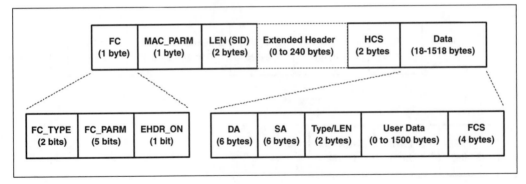

Figure 5.8   Ethernet packet PDU in MAC packet.

DOCSIS fundamentally is a variable length packet protocol. The intent is to transmit variable length Ethernet packets as efficiently as possible. Figure 5.8 illustrates the format of a MAC packet without an EHDR field that contains an Ethernet PDU. The total length of the packet is variable, from 70 to 1528 bytes. Note that this size accommodates all versions of Ethernet packets and the supplemental information required by the IEEE 802.1p and IEEE 802.1Q standards. Note in this example that the HCS value provides error detection coverage over the MAC header fields. The Ethernet Frame CheckSum (FCS) is carried in the packet and provides error detection of the Ethernet frame.

> **NOTE** DOCSIS V1.1 requires that the CM silently skip over any MAC packet whose type indicates ATM Cell.
>
> DOCSIS has provided for future growth by reserving a packet type that can be used for future extensibility.

Bandwidth Allocation Architecture

The DOCSIS system uses a downstream grant message called an Upstream Bandwidth Allocation message which is referred to as a MAP message. The CMTS periodically issues a MAP for each supported upstream channel. DOCSIS has five different types of allocation grants:

- Request interval (R), for CMs to transmit bandwidth requests upstream.
- REQ/Data interval (X), for CMs to transmit immediate mode data packets.

- Initial maintenance interval (I), for defining where new, not yet ranged, modems can attempt to send their first transmissions.

- Station maintenance interval (S), used for periodic station ranging adjustment.

- Data interval (D), allocated to one CM to transmit data. This is a direct grant of one or more minislots.

In addition, DOCSIS can provide acknowledgment (A) feedback to a CM. This feedback is used to let CMs know that their previous request was heard, but that no direct grant could be given in this interval. A special element in the MAC called the null information element (N) is used to indicate the last minislot allocatable by this MAP message.

DOCSIS uses a system very similar to the generic request and grant mechanism presented in Chapter 3. Figure 5.9 illustrates the DOCSIS mechanism of allocating upstream bandwidth. As shown here, the CMTS has issued a map message. Minislots 0, 1, 2, and 3 have been allocated at an Initial maintenance interval. Cable modem B has used this opportunity to transmit a packet. CM B must be a new station trying to come online with the CMTS. Minislots 4 and 5 are allocated for station maintenance. Minislots 6 and 7 are allocated for requests. CM A has been given a direct grant for minislots 8 through 14. CM C has received an acknowledgment but did not receive a direct grant in this MAP.

A MAP message is variable in length (this is described later under "DOCSIS Messages" on page 140.) The beginning of the MAP contains two important pieces of information: the Upstream Channel ID (UCI) number and the starting minislot number. The UCI indicates the upstream channel for which this MAP applies. DOCSIS uses an explicit labeling system for upstream channels, which are set by the CMTS. A CM knows the UCI of

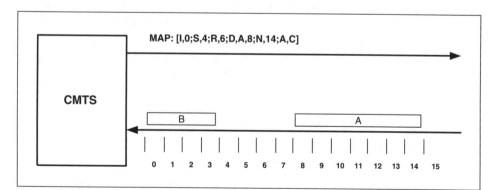

Figure 5.9   DOCSIS bandwidth allocation.

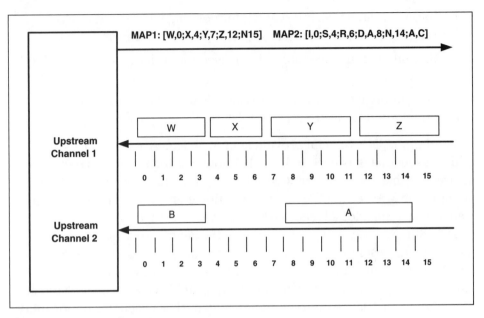

Figure 5.10   Example MAP messages.

the upstream channel, therefore, it listens for MAP messages that apply to that channel. The starting minislot number indicates when on the upstream the MAP becomes active.

Figure 5.10 illustrates a CMTS that has been configured with two upstream channels, 1 and 2. The CMTS has issued two MAP messages, one for each channel. The MAP for channel 1 allocates direct grants to stations W, X, Y, and Z. The MAP for channel 2 is the same from Figure 5.9. Each CM knows the channel ID number of its upstream channel; each CM, therefore, processes only MAP messages that correspond to the channel it is on.

The CMTS has flexibility to define if and when intervals will appear in a MAP. Each MAP need not have allocated each interval. For example, in one MAP, the intervals may all be direct grants; in a following MAP, the intervals might be R, I, and S.

It is the responsibility of the CMTS to send the next MAP downstream in time for each CM to process the MAP before the current MAP expires.

CM Quality of Service Scheduling and Queues

Upstream resources in DOCSIS are allocated to a CM on a SID-by-SID basis. Think of a SID as a queue within a cable modem. Any given CM can have one or more SIDs assigned to it. MAPs are sent downstream; the CM recognizes them by the UCI, then the CM scans the MAP to see if any grants are applicable to it.

This is the general procedure for allocating bandwidth in DOCSIS:

1. When a CM receives a packet in one of its upstream queues (either from the CM protocol stack or from the CMCI CPE interface), it calculates the number of minislots needed to transmit the packet, including all upstream burst profile overhead and guard time.

2. The CM constructs a Request MAC message packet for the SID, and waits for a Request opportunity to be allocated by the CMTS for the same SID.

3. When a request interval is available on the upstream, the CM transmits its request, hoping that the CMTS received it without collision. Request intervals are contention intervals. If the CM's request is heard by the CMTS, it will be allocated either a direct grant in a soon-to-be-coming MAP message, or it will receive an acknowledgment.

4. Upon reception, the CMTS scheduler will calculate when in the future it can allocate bandwidth for the CM's transmission.

5. When the allocation "future" arrives, the scheduler constructs a MAP message, and includes an allocation for the SID and number of minislots that were included in the Request message.

6. The MAP is sent downstream; the CM receives it and examines for either a direct grant or an acknowledgment. If it is a direct grant, the CM processes the packet and waits for the allocated minislot time to arrive for transmission. If an acknowledgment is received, the CM patiently waits to send the packet using a future-issued direct grant. If neither is received, the CM will time out, and enter a contention resolution algorithm and compute a backoff time similar to what was presented in Chapter 3.

NOTE In DOCSIS V1.1, the CMTS is not required to allocate as many minislots as requested by the CM. If at any time the CM is allocated fewer minislots than it requested, it must fragment the packet and transmit upstream the first fragment. Fragmentation is overviewed later in this chapter.

Service Flow and Service Flow Identifier

DOCSIS V1.1 has defined a term called *service flow* and *service flow identifier* (SFID). A service flow is unidirectional. There is a primary or default service flow in the downstream and a primary or default service flow in the upstream. Each service flow is directly related to a unique SID, which has been assigned to the CM. While SIDs are used for bandwidth allocation, each SFID is used to define the QoS parameters for the particular flow: for example, required data rate, delay, jitter, and others.

Service flows exist in three states in the DOCSIS system: *provisioned, admitted,* and *active.* The best example of a provisioned service flow is one in which the parameters for a given type of service are well known, such as packet voice or packet video. Admitted refers to the fact that the CMTS may be reserving resources for the flow, but is not actively scheduling bandwidth to and from the CM for that flow. Think of this state as standby. An active service flow is one where the CMTS is allocating upstream and downstream bandwidth resources. Each active SFID is assigned a SID so that the CMTS can schedule resources.

Service flows are assigned to a CM in one of two fashions: *static provisioning* or *dynamic creation.* Static provisioning is performed as part of the configuration file download procedure during CM initialization. Dynamic configuration is accomplished after the CM has completed registration and has been in operation. Several DOCSIS management messages facilitate dynamic service flow creation, modification, and deletion. (See the "DOCSIS CM Initial Operation Overview, and DOCSIS Messages" sections presented later in this chapter on pages 139 and 140 respectively.)

Figure 5.11 illustrates the general model of a CM with multiple queues. Each upstream queue is identified in the system as a separate service flow; it is assigned a unique SID by the CMTS as part of CM initialization. An active SFID is mapped to each SID. Multiple upstream queue capacity in a CM is an enhancement to DOCSIS V1.0 to handle QoS scheduling. In DOCSIS, each SID is allocated bandwidth using a request and grant mechanism for each SID.

1. When a packet arrives from a cable modem to customer premise equipment (CPE device), the DOCSIS CM will examine the packet; if the packet is to be forwarded on the upstream channel, the following steps take place: The packet is examined by the packet classifier. The classifier is configured with one or more packet pattern-matching criteria. Packets matching certain criteria are assigned to an SFID. If the service flow is active, the packet is transferred to a queue that belongs to the SID that was assigned to the active SFID. Otherwise, packets are transferred to the default SID queue.

2. Each SFID has QoS parameters associated with it. The CM upstream scheduler uses this information to decide when it is appropriate to

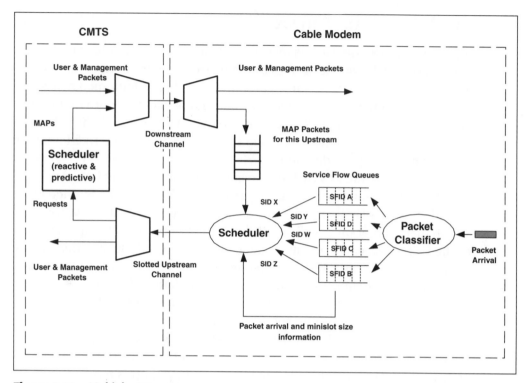

Figure 5.11   Multiple CM queues.

transfer a packet from the queue upstream. Note that the QoS settings may be set to *reactive,* in which case the CM must make a request to transmit the data. DOCSIS supports a predictive mode called the Unsolicited Grant Service (UGS) that is used typically to schedule constant bit rate (CBR) traffic without the need of the CM to send a request for bandwidth.

3. If the CM needs to send a request, it generates one, and sends it to the CMTS following the normal bandwidth request rules for the CM.

4. The CMTS scheduler receives the request, and allocates bandwidth in the next or several MAP messages on a SID-by-SID basis.

5. The CM receives examines the MAP message, and any SID allocations that belong to the CM are transmitted according to their direct grant for each SID.

This is a general description of the facilities for allocating bandwidth provided by the DOCSIS V1.1 protocol. Needless to say, DOCSIS V1.1 is very flexible for handling a variety of service flows.

Unsolicited Grant Service

As just mentioned, the UGS is provided to support constant bit rate (CBR) service flows (CBR service refers to fixed-sized packets at a regular periodic rate). Examples of this are real-time streaming or multimedia services, such as uncompressed packet voice and packet video. UGS does not require the CM to send packet requests to the CMTS; instead, the scheduler within the CMTS schedules grants for a UGS SID for the fixed number of minislots at the periodic interval.

The CM communicates UGS queue status condition to the CMTS using the Unsolicited Grant Synchronization Header (UGSH) in the Service Flow Extended Header (EH) (refer to the section "Extended MAC Headers" later in this chapter on page 142). If, for whatever reasons, the queue size for the UGS exceeds its transmit queue depth, the CM indicates this condition to the CMTS. The CMTS is expected to issue extra grants to bring the queue size back within expected size, after which the CM indicates *all is well* in the UGSH. This mechanism ensures that the effects of lost or corrupted MAP messages can be accommodated.

For service flows with real-time requirements but variable packet size or variable arrival rate, such as compressed packet voice or packet video, the UGS has an extension called *real time polling*. In this mode, the CMTS issues what are called *unicast requests*; that is request intervals specifically for the UGS SID. This mode is designed to offer a low-latency request mechanism when a UGS flow is active, but not running as a CBR service.

Fragmentation

Fragmentation is an upstream-only service. The CMTS may enable or disable fragmentation capability on a CM-by-CM basis, as part of the registration process. Fragmentation is then further enabled on a per-service flow basis. When enabled, fragmentation takes place whenever the CMTS issues fewer minislots in a direct grant than were requested by the CM.

Fragmentation is essentially an encapsulation of a portion of a MAC packet within a fixed-sized fragmentation header and a fragment CRC. Concatenated packets, as well as single packets, are encapsulated in the same manner. If Baseline Privacy is enabled, it is performed on each fragment rather the whole packet.

At the CMTS, the fragment is processed similarly to other received packets, with the additional requirement that it must reassemble all fragments back into the original packet. The CM sends fragment status information along with each fragmented packet so the CMTS can determine whether any fragment was dropped due to errors. If any errors are present, the CMTS drops all currently received fragments, as well as any trailing fragments received from the CM.

The main purpose of providing fragmentation in the upstream is so the CMTS can allocate UGS grants at their regular intervals. For example, for QoS reasons, UGS has priority over best-effort packets. If the number of minislots between UGS allocations is fewer than another CM's request, that CM can use the allocation to send at least part of the packet.

DOCSIS CM Initial Operation Overview

When a DOCSIS modem is powered up, it performs a Power On Self Test (POST), then begins to initialize the MAC. This requires an interaction between the CM and the CMTS to initialize various parameters within the CM, including:

- Downstream channel settings
- Upstream channel setting, including frequency, power, and other transmitter settings
- Ranging

At the end of the ranging process, the CMTS indicates success allowing the CM to move on to the next phase of powering up: initialization of the IP stack. The general procedure is:

1. Obtain IP address and configuration file name from cable operator using DHCP.
2. Set local clock using the Time of Day protocol.
3. Download configuration file using TFTP.

The configuration file for the CM contains settings and potential overrides for parameters already set in the initialization process. For example, if the configuration file contains new downstream or upstream frequency settings, the CM must change to the new channel(s) and redo ranging before continuing.

The next step in the process is for the CM to formally register with the CMTS. During this process, the CM informs the CMTS of the operational parameters and settings obtained within the configuration file. The CMTS responds to the CM by formalizing the settings or disallowing some of the settings. Only after the registration process is complete can the CM begin to forward user data, that is, Ethernet packets. Until this time, the CM only exchanges management packets with the CMTS and cable operator's servers.

To bring the CM to operational state and to enable subsequent reconfiguration, DOCSIS has implemented a comprehensive set of messages between the CM and CMTS. These are overviewed in the next section.

DOCSIS Messages

DOCSIS specifies several levels and many types of messages that are exchanged between the CMTS and the CM. The messages fall into three categories: MAC-Specific Messages, Extended MAC Headers, and MAC Management Messages.

MAC-Specific Messages are communicated using the values in the MAC Header without an Extended Header. The messages that have been defined in V1.1 are:

- Timing and Range Request
- MAC Management Header
- Request Frame
- Fragmentation Header
- Concatenation Header

Extended MAC Headers use the Extender Header option. The messages that have been defined in V1.1 are:

- Null
- Extended Request
- Acknowledgment requested
- Upstream Privacy element
- Upstream Privacy element with fragmentation
- Downstream Privacy element
- Service Flow EH element

NOTE MAC Management Headers and Extended MAC Headers have reserved values in their encoding, which permits future expansion, if needed.

MAC Management Messages are carried as Ethernet/LLC messages in the MAC packet data. These messages are exchanged between the Ethernet protocol stacks of the CMTS and each CM. The messages that are defined in V1.1 are:

- Time Synchronization
- Upstream Channel Descriptor
- Upstream Bandwidth Allocation (MAP)
- Ranging Request
- Ranging Response
- Registration Request
- Registration Response
- Upstream Channel Change Request
- Upstream Channel Change Response
- Telephony Channel Descriptor
- Termination System Information
- Privacy Key Management Request
- Privacy Key Management Response
- Registration Acknowledge
- Dynamic Service Addition Request
- Dynamic Service Addition Response
- Dynamic Service Addition Acknowledge
- Dynamic Service Change Request
- Dynamic Service Change Response
- Dynamic Service Change Acknowledge
- Dynamic Service Deletion Request
- Dynamic Service Deletion Response

The next three subsections give more background on each message.

MAC-Specific Messages

The following MAC-Specific Messages are communicated based on encodings in the MAC Header:

Timing and Range Request. In the downstream direction, the MAC-Specific Timing message is called a SYNC message, as it provides a global time reference that is used by all cable modems to synchronize to the 6.25 μsec Timebase Tick. The packet data contains a time stamp. In the upstream direction, this message is interpreted as a Ranging Request Message.

MAC Management. This type of packet indicates that the data contains a MAC Management Message.

Request Frame. This type of packet indicates a resource request sent upstream by a CM to the CMTS. It is used to request bandwidth on the upstream channel. The LEN field is replaced by the SID value. The SID uniquely defines a CM resource. The SID value was previously issued by the CMTS. A Request Frame has no data, just the MAC header. It is the minimum size packet used within DOCSIS; that is, 6 bytes.

Fragmentation Header. DOCSIS supports the fragmentation of packets in the upstream channel. Fragmentation refers to the capability to split a larger packet into two or more smaller pieces and transmit them separately rather than in one packet burst. This feature is required for maintaining tight adherence to packet scheduling from the CM in support of QoS.

Concatenation Header. DOCSIS supports the capability to send multiple MAC packets in one concatenated MAC packet; for example, sending two or more MAC packets in one upstream packet burst. When concatenation is used, the MAC_PARM field contains the number of user packets contained in the data portion of the packet. Nested concatenated MAC headers are not permitted.

Extended MAC Headers

Every MAC-Specific Message can support an EHDR, with the exception of Timing, Concatenation, and Request. When the EHDR_ON bit is set to 1 in the FC field, that indicates the presence of the EHDR. When this bit is set, the MAC_PARM value represents the length of the EHDR field (ELEN) in bytes. The allowable lengths of EHDR are from 1 to 240 bytes. The general format of a MAC packet with EHDR is shown in Figure 5.12.

The EHDR consists of three fields: the EH_TYPE field, which is 4 bits in length; the EH_LEN field, which is 4 bits in length; and the EH_VALUE field, which is 0 to 15 bytes long. The encoding of the EH_TYPE field is shown in Table 5.8.

NOTE Upstream and Downstream Privacy EH elements are described in the DOCSIS Baseline Privacy Specification.

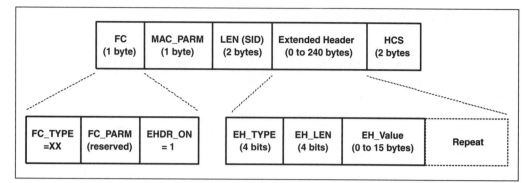

Figure 5.12 Extended MAC Header format.

Extended Requests

An Extended Request is often referred to as a "piggyback" request, because the CM can add this extended header to an existing data packet to convey the same information as a separate Request MAC-Specific Message. By using this, the CM can communicate bandwidth requests to the CMTS in a more timely manner.

Table 5.8 Extended Header Fields

EH_TYPE	EH_LEN	EH_VALUE
0	0	Null value. EH_VALUE field not present. Used to pad.
1	3	Extended Request: number of minislots (byte 1), SID (byte 2 and 3)
2	2	Acknowledgment requested; SID (byte 1 and 2) [CM –> CMTS]
3	4	Upstream Privacy EH element
	5	Upstream Privacy EH element with fragmentation
4	4	Downstream Privacy EH element
5	1	Service Flow EH Element: Payload Header Suppression (PHS) (1 byte)
	2	Service Flow EH Element: PHS (byte 1) Unsolicited Grant Synchronization (byte 2)
6-9		Reserved
10-14		Reserved [CM > CM]
15	XX	Reserved for future extensibility

Fragmentation Extended Header

The Fragmentation Extended Header is used to communicate details of the CM fragmentation process to the CMTS, so that the packet can be reassembled correctly. It is present only on those MAC packets that contain fragmented data.

The Fragmentation Extended Header is 6 bytes long, and contains the following pieces of encoded information for use by the CMTS for reassembly of the packet:

- Baseline privacy information, if security is turned on
- The SID, which is associated with the fragment
- Extended Request
- Flag, which indicates first fragment
- Flag, which indicates last fragment
- Fragment sequence counter

Service Flow Extended Header

The Service Flow Extended Header is used to enhance aspects of service flow operations. DOCSIS V1.1 has defined operators for Payload Header Suppression (PHS) and Unsolicited Grant Synchronization.

PHS is used to optimize the efficiency of the upstream channel by avoiding the repetitive retransmission of packet header information that rarely changes, such as Ethernet header information between the same two stations, or Ethernet and IP header information that remains relatively constant. PHS may be separately configured in the downstream or upstream.

Encoded within the PHS Extended Header is a Payload Header Suppression Index (PHSI), which is unique per SID. The value of the PHSI is a pointer into a table whose contents contain the repeated constant information.

The Unsolicited Grant Synchronization message is used by the CM to communicate status information to the CMTS regarding the Unsolicited Grant Service flow.

MAC Management Messages

All MAC Management Messages, with the exception of the Time Synchronization message, are transmitted in a MAC packet using the MAC Management Header. The data of the packet is encoded using a Logic Link Control (LLC) packet format, as defined in the ISO8802-2 standard (similar to Ethernet, but based on IEEE 802.3 packet formats).

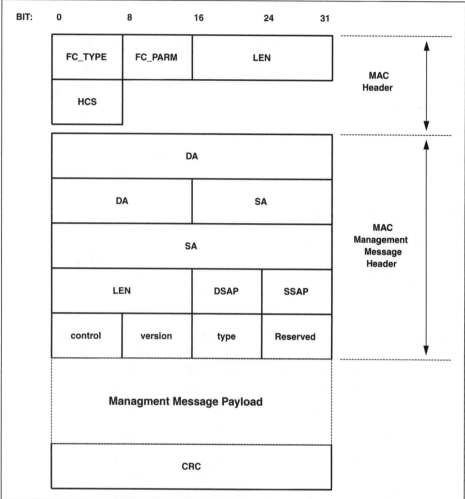

Figure 5.13   MAC management packet format.

Figure 5.13 illustrates the generic packet format. The MAC Header is encoded as a MAC Management Header, as follows:

- The Destination Address (DA) will be set to the 48-bit station address of the CM or to the DOCSIS Management Multicast Address.
- The Source Address (SA) is the address of the source CM or CMTS.
- The message length is variable.
- The Destination Service Access Point (DSAP) and Source Service Access Point (SSAP) fields are set to null (zeroes), as defined in ISO8802-2.

- The Control field is set to indicate an unnumbered information frame.
- The Version and Type fields are set to indicate which MAC Management Message is in the payload.
- The RSVD field is used to pad the start of the payload to the start of the next 32-bit word; it has a value of 0.
- The Payload is variable length.
- The CRC provides error detection over the packet from the DA to the end of the payload.

Time Synchronization

The Time Synchronization (SYNC) message is sent periodically by the CMTS to establish MAC sublayer timing. The MAC-Specific Header for this message is the Time MAC-Specific Header. The contents of the payload contain a time stamp that is set by the CMTS.

NOTE Regarding the construction of this message, the time stamp value is set within the downstream physical channel at the time the SYNC message is being encoded into an MPEG2-TS frame. The CMTS aligns the SYNC message so that it is always contained in one TS frame; that is, it never crosses the boundary into another frame.

Immediately after the CM extracts the packet from the MPEG2-TS frame, the MAC-Specific Header is easily decoded, and the processing of the time stamp synchronization is performed immediately, with low latency in the CM. In contrast, all other MAC Management Messages are forwarded up the protocol stack to the Ethernet/LLC sublayer, and processed. Depending on how loaded the CM central processor unit (CPU) is, forwarding up the protocol stack could introduce unacceptable jitter for the processing of the SYNC.

Upstream Channel Descriptor

Periodically, the CMTS transmits an Upstream Channel Descriptor (UCD) message per each active upstream channel per each downstream channel. The content of the UCD contains the following pieces of information:

Configuration Change Count. A counter that increments with a change to any of the information in the message.

Minislot size. The value of T.

Upstream Channel ID. A CMTS-assigned unique identifier for the upstream channel.

Downstream Channel ID. A CMTS-assigned unique identifier for the downstream channel on which the message was sent.

A list of Time-Length-Value (TLV) elements. These specify the attributes for the upstream channel (symbol rate, frequency, and preamble superstring pattern) and one or more burst descriptors. The burst descriptor sets the attributes of the burst profile listed in Table 5.4. In DOCSIS, there are several different types of packet bursts that may be used on the upstream channel:

- Request
- REQ/Data
- Initial Maintenance
- Station Maintenance
- Short Data Grant
- Long Data Grant

The UCD must contain a burst profile for each Interval Usage Code (IUC) that is used by the CMTS in the Upstream Bandwidth Allocation (MAP) message.

Upstream Bandwidth Allocation (MAP)

The MAP is the message that the CMTS uses to communicate the allocation of minislots in the upstream channel. The MAP is composed of the following pieces of information:

Upstream Channel ID. The ID of the upstream channel to which this MAP applies.

UCD Count. The configuration change count of the UCD message for this channel for which this MAP applies.

Number of MAP elements. Represents the number of information elements (IEs) that are contained in this map.

Allocation Start Time. Indicates the future minislot number where the allocation of this MAP begins.

ACK Time. Specifies a future time expressed as a minislot number that CMs use for collision-detection purposes.

Ranging Backoff Start. Sets the lower end of the backoff range for the contention procedure used in ranging.

Ranging Backoff End. Sets the upper limit of the backoff range for the contention procedure used in ranging.

Data Backoff Start. Sets the lower end of the backoff range for the contention procedure used when making a data request.

Data Backoff End. Sets the upper limit of the backoff range for the contention procedure used when making a data request.

MAP Information Elements. A list of information elements that is divided into two sublists. The first is a list of bandwidth allocation assignments the CMTS has made for the upstream channel, starting at the Allocation Start Time minislot number. Each IE is composed of a SID value, an IUC identifier, and a minislot offset number. The first IE has an offset value of 0, meaning start at the start of the MAP. Each subsequent IE specifies an incrementally larger offset. The amount of upstream resources allocated per IE is from the minislot number offset in the current IE to the minislot just before the offset in the next IE in the list. If the CMTS needs to send acknowledgments to one or more CMs, the first sublist will be terminated by a predefined null IE, and the second sublist will be one IE for each SID being acknowledged. Each IE is always the same length.

Recall that SID stands for service identifier, and represents a packet-receiving and -transmitting entity within the CM. A CM can have multiple SIDs assigned to it. All bandwidth allocation in DOCSIS is done on a SID-by-SID basis. Conceptually , the upstream channel in the CM might have two SIDs allocated, one for station management messages and general Ethernet packets, the other for packet voice. By using different SIDs the CMTS can schedule resources separately for packet voice and general data.

Each IE in the MAP specifies an Interval Usage Code (IUC), which defines the type of allocation for each IE. The following is a list of IUC types that have been defined:

Request. Defines the starting minislot of a region that is to be used for any station to send up requests for bandwidth allocation. This is a contention region for requesting stations.

REQ/Data. Start of region used for immediate data. The SID is a well-known multicast SID address.

Initial Maintenance. Start of region used by any new station entering the initial ranging procedure.

Station Maintenance. Start of the region used for periodic ranging of a single cable modem denoted by a unicast SID value.

Short Data Grant. A directed grant to a single CM, for transmitting short packets from the indicated SID.

Long Data Grant. A directed grant to a single CM, for transmitting long packets from the indicated SID.

In addition to the preceding IUCs, there are reserved values for a Null IE and the Data Acknowledgment IE. These IUC regions do not allocate upstream channel resources.

Ranging Request

This is a message sent by a new CM during initial and periodic ranging with the CMTS. It contains the SID of the sending CM, the downstream channel identifier from the last processed UCD message, and some state information used by the CM to communicate initialization status.

Ranging Response

This is a message sent by the CMTS in response to receiving a Ranging Request message. The message contains the SID that was in the Ranging Request, the upstream channel identifier on which the CMTS received the message, and a list of parameters and status encoded as TLVs:

Timing adjustment. To adjust the ranging delay of the CM.

Power adjustment. To tune the output power of the CM.

Frequency adjustment. To finetune the output frequency of the CM.

Ranging Status. To enable the CMTS to tell the CM to continue the ranging process—that is, send another Ranging Request, abort the process, and that ranging is successful.

CM Transmitter Equalization Information. Provides the equalization coefficients for the upstream transmitter preequalizer.

Downstream Frequency Override. If present, directs the CM to change to the specified downstream frequency. This effectively resets the CM and the procedure for listening for UCD and MAP messages are repeated on the new downstream channel when the CM reboots. The CM will likely do reranging on a new upstream channel.

Upstream Channel ID Override. If present, directs the CM to tune to a new upstream channel and redo initial ranging. The CM continues to use the same downstream channel.

When a CM is directed to change to a different downstream or upstream channel, it must repeat the ranging procedure.

Note that if multiple channels are in operation, a CM selects an upstream channel for initial ranging out of the set of channels, based on receiving multiple UCD messages. The CM merely selects a UCD to use to attempt ranging.

Registration Request

A Registration Request is send by the CM to the CMTS after the CM has downloaded and processed its configuration file. The following settings may be contained in the message:

- SID
- Downstream frequency setting
- Upstream channel ID setting
- Network access control object
- Upstream packet classification configuration
- Downstream packet classification configuration
- Class of service configuration
- Upstream service flow configuration
- Downstream service flow configuration
- Baseline privacy configuration
- Maximum number of CPE devices supported
- Maximum number of classifiers
- Privacy enable configuration
- Payload header suppression
- TFTP server timestamp
- TFTP server-provisioned modem address
- Vendor-specific information configuration
- CM MIC configuration
- CMTS MIC configuration
- Vendor ID configuration setting
- Modem capabilities encoding
- Modem IP address

Registration Response

The CMTS sends a Registration Response after it receives a Registration Request message from a CM. In addition to a SID and Response indicator, the CMTS will include feedback for Service Flow Configuration, Classifier Configuration, and Payload Suppression Configuration, if these were present in the Registration Request.

> **Classifier Configuration.** The CMTS will repeat what was sent, along with classifier identifier assignments.

> **Service Flow Configuration.** The CMTS provides a full set of TLVs, which configure each service flow specified in the request and any additional service flows. At a minimum, this includes a SID assignment for each service flow and QoS configuration. Other service flow configurations may be included.

> **Payload Header Suppression Configuration.** The CMTS returns the PHS configuration and PHS index assignments.

If the Registration Request fails, DOCSIS has defined a mechanism by which the CMTS can provide error feedback in the Registration Response message.

The CMTS will also echo the vendor-specific data and the modem capabilities in the response. For the modem capabilities, the CMTS will specifically state which capabilities are on or off. Only those capabilities that were on in the request can be set to on in the response.

Registration Acknowledge

After processing the Registration Response, the CM transmits a Registration Acknowledge to the CMTS. This message confirms acceptance of the settings specified in the Registration Response. If the CM is unable to support any of the settings, it sends a detailed error report back to the CMTS in this message.

Upstream Channel Change Request

The Upstream Channel Change Request may be sent by the CMTS to direct a CM to change to another upstream channel. Included in this message is the Upstream Channel ID of the new channel, as well as information pertaining to the level of reranging the cable modem will need to do, from the following choices:

- Perform initial ranging on the new channel.
- Perform station maintenance on the new channel.
- Perform initial or station maintenance, whichever comes first.
- Use the new channel without reranging.

Upstream Channel Change Response

After receiving an Upstream Channel Change Request, the CM transmits an Upstream Channel Change Response on the current channel before switching to the new channel. The message includes the Upstream Channel ID of the new channel to which it is switching.

Dynamic Service Addition Request

The Dynamic Service Addition Request may be sent by a CM or the CMTS to request that a new service flow be created. The message contains a unique transaction ID that is created by the sender, in addition to service flow parameters, classifier parameters, and PHS parameters.

Each service flow is defined by a SFID in the system, and the classifier and PHS parameters are assigned per SFID. The CMTS binds a SFID to a SID when the SFID become active. If the CM initiates this message, it substitutes a generic service flow reference value for the SID. If the CMTS initiates this message, it can assign SID values.

Dynamic Service Addition Response

The Dynamic Service Addition Response is sent in response to the Dynamic Service Addition Request. Included in this message is the transaction ID, plus other information similar to the Registration Response message.

If the CMTS is transmitting this message, it makes SID assignments as well as other assignments similar to the Registration Response message.

Dynamic Service Addition Acknowledge

The Dynamic Service Addition Acknowledge message is sent in response to the Dynamic Addition Response message to confirm that the new service additions could be implemented. Any errors are returned in this message; this is similar to the operation of the Registration Acknowledge message.

Dynamic Service Change Request

The Dynamic Service Change Request may be transmitted either by the CM or the CMTS. This message includes a unique transaction ID generated by the sender of the message. Included in this message are classifier, service flow, and PHY parameter configuration information. In addition, for classifier and PHS items, on a per-item basis is a directive to add, replace, or delete. For service flow parameters, it is a replacement operation.

Dynamic Service Change Response

Similar to the Dynamic Service Addition Response message, the Dynamic Service Change Response provides a response to the Dynamic Service Change Request message.

Dynamic Service Change Acknowledge

Similar to the Dynamic Service Addition Acknowledge message, the Dynamic Service Change Acknowledge provides a confirmation response to the Dynamic Service Change Response message.

Dynamic Service Deletion Request

The Dynamic Service Deletion Request message is sent from either the CM or the CMTS to request that a service flow be deleted. Included is a unique transaction ID generated by the sender and the SID.

Dynamic Service Deletion Response

The Dynamic Service Deletion Response message is sent in response to a Dynamic Service Deletion Request. The message includes confirmation feedback indicating the success of the deletion operation.

Baseline Privacy

The suite of DOCSIS specifications includes Baseline Privacy Interface Plus (BPI+). The public version of this specification referenced in this book is SP-BPI+-I04-000407.

Baseline privacy has two components, excerpted from the preceding spec:

An encapsulation protocol for encrypting packet data across the cable network: This protocol defines (1) the frame format for carrying encrypted packet data within DOCSIS MAC frames, (2) a set of supported cryptographic suites, i.e., pairings of data encryption and authentication algorithms, and (3) the rules for applying those algorithms to a DOCSIS MAC frame's packet data.

A key management protocol (Baseline Privacy Key Management, or "BPKM") providing the secure distribution of keying data from CMTS to CMs: Through this key management protocol, CM and CMTS synchronize keying data; in addition, the CMTS uses the protocol to enforce conditional access to network services. Baseline Privacy was designed to support the following types of communications with DOCSIS:

- Best-effort, high-speed, IP data services

- QoS (e.g., constant bit rate) data services

- IP multicast group services

BPI+ uses public key cryptography to establish a secret shared by the CM and the CMTS. Each CM has an embedded security certificate provided by its manufacturer. During the CM BPI+ initialization process, the CM's digital certificate includes the MAC address, serial number, and manufacturer identifier as passed to the CMTS. The CMTS associates this information to a paying subscriber.

In operation, a security association between the CM and CMTS is on a SID-by-SID basis. Different SIDs in the upstream or downstream carry their own security relationship. This is useful for two main reasons:

- Unicast traffic exchanged between the CMTS and CM can be uniquely secured.

- Multicast traffic in the downstream can be secured for each member of the multicast group; that is, if a CM is not a member of the group, it will not have the security information needed to decode the messages.

When BPI+ is being used, initialization of security happens after the CM finishes registration with the CMTS. If a CM is to use BPI+, the downloaded configuration file will contain BPI+ configuration information. The procedure for security registration and key exchange is specified in SP-BPI+-I04-000407.

After BPI+ is initialized, all user data packets exchanged between the CM and CMTS, and vice versa, are encrypted. MAC Management Messages are sent unencrypted.

A Closer Look at CM Initialization

We have already described DOCSIS messages, enabling us to fill out the procedure for bringing a new CM online with a CMTS. These are the general steps for initializing a CM for successful operation:

1. CM is powered on and completes POST.
2. Downstream frequencies are scanned for an active DOCSIS digital channel. An active DOCSIS channel consists of:
   - 64 QAM or 256 QAM modulation
   - MPEG2-TS frames present with DOCSIS PID
   - Periodic receipt of UCD and MAP messages
3. The CM examines UCD messages, and selects an appropriate one for using for the initial ranging request.
4. The CM examines MAP messages and waits for an Initial Management interval.
5. The CM transmits a Ranging Request message.
6. If received, the CMTS transmits a Ranging Response message.

   NOTE Steps 5 and 6 are repeated until the CMTS indicates success.

7. The CM issues a DHCP request to obtain its IP address, configuration file name, and the TFTP server to use.
8. A DHCP server operated by the cable operator responds with this information to the requesting CM.
9. The CM sets it Time of Day.
10. The CM downloads its configuration file, using TFTP from the indicated server.
11. The CM processes its configuration file.
12. The CM sends a Registration Request to the CMTS.
13. The CMTS responds with a Registration Response.
14. The CM processes the Registration Response and responds with a Registration Acknowledgment.
15. If the configuration file contains Baseline Privacy settings, the CM and the CMTS exchange security information, following the procedures in the Baseline+ Privacy specification SP-BPI+-I04-000407.
16. The CM is now online and is allowed to forward subscriber packets.

NOTE The initialization steps presented here comprise an example of a generic series of steps, in which no errors or negotiation occur between the CM and the CMTS. The DOCSIS specification contains detailed flowcharts for each step in the initialization and registration process.

DOCSIS and the Simple Network Management Protocol

As mentioned earlier in this chapter, DOCSIS requires that both the CM and the CMTS support the Simple Network Management Protocol (SNMP) for managing Ethernet/LLC and IP protocol facilities of operation. These facilities are in addition to the requirements stated in the DOCSIS RFI specification.

SNMP provides two basic operations for accessing and, potentially, changing management information. A read operation is called a GET. A write operation is called a SET. In addition, the particular object being accessed may be read-only or read-write. It is not possible to SET a read-only object. The MIB specifies how objects are defined and related to one another. Frequently, objects are arranged in tables within the MIB hierarchy.

NOTE This section does not go into detail on how the MIB is constructed; rather, the intent is to highlight the manageability of DOCSIS via the SNMP interfaces.

There are two MIB specifications: a Cable Device MIB and a DOCSIS RF Interface MIB, described in the following subsections.

Cable Device MIB

Each compliant CMTS and CM must implement the "DOCSIS Cable Device MIB: Cable Device Management Information Base for DOCSIS-compliant Cable Modems and Cable Modem Termination Systems," which is defined in the IETF document RFC2669.

NOTE The information in this section is current to the August 1999 release of the MIB specification document. The material in this section is meant to convey the power of DOCSIS SNMP management, not to teach the implementation elements of the MIB. For comprehensive information, refer to RFC2669.

This MIB is divided into seven groups:

- Cable device system management
- SNMP access security
- Network-downloadable software upgrades
- Provisioning server interaction
- Event reporting and logging
- Filter configuration for IP Layer 3 and Bridging Layer 2 data traffic
- CPE address management (CM only)

The updating of CM operating software is controlled via SNMP. The cable operator accesses a CM's MIB via SNMP and configures the TFTP server address for the new software, the file name, and directive to the CM to upgrade. The CM attempts to run the new software only if the download completes, the contents are not damaged, and the software is intended for its hardware. After determining these requirements, the CM reboots using the new software image. If for any reason the download is not assured, the CM continues running its existing software.

A CM uses the TRAP facility of SNMP to send error and logging messages to the SNMP TRAP server. The messages in such traps are human-readable text strings with a time-of-day stamp. Messages are vendor-specific.

The Cable Device MIB provides management of CM Layer 2 Ethernet/LLC and Layer 3 IP protocol filters. The Ethernet/LLC filters limit CM forwarding to a restricted set of network-layer protocols, such as IP, IPX, NetBIOS, and EtherTalk (AppleTalk). The IP filters can be used to restrict upstream and downstream traffic based on source and destination IP addresses, as well as limit to Layer 4 transport protocols, such as TCP, UDP, ICMP, in addition to source and destination TCP and UDP source and destination ports.

Protocol filtering is per-interface and -direction (in or out). The CM has two interfaces: the cable RF interface and the CPE Ethernet interface. The order in which the filters are processed is as follows:

1. Ethernet/LLC In.
2. IP Spoof and/or SNMP Access.
3. IP Filter In and Out.
4. Ethernet/LLC Out.

Ethernet/LLC In. Examines the Type field in Ethernet/LLC packets received from an interface. Packets are accepted or rejected based on the rules for Ethernet/LLC In. The specific goal of this filtering is to allow certain protocols to be further processed while rejecting others. For example, it is possible to use this facility to forward IP and ARP traffic from the home network while rejecting NetBIOS and EtherTalk.

IP Spoof. This filter is applied to the CPE In interface; if enabled, it is used to validate IP source addresses received from the CPE. For example, the cable operator may use this to restrict IP source addresses from the CPE to only those addresses that have been allocated to the subscriber (and paid for).

SNMP Access. This filter restricts which IP source addresses may access the SNMP process in the cable modem. Typically, the cable operator will set this filter so that only its management servers can access SNMP.

IP Filter In and Out. This filter is much like a packet classifier. Each IP packet received from an interface is compared with entries in the filter table. Each filter rule may include IP source address, IP destination address, source subnetwork netmask, destination subnetwork netmask, IP type of service (TOS) values and mask, UDP or TCP source and destination port values and mask. The cable operator can set the order in which entries are processed in the filter table. Each filter in the table has an action: deny, permit, or process, based on a policy. The cable operator can also specify a set of policies that may be applied to a packet, which include modifying the TOS field and/or assigning the packet to a particular queue. In the CM, this filter works in conjunction with the packet classifier, and allows a packet to be assigned to a particular queue. In the CMTS, this may be used to assign downstream packets to priority queues based on the contents; for example, packet voice might receive priority treatment on the downstream over all other types.

Ethernet/LLC Out. The MIB has required this filter for examining outbound Ethernet/LLC packets but has not specified any requirements at this time. Based on the implementation directives, in the future, this filter may be activated in any compliant CM.

Radio Frequency Interface MIB

Each compliant CMTS and CM must implement the "Radio Frequency (RF) Interface Management Information Base for MCNS/DOCSIS-compliant RF Interfaces," which is defined in the IETF document RFC2670. This MIB is structured into three management groups:

- Covering both CM and CMTS operation, including active downstream and upstream channels, QoS profiles, and RF signal quality.
- Covering CM operation, including monitoring of the DOCSIS MAC interface and the upstream service queues.
- Covering CMTS operation, including a table of "rolled up" values that summarize events on all interfaces, a table of known (registered) CMs serviced by this CMTS, upstream service queues, modulation profiles for downstream and upstream channels, and MAC-address fast access for gathering information on a registered CM.

NOTE The information in this section is current to the August 1999 release of the MIB specification document. The presentation in this section is meant to convey the power of DOCSIS SNMP management and will not provide a teaching of the implementation elements of the MIB. For precise information, refer to RFC2670.

Downstream Channel Table

On a per-downstream channel basis, both the CM and CMTS provide the following information objects:

Channel ID. Provided by the CMTS to identify the downstream channel.

Channel Frequency. The center of the downstream frequency associated with this channel.

Channel Width. The RF bandwidth of this downstream channel.

Modulation. Selected from the set: unknown, other, 64 QAM, 256 QAM.

Interleave. Adjusts the amount of interleaving used by the downstream PHY FEC process.

Power. At the CMTS, the operational transmit power of the transmitter; at the CM, the received power level.

For the CM, these objects are all read-only; for the CMTS, except for the Channel ID, these objects are read-write.

Upstream Channel Table

On a per-upstream channel basis, both the CM and CMTS provide the following information objects:

Channel ID. CMTS-provided channel ID.

Frequency. The center frequency of this upstream channel.

Width. The RF bandwidth of this channel.

Modulation Profile. The modulation profile for the channel.

Slot Size. The number of Timebase Ticks (6.25 µsec) in each upstream minislot.

Transmitter Timing Offset. A measure of the current round-trip time at the CM, or the maximum round-trip time as seen by the CMTS.

Ranging Backoff Start. The low end of the ranging backoff window.

Ranging Backoff Stop. The high end of the ranging backoff window.

Request Backoff Start. The end of the request backoff window.

Request Backoff Stop. The high end of the request backoff window.

For the CM, these objects are all read-only; for the CMTS, except for the Channel ID, these objects are read-write.

QoS Profile Table

The QoS Profile Table is implemented in both the CM and CMTS. It contains service profiles that can be assigned to service flow or SID, as described here:

Priority. A relative priority between 0 (lowest) and 7 (highest) assigned to the service when allocating bandwidth.

Maximum Upstream Bandwidth. The maximum upstream bandwidth for any service flow that uses this profile.

Guaranteed Upstream Bandwidth. The minimum guaranteed upstream bandwidth for any service flow that uses this profile.

Maximum Downstream Bandwidth. The maximum downstream bandwidth for any service flow that uses this profile.

Maximum Transmission Burst. That maximum number of minislots that may be requested for a single upstream transmission.

Baseline Privacy. Indicates whether BPI+ is enabled for this profile.

CMTS Interface Management Objects

The following information is managed for each CMTS downstream channel:

- Raw speed in bits/second
- Administrative status
- Operational status
- Maximum transmission unit (MTU) size for transmitted packets

- Number of transmitted bytes
- Number of unicast packets
- Number of multicast packets
- Number of broadcast packets
- Number of discarded packets (e.g., buffer shortage)
- Number of packets that could not be transmitted due to errors

The following information is managed for each CM downstream channel:

- Raw speed in bits/second
- Administrative status
- Operational status
- Maximum transmission unit (MTU) size for received packets
- Number of received bytes
- Number of unicast packets
- Number of multicast packets
- Number of broadcast packets
- Number of discarded packets (e.g., buffer shortage)
- Number of packets received that were discarded due to errors (e.g., CRC check failed on MAC header or user data)
- Number of frames received with unknown packet type

The following information is managed for each CMTS upstream channel:

- Raw speed in bits/second
- Administrative status
- Operational status
- Maximum transmission unit (MTU) size for received packets
- Number of received bytes
- Number of unicast packets
- Number of multicast packets
- Number of broadcast packets
- Number of discarded packets (e.g., buffer shortage)
- Number of packets received that were discarded due to errors (e.g., CRC check failed on MAC header or user data)
- Number of frames received with unknown packet type

The following information is managed for each CM upstream channel:

- Raw speed in bits/second
- Administrative status
- Operational status
- Maximum transmission unit (MTU) size for transmitted packets
- Number of transmitted bytes
- Number of unicast packets
- Number of multicast packets
- Number of broadcast packets
- Number of discarded packets (e.g., buffer shortage)
- Number of packets which could not be transmitted due to errors

The following information is managed for the CM MAC layer:

- Physical address of the interface
- Administrative status
- Operational status
- Maximum transmission unit (MTU) size
- Number of received bytes
- Number of received unicast packets
- Number of received multicast packets
- Number of received broadcast packets
- Number of received discarded packets (e.g., buffer shortage)
- Number of packets received that were discarded due to errors (e.g., CRC check failed on MAC header or user data)
- Number of frames received with unknown packet type
- Number of transmitted bytes
- Number of transmitted unicast packets
- Number of transmitted multicast packets
- Number of transmitted broadcast packets
- Number of output packets that were discarded (e.g., buffer shortage)
- Number of packets that could not be transmitted due to errors

CM Management Objects

The following information is managed per CM:

- CMTS MAC address—(MAC address of the CMTS that is believed to be managing the CM)
- Capabilities—(ATM cell support, concatenation support)
- Ranging response timeout and ranging timeout—(waiting time for a Ranging Response packet)
- Status Value—(other, not ready, not synchronized, PHY synchronized, user parameters acquired, ranging complete, IP complete, time of day established, security established, parameter transfer complete, operations, and access denied)
- Transmit power
- Number of resets
- Number of lost syncs
- Number of invalid MAPs
- Number of invalid UCDs
- Number of invalid ranging responses
- Number of invalid registration responses
- Number of ranging aborts

The following information is managed on a per-upstream queue basis:

- Service ID (SID value)
- QoS profile index
- The number of upstream minislots used to transmit packets in REQ/Data mode
- The number of upstream minislots used to transmit packets in response to direct grants
- The number of attempts to transmit packets in REQ/Data mode that did not result in acknowledgment
- The number of packets discard due to excessive retries in REQ/Data mode
- The number of transmitted requests that did not result in acknowledgment
- The number of requests for bandwidth that failed due to excessive retries without acknowledgment

CMTS MAC Management Objects

At the CMTS, the MAC interface consists of a downstream channel and one or more upstream channels. The following information is managed per CMTS for each MAC interface:

- CMTS capabilities—(ATM cells, concatenation)
- SYNC interval—(interval between successive SYNC messages)
- UCD interval—(interval between successive UCD messages)
- Maximum service IDs—(maximum number of SIDs that may be simultaneously active)
- Insert interval—(amount of time elapsed between each initial management interval for new cable modems to begin ranging)
- Number of invalid ranging requests
- Number of aborted ranging attempts
- Number of invalid registration requests
- Number of failed registration requests
- Number of invalid data requests

The CMTS implements a CM status table. The following information is kept on a per-CM basis:

- MAC address
- IP address
- Downstream channel number
- Upstream channel number
- Received power level
- Ranging timing offset
- Equalization data
- Status value
- Number of FEC codewords received without error
- Number of FEC codewords received with correctable errors
- Number of FED codewords received with uncorrectable errors
- Signal-to-noise ratio as perceived for upstream data from this CM
- Total microreflections perceived on this interface

The CMTS implements an upstream service queue status table. The following information is kept on a per-SID basis:

- SID value
- CM status
- Administrative status
- QoS profile
- Creation time
- Number of user bytes received
- Number of packets received

The CMTS implements an upstream channel modulation table. The following information is kept on modulation index basis:

- Modulation index
- Interval usage code
- Modulation type
- Preamble length
- Differential encoded (yes/no)
- FEC
- FEC codeword length
- Scrambler seed
- Maximum burst size (in minislots)
- Guard time size (in symbols)
- Shortened last codeword (yes/no)
- Scrambler used (yes/no)

The CMTS maintains a fast CM lookup table based on MAC address. Each entry has a pointer to the cable modem status table.

IP Multicast and IGMP Management

Requirements were added in the DOCSIS V1.1 release to improve handling of IP multicast packets as well as the Internet Group Management Protocol (IGMP), which is the signaling protocol used for IP stations to communicate their joining and leaving multicast groups. Both the CMTS and CM have been augmented with new services to facilitate operating IGMP in a controlled manner on a shared media cable network.

Recall that in a high-speed data-over-cable network, the downstream channel is a point-to-multipoint broadcast network; one transmitter at the

CMTS and many receivers in all the CMs. This is a natural multicast environment, as one copy of a packet need be sent downstream to be received by all members of the multicast group. Whether there is one or more members of a group, the headend router (either the CMTS or a router connected to the CMTS) must forward multicast packets downstream toward the subscribers. If there are no members of a group, or when the last member leaves, IGMP invokes a procedure that allows the multicast router to stop forwarding a particular multicast group.

Quick Overview of the IGMP Protocol

IGMP is used to report multicast group management status on a physical network to any immediate neighboring multicast routers. All IP hosts that want to use IP multicast are required to run the IGMP protocol. IGMP V2, documented in IETF RFC2236, provides the implementation specifications. This overview describes the generalities of the protocol operation.

Three messages make up the IGMP protocol:

Membership Query. Sent by the multicast router, this comes in two flavors: a general query or a group-specific query.

Membership Report. Sent by one or more IP hosts regarding its membership in a particular multicast group.

Leave Group. Sent by the last IP hosts to leave a specific group.

The multicast router uses IGMP to discover those multicast groups that have membership on each physical network to which it is connected. The router only needs know whether there is at least one member active in the group. If there is more than one multicast router connected to the same physical network (e.g., an IP subnetwork), IGMP provides a mechanism for them to decide which one is the querying router.

The querying router sends out general Membership Query messages over a random time period on each physical interface. Upon reception of this message, an IP multicast host sets a timer with a random time selected from a predefined range for each group for which it is a member. If a timer expires on a host for a group, it sends a Membership Report (hereafter, Report) to that mulitcast group. If a host is delaying (timer has not expired) upon reception of a Report from another host, it deactivates its timer for the particular group and does not send its own Report. The multicast router receives the Report from at least one member in this scheme.

When a router receives a Report, it records that it has membership for that multicast group on the physical network from which the Report was received. The router sets a random timer each time a Report is received for the group and the physical interface. The timer value is called the *Query Response Interval*. If no new reports are received, and the timer expires, the router concludes that there is no need to forward that multicast group on that physical interface.

When a host joins a multicast group, it sends an unsolicited Report to the all-systems group address (IP address 224.0.0.1), sets its random timer, and starts delaying.

When a host leaving a group is the last host to send the Report in response to a query, it sends a Leave Group message to the all-routers group address (IP address 224.0.0.2). If it is not the last host, it can leave quietly or send a Leave Group message to the group.

When a router receives a Leave Group message, it sends one or more group-specific queries. If no reports are received, the router concludes that there are no members left in that group and terminates forwarding of that group on that physical interface.

Multicast Addressing

IP multicast addresses are assigned out Class D IP address spaces. For the 32-bit IP address, this is the set of addresses that have the binary value of 1110 as their high-order 4 bits. In Internet dotted-quad notation, this is the range from 240.0.0.0 to 239.255.255.255. The address of 224.0.0.0 is never assigned to any group. The address 224.0.0.1 is assigned to all multicast hosts, including multicast routers. The address 224.0.0.2 is assigned to all multicast routers.

NOTE The rules for mapping IP multicast addresses to Ethernet multicast addresses are defined in IETF RFC1112 "Host Extensions for IP Multicasting."

IP multicast addresses are mapped to Ethernet multicast addresses following the specification contained in the IETF RFC1700 "Assigned Numbers." Note: RFC1700 is the last Request for Comments (RFC) document (see Figure 5.14). The text from this document is maintained on the Web site of the Internet Assigned Numbers Authority (IANA),www.isi.edu /in-notes/iana/assignments/ethernet-numbers.

The procedure for mapping IP multicast is as follows:

1. Number the bits of an Ethernet address from 0 to 47, left to right.

2. In hex format, set the leftmost bits to 01:00:5E. Set bit 24 to 0.

3. Map the lower 23 bits of the IP multicast address into the lower 23 bits of the 48-bit address. This gives a range of Ethernet address values from 01:00:5E:00:00:00 to 01:00:5E:7F:FF:FF.

A CMTS or CM recognizes that an Ethernet multicast packet contains an IP multicast packet by acknowledging that the top bits are 01:00:53. The rest of the address indicates the bottom 23 bits of the IP multicast address. There are 32 bits minus 4 bits (for Class D bits) minus 23 bits equals 5 bits in an IP address that are not mapped into the Ethernet address. This means that the address in the Ethernet packet can be from 32 (2 raised to power of 5) different IP multicast addresses. Extracting the IP packet from the Ethernet packet allows the CMTS or CM to examine the entire 32 bits of the IP multicast address.

CMTS Rules for IGMP and Multicast Forwarding

Clearly, there is a need to conserve both downstream and upstream bandwidth in a cable modem system. Having the capability to turn on and shut off multicast packets based on actual group membership is essential. DOCSIS permits a CMTS to operate as either a Layer 2 bridge or a Layer 3 router. The rules for IGMP message forwarding are slightly different in each mode.

CMTS AS A BRIDGE

- Forwards all membership queries on all downstream channels.
- Forwards the first copy of a solicited or unsolicited Report to all downstream channels.
- Suppresses the forwarding of additional Reports on the downstream for at least the Query Response Interval.
- Suppresses the downstream transmission to any mulitcast group that does not have subscriber membership, subject to administrative controls.

CMTS AS A ROUTER

- Forwards the first copy of a solicited or unsolicited Report to all downstream channels.
- Forwards the first copy of a solicited or unsolicited Report to all downstream channels.
- Suppresses the forwarding of additional Reports on the downstream for at least the Query Response Interval.
- Suppresses the downstream transmission to any mulitcast group that does not have subscriber membership, subject to administrative controls.

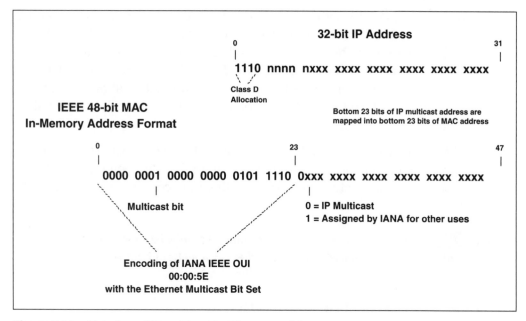

32-bit IP Address

0
31

1110 nnnn nxxx xxxx xxxx xxxx xxxx xxxx

Class D
Allocation

Bottom 23 bits of IP multicast address are
mapped into bottom 23 bits of MAC address

**IEEE 48-bit MAC
In-Memory Address Format**

0
23
47

0000 0001 0000 0000 0101 1110 0xxx xxxx xxxx xxxx xxxx xxxx

Multicast bit

0 = IP Multicast
1 = Assigned by IANA for other uses

**Encoding of IANA IEEE OUI
00:00:5E
with the Ethernet Multicast Bit Set**

Figure 5.14   Mapping of IP multicast to Ethernet multicast.

- Performs the multicast router functions in RFC2236, and acts as the only querier on the downstream interface.

CM Rules for IGMP and Multicast Forwarding

In DOCSIS, the CM has specific requirements for handling IGMP packets. These requirements are listed in precedence order:

- Does not forward queries from the CPE interface to the RF interface—that is, upstream.
- Does not forward Report or Leave Group messages from the RF interface to the CPE interface—that is, downstream.
- Does not forward multicast packets from the RF interface to the CPE interface unless a CPE device is a member of that group.
- Forwards multicast packets received on the CPE interface to the RF interface (upstream) unless administratively prohibited, except as noted.
- Forwards multicast packets sent to the all-hosts address, except as noted, from the RF interface to the CPE interface—that is,downstream.

- Forwards multicast packets from all-host queries or group-specific queries from the RF interface to the CPE interface. Or, if the CM implements the host portion of RFC2236 on its RF interface, it does not act as a querier on the RF interface, it is a querier on the CPE interface, and derives its timer values as described shortly. (Note: There may be a CM configuration control that overrides these values.)

Though the details of a CM operating as an RFC2236 host are beyond the scope of this chapter, we do point out here that the requirements on the CM were constructed to enforce limiting unnecessary upstream IGMP traffic as much as possible.

NOTE The DOCSIS specification states that a CM may be specifically configured to *not* forward multicast packets as a matter of network policy.

Fee, PHY, Foe, Fumble

In a press release titled "CableLabs Selects Broadcom and Terayon to Author Advanced Modem Technology Proposals," on November 13, 1998, CableLabs announced it had started an update project to DOCSIS V1.1 called DOCSIS V1.2. The idea at the time was that Broadcom's Frequency Agile Time Division Multiplexed Access (FA-TDMA) system and Terayon's Synchronous Code Division Multiplexed Access (S-CDMA) sys-

CABLELABS CERTIFICATION PROGRAM

CableLabs, located in Louisville, Colorado, runs a DOCSIS certification program for vendors. Before a vendor can claim a cable modem to be DOCSIS-compatible, the modem hardware and software version must have been certified by CableLabs. CableLabs program runs in the form of "waves" that last approximately five weeks. Vendors may enter a certification wave only when they have completed the necessary documentation that overviews their testing of every item in the DOCSIS test plan. CableLabs then runs the cable modem through real-time tests to validate many key points of operation, including interoperability with several different vendors' CMTSs. If the cable modem meets approval, it is certified. Later, if the vendor changes hardware or software, the cable modem must be recertified.

Similarly, CMTS products are certified in waves. After passing, the CMTS is qualified for DOCSIS operation.

tems could be brought into convergence technically and released as one specification. Much of the work that led to this decision came out of the efforts of the IEEE 802.14 High Performance PHY (HiPHY) working group, a second working group started to develop a joint HiPHY specification for both DOCSIS and IEEE 802.14. Shortly after the work began, CableLabs agreed to have IEEE 802.14 help the DOCSIS V1.2 process along.

On September 8, 1999, the DOCSIS Certification Board, via letter to the IEEE HiPHY Working Group, expressed that they were intent at putting FA-TDMA on a fast-track schedule, to include features into the DOCSIS V1.1 release. Terayon had been asked to produce a prototype with a modification for clock recovery and other aspects; after evaluation of the prototype, DOCSIS would decide if it wanted to include S-CDMA in the DOCSIS specifications. The DOCSIS Certification Board had decided to approach HiPHY additions differently from their original intent. Thus, part of the closing statement in the letter stated: "Given this, we do not require that the 802.14 perform any additional work in this area." In this way, the joint work between IEEE 802.14 HiPHY and DOCSIS was concluded. IEEE 802.14 formally shut down its working groups in November 1999.

On February 25, 2000, the DOCSIS Certification Board released another statement to the public, announcing that work on FA-TDMA would be put on a shorter and different timeline from that for S-CDMA, and so they would no longer be paired; the statement further announced that S-CDMA had to be prototyped and proven to meet the anticipated advantages and low incremental cost considerations; that before anything was added to the DOCSIS specification, the vendor contributing the technology to the specification had to agree to include it in the DOCSIS royalty-free IPR pool; and, finally, the label "DOCSIS V1.2" was no longer valid for FA-TDMA or S-CDMA. Moreover, the statement announced that it would be "unlikely that any of the other techniques considered by 802.14 (e.g., OFDM [Orthogonal Frequency Division Multiplexing], DMT [Discrete Multi-Tone] or S-TDMA [Synchronous TDMA]) would be included in any near-term DOCSIS release."

In summary, the work launched in November 1998 for a combined FA-TDMA and S-CDMA-advanced PHY was reevaluated in the second half of 1999 by the DOCSIS Certification Board. The DOCSIS V1.2 number was removed from consideration for an advanced PHY specification update. However, work is proceeding on some advanced PHY prototypes. If any meet the specifications and expectations, they may be considered for future addition to DOCSIS.

Summary

This chapter presented an overview of the DOCSIS RFI Version 1.1 specification. It was not meant to detail the complete specification, rather to provide a basic understanding of the protocol and to allow straightforward navigation into the specification. Readers who would like to understand the specification in greater detail should download the specification from CableLabs.

For Further Information

More information about CableLabs' activities, DOCSIS, and OpenCable can be found at the following Web sites:

www.cablelabs.com

www.cablemodem.com

www.opencable.com

Topical information about cable modem system news, user experiences, cable operator and ISP deployments, cable modem technology, cable telephony, and general cable industry information can be found at Broadband Bob's Website at www.catv.org.

The Internet Engineering Task Force (IETF) documents and reports of the IP over Cable Data Networks (ipcdn) working group can be found at www.ietf.org.

This chapter referenced directly or indirectly many IETF documents:

RFC791. Postel, J., "Internet Protocol," IETF RFC-791 (MIL STD 1777), September 1981.

RFC826. Plummer, D., "Ethernet Address Resolution Protocol: On Converting Network Protocol Addresses to 48-bit Ethernet Address for Transmission on Ethernet Hardware," November 1982.

RFC868. Harrenstien, K., and Postel, J., "Time Protocol," May 1983.

RFC1042. Postel, J., and Reynolds, J., "A Standard for the Transmission of IP Datagrams over IEEE802 Networks," February 1988.

RFC1058. Hedrick, C., "Routing Information Protocol," June 1988.

RFC1123. Braden, R., "Requirements for Internet Hosts—Application and Support," October 1989.

RFC1157. Schoffstall, M., Fedor, M., Davin, J. and Case, J., "A Simple Network Management Protocol (SNMP)," May 1990.

RFC1350. Sollings, K., "The TFTP Protocol" (Revision 2), July 1992.

RFC1493. Decker, E., Langille, P., Rijsinghani, A., and McCloghrie, K. "Definitions of Managed Objects for Bridges," July 1993.

RFC1633. Braden, R., Clark, D., and Shenker, S., "Integrated Services in the Internet Architecture: An Overview," June 1994.

RFC1812. Baker, F., "Requirements for IP Version 4 Routers," June 1995.

RFC2104. Krawczyk, H., Bellare, M., and Canetti, R., "HMAC: Keyed-Hashing for Message Authentication," February 1997.

RFC2131. Droms, R., "Dynamic Host Configuration Protocol," March 1997.

RFC2132. Alexander, S. and Droms, R., "DHCP Options and BOOTP Vendor Extensions," March 1997.

RFC2210. Wroclawski, J., "The Use of RSVP with the IETF Integrated Services," September 1997.

RFC2211. Wroclawski, J., "Specification of the Controlled-Load Network Element Service," September 1997.

RFC2212. Shenker, S., Partridge, C., and Guerin, R., "Specification of Guaranteed Quality of Service," September 1997.

RFC2236. Fenner, W., "Internet Group Management Protocol, Version 2," November 1997.

RFC2349. Malkin, G. and Harkin, A., "TFTP Timeout Interval and Transfer Size Options," May 1998.

RFC2669. M. St. Johns, Ed., "DOCSIS Cable Device MIB Cable Device Management Information Base for DOCSIS-Compliant Cable Modems and Cable Modem Termination Systems," August 1999, www.ietf.org.

RFC2669. M. St. Johns, Ed., "Radio Frequency (RF) Interface Management Information Base for MCNS/DOCSIS-compliant RF interfaces," August 1999, www.ietf.org.

The following International Standards Organization specifications were referenced in this chapter:

ISO8802-2, ISO/IEC 8802-2: 1994 (IEEE Std 802.2: 1994) – Information technology –Telecommunications and information exchange between systems – Local and metropolitan area networks – Specific requirements – Part 2: Logical link control, www.iso.ch.

The following ITU standards were referenced in this chapter:

ITU-T H.222.0, ITU-T Recommendation H.222.0 (1995) | ISO/IEC 13818-1:1996. Information technology–generic coding of moving pictures and associated audio information systems, www.itu.int.

ITU-T J.83-B, Annex B to ITU-T Recommendation J.83 (4/97). Digital multi-programme systems for television sound and data services for cable distribution, www.itu.int.

ITU-T J.112, Annex B to ITU-T Recommendation J.112 (3/98). Transmission systems for Interactive Cable Television Services, www.itu.int.

CHAPTER

6

PacketCable Overview

At CableLabs, a project called PacketCable is underway to develop specifications for packet voice, video, and other multimedia services over cable networks using the IP protocol family. The project is similar to the DOCSIS program in that the specifications work is being performed by a number of vendor authors and members of the North American cable industry. This chapter presents an overview of the architecture and services that are targeted for the first deployment of PacketCable.

NOTE PacketCable services require the QoS facilities provided by DOCSIS V1.1.

The effort to create packet voice services to replace traditional circuit-switched plain old telephone service (POTS) is being fueled by the worldwide growth of IP packet networks and the emergence of many competitive local exchange carriers (CLECs) that want to break into the local telephone business. Cable operators are especially motivated, because, with the deployment of DOCSIS and PacketCable services, their cable networks are becoming packet voice-ready.

The first public PacketCable documents were released in December 1999. This first release focused on the development of low-cost subscriber-side equipment and on the interfaces of that equipment to packet voice services.

Similar to DOCSIS, PacketCable has produced a suite of specifications and reports:

- Audio Video Codecs (PKT-SP-CODEC)
- Dynamic Quality of Service (PKT-SP-DQOS)
- Network-Based Call Signaling (NCS) (PKT-SP-EC-MGCP)
- Event Messages (PKT-SP-EM)
- Internet Signaling Transport Protocol (ISTP) (PKT-SP-ISTP)
- MIB Framework (PKT-SP-MIBS)
- MTA MIB (PKT-SP-MIBS-MTA)
- NCS MTA MIB (PKT-SP-MIBS-NCS)
- MTA Device Provisioning (PKT-SP-PROV)
- Security (PKT-SP-SEC)
- PSTN Gateway Call Signaling Protocol (PKT-SP-TGCP)
- Call Flows (PKT-TR-CF)
- Architecture Framework (PKT-TR-ARCH)
- OSS Overview (PKT-TR-OSS)

PacketCable Goals

PacketCable is designed to provide comparable or better than PSTN toll-quality voice services; to scale up to millions of users; and to offer competitive features as compared to PSTN services.

To meet these high-level goals, the system must transparently interface the MTA to the PSTN so that calls can be made outbound as well as be received inbound from any domestic or international phone number. In addition, the system must support the normal suite of features, such as:

- Call waiting
- Cancel call waiting
- Call forwarding
- Three-way calling
- Voice mail message-waiting indicator

It must also support Custom Local Area Signaling Services (CLASS), such as:

- Calling number delivery
- Calling name delivery
- Calling identity delivery on call waiting
- Calling identity delivery blocking
- Anonymous call rejection
- Automatic callback
- Automatic recall
- Distinctive ringing/call waiting
- Customer originated trace

PacketCable Architecture Framework

The PacketCable architecture spans three networks: the DOCSIS HFC network, the managed IP network of the cable operator, and the interconnection to the Public Switched Telephone Network (PSTN). Figure 6.1 illustrates the general components of the PacketCable service architecture, which is composed of the following elements:

Multimedia Terminal Adapter (MTA). Located in the subscriber's home, the MTA works in conjunction with the DOCSIS CM and CMTS. The MTA provides the subscriber-side interfaces (e.g., RJ11 jacks) to existing CPE (e.g., telephone). The MTA also includes a network-side signaling interface, call processing, and media data processing facilities.

CMTS. Interfaces the HFC network to the managed IP backbone.

Managed IP Network. PacketCable servers are interconnected to a managed IP network. Managed means that the network is able to provide long-haul packet voice services, as well as support QoS, signaling, and management.

Operational Support System (OSS) and Back-Office Servers. Provide Simple Network Management Protocol (SNMP) management stations, Dynamic Host Configuration Protocol (DHCP) servers, Domain Name Service (DNS) servers, Trivial File Transfer Protocol (TFTP) servers, Web servers, record-keeping servers, provisioning servers, and cryptographic ticket-granting servers.

Call Management Server (CMS). Also referred to as Call Agent (CA). Responsible for call control and signaling-related services.

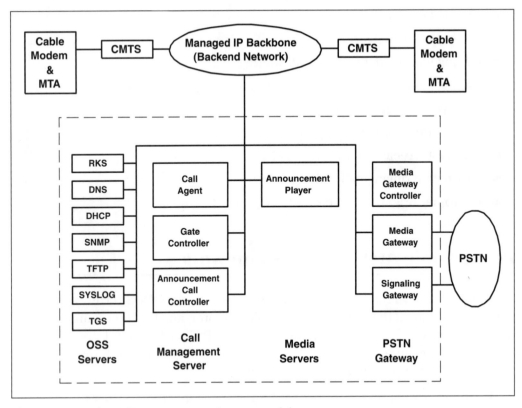

Figure 6.1 PacketCable component reference model.

Gate Controller (GC). A logical component of the CMS that coordinates QoS authorization and control.

Announcement Controller (ANC). A logical component of the CMS; used to control media announcement services to provide information tones and messages.

Announcement Player (ANP). A media server, under control of the ANC; provides the actual media streams for the Announcement function.

Media Gateway Controller (MGC). A logical component of the PSTN gateway; used to control PSTN Media Gateways.

Signaling Gateway (SG). Provides an interconnection between PacketCable signaling and PSTN SS7 signaling.

Media Gateway (MG). Provides the translation of media streams between the circuit switches PSTN world and the PacketCable packet voice network.

Multimedia Terminal Adapter and the CM

The MTA will come in two forms: *standalone* and *embedded*. The stand-alone MTA will be a separate box that will interconnect to the CM. The embedded MTA is co-resident with the CM in the same box. The focus of PacketCable V1.0 is on the embedded MTA.

Figure 6.2 illustrates an example protocol stack for an embedded MTA. The basic functionality is a DOCSIS V1.1 CM with enhancements to support packet voice applications. The PacketCable enhancements include support for PacketCable Network-based Call Signaling (NCS), Real-Time Protocol (RTP), and the MTA Functions including POTS interfaces and

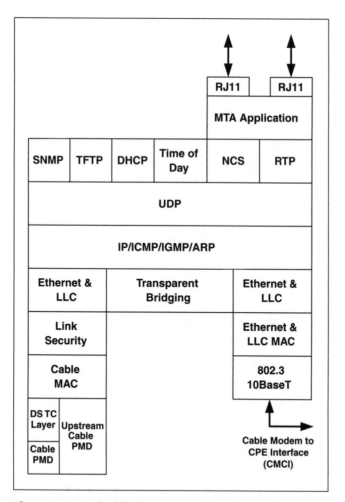

Figure 6.2 Embedded MTA protocol stack example.

voice coder/decoders (CODECs). The base function set of MTA includes the following:

- NCS call signaling with the CMS.

- QoS signaling with the CMS and the CMTS.

- Authentication, confidentiality, and integrity of some messages between the MTA and other PacketCable network elements.

- Mapping media streams to the MAC services of the DOCSIS access network.

- Encoding/decoding of media streams.

- Providing multiple audio indicators to phones, such as ringing tones, call-waiting tones, stutter dial tone, dial tone, and others.

- Standard PSTN analog line signaling for audio tones, voice transport, caller-ID signaling, DTMF, and message-waiting indicators.

- The G.711 audio CODEC.

- One or more RJ11 analog interface(s), as defined by Bellcore TR-909.

Within the MTA there will be two IP protocol stacks, each identified with its own MAC address and IP address. The DOCSIS CM stack will have its own IP address, as will the MTA application and stack. The IP addresses need not be issued from the same IP subnetwork.

CMTS

The CMTS in the PacketCable Network is delegated the following tasks for PacketCable:

- Providing the required QoS to the CM, based upon policy configuration.

- Allocating upstream bandwidth in accordance to CM requests and network QoS policies.

- Classifying each arriving packet from the network-side interface and assigning it to a QoS level based on defined filter specifications.

- Policing the TOS field in received packets from the cable network to enforce TOS field settings per network operator policy.

- Altering the TOS field in the downstream IP headers based on the network operator's policy.

- Performing traffic shaping and policing as required by the flow specification.

- Forwarding downstream packets to the DOCSIS network using the assigned QoS.

- Forwarding upstream packets to the backbone network devices using the assigned QoS.

- Converting and classifying QoS gate parameters into DOCSIS QoS parameters.

- Signaling and reserving any backbone QoS necessary to complete the service reservation.

- Recording usage of resources per call using PacketCable Event messages.

Call Management Server

The CMS provides call control and signaling-related services for the MTA, CMTS, and PSTN gateways. The PacketCable 1.0 CMS includes the following logical components:

Call Agent (CMS/CA). Responsible for NCS services to each MTA, including call features; tracking call progress state; selecting of CODECs; collecting and preprocessing dialed digits; collecting and classifying user actions.

Gate Controller. Responsible for establishing QoS management with CMTSs and other PacketCable components.

Announcement Controller. Controls network announcement media servers.

The CMS may be implemented as separate servers running as a coordinate CMS, or as separate processes running on one CMS server.

PSTN Gateway

The main functions of a PSTN gateway are: to participate with the signaling in the PacketCable network and the signaling in PSTN network via SS7, and to convert media streams between PacketCable and the PSTN. The PSTN gateway consists of the following three functional components:

Media Gateway Controller (MGC). Processes signaling messages and mediates between the PacketCable network and the PSTN. It maintains and controls the overall state for calls interconnecting with the PSTN. The MGC controls the Media Gateway (MG) for creating, modifying, and deleting calls, as well as control of operational maintenance and testing.

Media Gateway (MG). Provides the conversion facility for user voice streams between the PSTN and the PacketCable IP network. In essence, it converts Time Slot Interchange (TSI) voice circuits to voice over IP packets, and vice versa, under direction of the MGC.

Signaling Gateway (SG). Responsible for interfacing between the SS7 network and the PacketCable signaling network.

OSS and Back-Office Components

A number of services in the cable operator backend network are required for support of PacketCable services. They are as follows:

Ticket Granting Server (TGS). Provides cryptographic key management services to the PacketCable network. The TGS is based on a Kerberos server. MTAs are granted tickets to set up authentication, privacy, integrity, and access control for call signaling between the MTA and the CMS.

DHCP Server. As with DOCSIS V1.1 deployment, a DHCP server is required to assign IP addresses to CMs and MTAs.

DNS Server. Provides server support for the Domain Name System protocol.

TFTP/HTTP Server. Provides configuration file download facilities to MTAs. The HyperText Transport Protocol (HTTP) is available as an alternative to TFTP.

Syslog Server. Used to collect events and trap reports from MTAs within PacketCable. Syslog is a well-known logging daemon, which traditionally ran on UNIX-based platforms. It has the ability to listen on a well-known network port and logs messages to files.

Record-Keeping Server (RKS). Receives PacketCable events from the non-MTA components of the network, for example, CMS, CMTS, and MGC. The RKS may convert event messages into Call Detail Records (CDRs), which can then be made available to billing and other systems.

Call-Signaling Interfaces

The PacketCable architecture specifies eight different call-signaling interfaces for use within the system: Pkt-c1 trough Pkt-c8 (see Figure 6.3). This

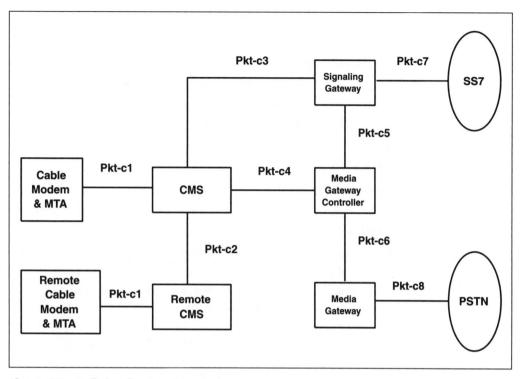

Figure 6.3 Call-signaling interfaces.

section defines the interfaces; it is beyond the scope of this chapter to detail the operation of the protocols.

Pkt-c1. NCS messages between MTA and CMS. NCS is a profile of MGCP.

Pkt-c2. Future CMS-to-CMS call-signaling protocol.

Pkt-c3. Call signaling between CMS and SG, based on ISTP/TCAP.

Pkt-c4. Future call-signaling protocol between CMS and MGC.

Pkt-c5. Call signaling between SG and MGC, using the ISTP/ISUP and ISTP/TCAP protocols.

Pkt-c6. Call signaling between MGC and MG, using the TGCP protocol. TGCP is a profile of MGCP.

Pkt-c7. Call signaling between SG and SS7, using ISUP and TCAP.

Pkt-c8. Bearer channel call signaling between MG and PSTN, using in-band MF signaling. (A future version of PacketCable may support ISDN PRI.)

To clarify the numerous acronyms used in the preceding list, note the following:

- ISTP is the PacketCable Internet Signaling Transport Protocol.

- TCAP is the Transaction Capabilities Application Protocol, which is a protocol within the SS7 stack used for performing remote database transactions with a Signaling Control Point.

- ISUP is the ISDN User Part, which is a protocol within SS7 used for call signaling within an SS7 network.

- ISDN stands for Integrated Services Digital Network.

- SS7 is the Signaling System 7 protocol developed for out-of-band call signaling within the PSTN.

- The PacketCable-defined NCS protocol is an extended variant of the IETF's call-signaling Media Gateway Control Protocol (MGCP). In the MGCP model, call state and features are implemented in a centralized location called the Call Management Server (CMS). Device control intelligence resides in the MTA. The MTA exchanges device events with the CMS and responds to commands (as a "slave") from the CMS. The CMS is responsible for setting up and tearing down calls, providing advanced services, authorizing calls, and generating billing records.

The interaction between the CMS and the MTA is flexible. For example, the CMS can instruct the MTA to notify it when the phone is taken off-hook and after seven digits have been dialed. The CMS then instructs the MTA to create a connection and to reserve QoS resources from the CMTS. The MTA may also be told to play a locally generated ring-back tone. The CMS in turn communicates with a remote CMS or MGC to finish the call setup. When the CMS detects an answer from the far end, it instructs the MTA to stop the ring-back tone and to activate the media stream connection.

The CMS and MGC may send routing queries (e.g., 800-number lookup) to an SS7 Service Control Point (SCP) via the SG (Pkt-s3 and Pkt-s5). The MGC, via the SG, exchanges ISUP signaling with the PSTN's SS7 entities for trunk management and control. The ISTP protocol provides the signaling interface for call control between the PacketCable network and the PSTN SS7 signaling network. ISTP contains the features necessary for address mapping between SS7 and IP, as well as other messaging features. ISTP emulates some functions of the SS7 protocol, allowing the IP network to interact and receive services from the PSTN.

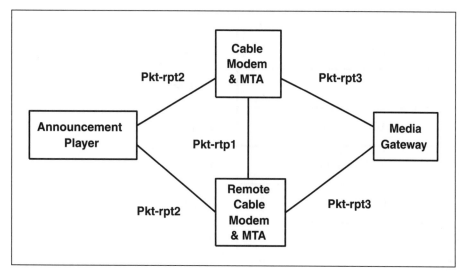

Figure 6.4 Media stream interfaces.

Media Stream Interfaces

The PacketCable architecture specifies three different bidirectional media streams for use within the system: Pkt-rtp1 through Pkt-rtp3 (see Figure 6.4). This section defines the interfaces; it does not detail the operation of the protocols.

Pkt-rtp1. Responsible for media flow between MTAs. Includes voice, video, and fax.

Pkt-rtp2. Responsible for media flow between the ANP and MTA for playback of tones and announcements.

Pkt-rtp3. Responsible for media flow between the MG and the MTA. Includes tones, announcements, and voice media flow exchanged with the PSTN.

All media stream interfaces are based on the IETF Real-Time Protocol, which is specified in RFC1899. The packet format for RTP is shown in Figure 6.5.

RTP encodes a single channel of multimedia information. RTP uses UDP and IP to get from place to place. The RTP header contains information about the type of media that is in the RTP payload, including which CODEC to use. From that information, the size of the packet and the frequency at which packets are sent are determined.

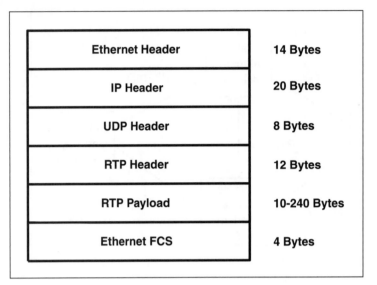

Ethernet Header	14 Bytes
IP Header	20 Bytes
UDP Header	8 Bytes
RTP Header	12 Bytes
RTP Payload	10-240 Bytes
Ethernet FCS	4 Bytes

Figure 6.5   RTP packet format.

QoS Interfaces

The PacketCable architecture specifies seven different QoS signaling interfaces for use within the system: Pkt-q1 through Pkt-q7 (see Figure 6.6). This section defines the interfaces; it does not detail the operation of the protocols.

Pkt-q1. This MTA-to-CM interface is defined only for the embedded MTA. The interface is used to: manage DOCSIS service flows and their associated QoS traffic parameters and classification rules; synchronize packet and scheduling for minimization of latency and jitter; and process packets in the media stream and perform appropriate per-packet QoS processing

Pkt-q2. This CM-to-CMTS interface is the DOCSIS QoS interface (control, scheduling, and transport).

Pkt-q3. This MTA-to-CMTS interface is used for request of bandwidth and QoS resources related to the bandwidth. The interface runs on top of Layer 4 protocols that bypass the CM. As a result of message exchanges between the MTA and CMTS, service flows are activated using CMTS-originated signaling on interface Pkt-q2. An enhanced version of RSVP is utilized for this signaling.

Pkt-q4. This MTA-to-CMS/GC signaling interface is used to communicate parameters such as media stream, IP addresses, and CODEC selection.

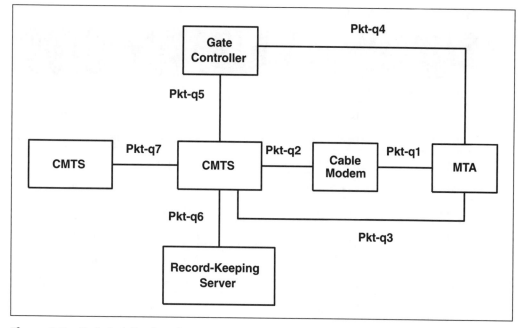

Figure 6.6 QoS signaling interfaces.

Pkt-q5. This CMS/GC-to-CMTS interface is used to manage the dynamic gates for media stream bearer channels. This interface enables the PacketCable network to request and authorize QoS changes without requiring any Layer 2 DOCSIS access network QoS control functions in MTA. When supporting standalone MTAs, no new client-side QoS signaling protocol needs to be designed. The CMS/GC takes responsibility for requesting policy, and the CMTS takes responsibility for access control and quickly setting up QoS on the DOCSIS access link.

Pkt-q6. This CMTS-to-RKS interface is used by the CMTS to signal to the RKS all changes in call authorization and usage. This interface is defined in the Event Messages specification.

Pkt-q7. This CMTS-to-CMTS interface is used to coordinate resources between the CMTS of the local MTA and the CMTS of the remote MTA. The CMTS is responsible for the allocation and policing of local QoS resources.

Security

The PacketCable architecture specifies 16 different security interfaces for use within the system, starting at Pkt-s0. Table 6.1 enumerates the interfaces.

Table 6.1 Security Interfaces

INTERFACE	PACKETCABLE FUNCTIONAL COMPONENTS	DESCRIPTION
Pkt-s0	MTA <> Provisioning Server	SNMP, MTA signature
Pkt-s1	MTA <> TFTP or HTTP server	MTA configuration file download
Pkt-s2	MTA <> Provisioning Server	SNMP, v3 security
Pkt-s3	CM <> CMTS	BPI+ privacy
Pkt-s6	MTA <> MTA	End-to-End media packets
Pkt-s7	MTA <> MTA	RTCP protocol for RTP
Pkt-s10	MTA <> CMS	MTA-CMS signaling for RTP
Pkt-s12	CMS <> RKS	Radius, Radius billing events
Pkt-s13	CMTS <> RKS	Radius events from CMTS to RKS
Pkt-s14	GC <> CMTS	GC to CMTS messaging
Pkt-s15	GC <> CMTS	Gate coordination messages
Pkt-s16	N/A	N/A
Pkt-s17	MGC <> MG	PacketCable interface to PSTN media gateway
Pkt-s18	MGC <> SG	PacketCable interface to PSTN signaling gateway
Pkt-s19	MTA <> TGS	Kerberos/PKINIT key mgmt protocol
Pkt-s20	CMS <> SG	CMS queries to PSTN gateway for local number portability

The acronyms used in the table are defined as follows:

- IPsec (IP Security) is the collection of IETF protocols for protecting IP packets with encryption and authentication.

- IKE is the Internet Key Exchange, a key management mechanism used to negotiate and derive keys for security associations in IPsec. IKE- indicates keys using preshared keys.

- MGCP is the Media Gateway Control Protocol.

- RADIUS stands for the Remote Access Dial-in User Service, as defined in RFC2138 and RFC2139.

- RC4 is a variable-length stream cipher used to encrypt media traffic in PacketCable.
- RTCP is the Real-Time Control Protocol.

Compliance Testing

On July 21, 2000, CableLabs announced it was developing compliance test plans for PacketCable. At the time, between 15 and 35 vendors were participating, with some vendors doing limited interoperability testing. The initial focus of the test plan was on the MTA, CMS, and CMTS. The compliance test plan will expand in subsequent test waves to include more elements of the PacketCable backend system, CableLabs intends to start formal compliance testing by the end of 2000.

Summary

This chapter introduced the PacketCable architecture, in order to illustrate that CableLabs, together with its vendor authors, is creating a very complete and fully featured packet voice system for the cable network that will play well with DOCSIS V1.1. Furthermore, compliance test plans with a large number of vendors are in the works. That is the good news.

The not so good news is that the PacketCable is a very large and complex suite of specifications with over 34 protocol interfaces. That means it will take some time to reach its full potential. As it grows, expect to see additional specifications and protocols, as well as updates and changes based on experience.

For Further Information

The PacketCable specifications described at the beginning of this chapter can be obtained from the public area of the PacketCable Web site, www.packetcable.com, as they are released.

The following documents from the IETF can be obtained from the organization's Web site, www.ietf.org:

RFC1889. Schulzrinne, H., Casner, S., Frederick, R., and V. Jacobson, "RTP: A Transport Protocol for Real-Time Application," www.ietf.org, January 1996.

RFC1890. Schulzrinne, H., "RTP Profile for Audio and Video Conferences with Minimal Control," www.ietf.org, January 1996.

RFC2138. Rigney, C., Rubens, A., Simpson, W., and Willens, S, "Remote Authentication Dial-in User Service (RADIUS)," www.ietf.org, April 1997.

RFC2139. Rigney, C., "RADIUS Accounting," www.ietf.org, April 1997.

RFC2327. Handley, M. and Jacobson, V., "SDP: Session Description Protocol," www.ietf.org, April 1998.

RFC2474. Nichols, K., Blake, S., Baker, F., and Black, D., "Definition of the Differentiated Services Field (DS Field) in the Ipv4 and Ipv6 Headers," www.ietf.org, December 1998.

RFC2475. Blake, S., Black, D., Carlson, M., Davies, E., Wang, Z., and Weiss, W., "An Architecture for Differentiated Services," www.ietf.org, December 1998.

Not Your Grandparent's Ethernet

The primary purpose of high-speed data cable modem systems today is to connect the subscriber with Internet services using Internet Protocol (IP) over Ethernet. Digital subscriber line (DSL) modems have pretty much the same goal. IP over Ethernet is becoming the common user's interface to the global Internet. For almost two decades, the use of Ethernet has been concentrated for use in business as a local area network (LAN) technology. Today, the emergence of high-speed broadband access services is pushing Ethernet into the home.

The term Ethernet encompasses both the packetization of data within an Ethernet frame and the LAN protocol used to arbitrate exchanges of frames between stations on the Ethernet network. Too often, and in error, cable modem systems are thought of and deployed as big Ethernet LANs. This chapter will explain why cable modem LANs are a bad idea for use in today's residential public access networks.

The Socialization of Cable Modems

The "socialization" of Ethernet into the home via a cable modem is dependent on a number of factors, which relate to how people perceive Ethernet service and whether it is of value to them.

NOTE For most socialization issues regarding cable modems there is a corresponding issue for DSL modems. DSL technology doesn't escape the need to be socialized. However, the focus of this is book is on cable modems, and precludes a lengthy discussion of DSL technology.

The socialization of broadband access technology is geared primarily to the subscriber, specifically, how well cable modems fit into their lives. People judge cable modems by a number of criteria:

- Can I get the service in my area?

- Do I have a choice of ISP with my cable modem service?

- Can I buy it off the shelf at my favorite e-commerce site?

- Can the cable modem be upgraded. or do I have to keep sinking money into each major upgrade?

- Will it be easy for my home computer to connect to the cable modem?

- How do cable modems really use Ethernet?

- Are there any hidden surprises?

- Am I receiving the service I think I'm paying for? I've heard that, as more of my neighbors sign up for cable modem service, my access will become slower.

Where cable modems get deployed is very much dependent on where a cable operator's home office decides they'll get deployed. It appears that the first target markets for cable modems are cities where there is an existing population of high-end Internet users, meaning numerous existing Internet users or a predictable source of income. In less dense areas, or those deemed less willing to spend on the new technologies, cable modem service will be slower in appearing. All that said, in some situations, cable modem deployment is prey to time and money constraints of the cable operators themselves. Another cause for delay may be a dearth of qualified installers.

NOTE The issue of being able to select an ISP for cable modem service is called *open access*. This is an extremely important topic, to which the next chapter is devoted.

One of the main goals of the North American DOCSIS project is to produce interoperable products from multiple vendors, such that cable modems can be sold via retail channels. The ideal is that everyone will be able to purchase a DOCSIS-certified cable modem, take it home, hook it up to the cable, then hook their computer up via Ethernet, load up some software, call up the cable operator, and have service turned on— all without having to dispatch a cable technician to the home. In practice, we're a far from this, although it is seen as an achievable goal. Still, today, usually at least one technician must come out to the subscriber's home. Typically, the CATV drop cable from the pole or box needs to be replaced with higher-quality cable and connectors. The grounding block, the demarcation between the cable operator's network and the home wiring, also may need to be relocated. Ethernet is still too new for a large number of people, and they need help to install the interface in a PC and properly configure the networking software. However, already, Apple Macintosh computers are Ethernet-socialized, and come standard with built-in Ethernet. PCs, too, are getting more socialized: Some have embedded Ethernet; others may be sold in the future that have embedded cable modems (or DSL modems).

Ethernet is a very convenient and easy-to-use, plug-and-play networking technology. The 10BaseT interface was the first customer networking equipment connection specified for DOCSIS cable modems. With Ethernet, one or more computers can easily share Internet access via the same cable modem. Expect to see external cable modems supporting a Universal Serial Bus (USB) connection. USB is an easy-to-use, plug-and-play extended I/O bus technology for both PCs and Macintoshes. (A USB port supports only a connection to one host computer; it is not a networking connection like Ethernet.) The DOCSIS project appears to be interested in a future internal DOCSIS modem. An Ethernet interface is not required when a personal computer has an internal cable modem.

One for All, All for Ethernet

Ethernet is a universal networking protocol and connection technology. It has been around since the late 1970s, which is almost ancient in computer networking time. Today, Ethernet is inexpensive and comes in several different flavors of speeds and cabling. The most typical speed is 10Mbps, using Category 5 twisted-pair wiring, also known as 10BaseT. Due both to dropping costs and the ease of combining with 10BaseT transceivers, 100Mbps over twisted-pair (known as 100BaseT) is being rapidly deployed. Today, many low-cost Ethernet network interfaces support 10/100, which means the transceiver can run at 10Mbps or 100Mbits. The speed is determined through a negotiation process between the transceivers at each end of the twisted-pair cable. From the point of the user, it's just plug-and-play.

Ethernet Refresher Course

Before going into the nuances of Ethernet behavior with DOCSIS and cable modems, a brief review is the Ethernet protocol is in order.

Ethernet packets are called *frames*. Frames are composed of five data fields: the Destination Address (DA), the Source Address (SA), the Ethernet Type (Type) value, the User Data, and the Frame CheckSum (FCS). Frames have a size range of 64 bytes up to approximately 1500 bytes. The Ethernet Type field allows multiple protocols to run over an Ethernet LAN network. For example, the Internet Protocol (IP) runs very nicely over Ethernet, as do other network protocols such as Novell's IPX, AppleTalk (as EtherTalk), Microsoft Networking (NETBEUI), and others.

Ethernet Addresses

Ethernet stations identify themselves on a LAN using a 48-bit identifier called a MAC address. The source address and destination address in the Ethernet frame are each 48-bit values. The Ethernet protocol uses special bit combinations to determine whether the address is an Individual (I) or Group (G) address. Individual addresses are also called *unicast addresses*. The protocol requires that a unique Individual address be programmed into the interface at manufacturing time. The Institute of Electrical and Electronic Engineers (IEEE) sells large blocks of MAC addresses to vendors, and it is possible to tell the manufacturer of the transmitting interface by observing the source address in packets. A Group address is either a *Broadcast* or a *Multicast*. The Broadcast address has only one value, whereas a Multicast address has many different address values, each of which is called a *multicast group*.

The source address in an Ethernet frame is always an individual address that identifies the sending station. The destination address can either be an Individual or Group address. Each Ethernet station receives every Ethernet frame transmitted on the network. Whether a station processes that frame is based on the following rules:

- A Broadcast address is processed by all stations connected to the Ethernet network.

- A Multicast address is processed only by those stations belonging to the multicast group.

- An Individual address is processed only by the single station corresponding to that unicast address.

NOTE It is possible to put an Ethernet interface into what's called *Promiscuous Mode*, causing the station to receive and process all frames received on the interface, but special software is required to do this. This mode is used by LAN analyzers, packet sniffers, and some hacking software.

The Ethernet LAN Protocol

The Ethernet LAN-sharing protocol is in a class of protocols called Carrier Sense, Multiple Access with Collision Detection, or CSMA/CD for short, defined as follows:

Carrier Sense. Refers to the fact that when a station has a frame to transmit, it can listen to the shared Ethernet network and determine whether another station is already transmitting. A station will only transmit if it detects that no other station is transmitting.

Multiple Access. Means that many stations are sharing the same communications media. In an Ethernet network, for any giving successful frame transmission, there is one sending station and multiple receiving stations.

Collision Detection. The process of the station monitoring the electrical signal on the Ethernet cable when it is transmitting its frame. Transmission signals in copper wire travel more slowly than the speed of light. Because of this, it is possible for two or more stations to begin transmitting at nearly the same time, thereby interfering with one another. This interference can be sensed electrically, triggering a collision detection event. Any station sensing a collision detection sends out a short "jabber" signal, to ensure that all colliding stations actually detect a collision; then each station goes into Backoff mode. Ethernet uses a scheme called Truncated Binary Exponential Backoff. Simply stated, if a station collides, it computes a random number. If it collides on the next transmission attempt, it doubles the number of possible values it can use, and computes another random number. For each subsequent collision, it doubles the number of possible values. But when the algorithm has doubled 15 times, it does not double again; it computes a random number of that maximum range. So, for each colliding station, it is expects that the random attempts of each station will sort out, to allow each colliding station to eventually transmit its frame in the clear.

Ethernet Switches and Bridges

Ethernet was originally designed for stations sharing a single coaxial cable, where only one station could be transmitting at a time. For the past half-decade, the Ethernet protocol has been enhanced through the use of twisted-pair cabling and so-called intelligent Ethernet switches and bridges. With a twisted-pair cable, each Ethernet interface has a pair for receiving frames and a pair for transmitting frames. Original-style 10BaseT interfaces would only work in half-duplex mode, meaning the station or the port on the Ethernet switch could be either transmitting or receiving, but not both at the same time. Collision detection was managed by each individual station. Some modern switches and interfaces support full-duplex operation, where the station and switch/hub can be simultaneously transmitting and receiving. In addition to full-duplex operation, the use of sophisticated circuitry and memory has enabled Ethernet switches to manage collision detection.

Ethernet switches provide multiple ports, each port connecting to either a single station or another Ethernet switch. Each switch keeps track of which individual source addresses it hears on each port. The switch builds a table or other memory structure to keep track of source addresses and ports. When a switch receives a frame from one port, it examines the addresses, and transmits the frame to one or more other ports depending on the following general algorithm, called a *learning bridge algorithm*:

- If the destination address is a Group (Broadcast or Multicast) address, the frame is transmitted on all other ports on the switch.

- If the destination address is an Individual (unicast) address and matches a source address it learned on another port, the frame is transmitted only to that single port.

- If the destination address is an Individual address and doesn't match a previously learned source address, it is transmitted on all ports.

- If the destination address is an Individual address and matches a source address it learned on the same port on which it was just received, the frame is discarded.

NOTE The algorithm described here is necessarily general. The numerous details of learning bridges are beyond the scope of this book.

Learning bridges were originally designed to join two or more Ethernet network segments to build a bigger network. However, bridges only permit the transmission of individually addressed frames that need to be transmitted. In contrast, an Ethernet hub or repeater also links Ethernet segments, and transmits all frames heard. Ethernet switches further refine the process by transmitting only individually addressed frames to the single port on which they need to be transmitted, not to all ports. Further, an Ethernet switch can do this simultaneously among multiple sets of transmitting and receiving ports.

Ethernet hubs and repeaters typically don't have much internal memory for storing frames. In the past, sometimes there was no memory at all, and the signals were just electrically repeated. Ethernet repeaters were usually two-port devices.

Ethernet switches always have frame memory. Some begin transmitting the frame on another port, if possible, based on other traffic, before receiving the end of the frame from the source port. This is called *cut-through*. Other Ethernet switches always buffer the entire frame before transmitting on the destination port(s).

Another configuration of Ethernet bridges and switches is called a *half-bridge*. In this configuration, the switch or bridge is, in effect, split down the middle with the halves separated by a slower-speed point-to-point connection. For example, a T1 line (1.44Mbps) might be used to bridge traffic between a home office and a remote office in another part of the same town by using half-bridges. Each half of the bridge implements a modified learning bridge algorithm so as to only send the necessary packets over the slower-speed link.

Ethernet LAN Attributes

A number of Ethernet LAN attributes shared by all Ethernet LAN stations need to be highlighted:

- The Ethernet protocol is a local area network technology that provides for the transfer of Ethernet frames from one station to another.

- Ethernet framing supports multiple higher-layer protocols.

- Every station has equal access and opportunity to the shared network via the Ethernet protocol.

- The Ethernet protocol shares bandwidth by allowing a station's transmission to collide, recognize it, and then randomly back off in time, until the colliding stations don't collide anymore. For this to work, every station has to be able to hear every other station in the Ethernet network. In an Ethernet LAN that is connected via Ethernet switches, the switches themselves buffer packets and provide collision detection and avoidance.

- If more bandwidth or stations are needed, network administrators can segment their network by using one or more Ethernet switches.

- If more bandwidth is needed for QoS, the network administrator can upgrade the network from 10Mbps to 100Mbps; (that is, in order to get better quality of service, more link bandwidth can be thrown at the problem.

- Typically, every station on the network belongs to the same organization.

Now we can delve into the use of Ethernet in the cable modem environment.

Oops, There Goes the Neighborhood

As explained earlier, Ethernet has been a fundamental part of cable modem history and deployment. Most external cable modems ever made have had an Ethernet interface to connect to the home computer. But for this discussion, it's very important to observe the distinction between the cable modem over-the-RF MAC protocol from the end-to-end Ethernet service. The Ethernet service runs over the cable modem system's MAC protocol. The end-to-end Ethernet service is what the subscriber's PC experiences directly.

Two chief architectural aspects distinguish legacy cable modem systems from modern cable modem systems: *dumb headend transverter* and *intelligent headend controller*. Though there are examples of intelligent headend controller designs and some implementations from the 1980s, most widely deployed data-over-cable systems were likely to use a dumb transverter.

In almost all legacy cable modem systems, the Ethernet service was implemented as a LAN service. That is, the CATV network became a transparent replacement for a shared Ethernet coaxial cable. Every cable modem shared every Ethernet LAN attribute, listed earlier. Any ISP for the network connected up via another cable modem and provided service through that cable modem to the other cable modems. Every cable modem could exchange Ethernet frames with every other modem.

Modern cable modem systems use an intelligent headend controller. The chief distinction is that the Ethernet service connects to the ISP over a WAN interface in the controller. The ISP is *not* located on the other side of a cable modem; only subscribers attach to cable modems. In this architecture, the Ethernet service is best described as a large distributed Ethernet switch or as a set of half-bridges connected by the CATV network. The headend controller, the "master," plays the role of the other half of the learning bridge for the half-bridge located in every cable modem. If the Ethernet service in the intelligent controller allows the Ethernet frames received from one cable modem to be transmitted back down the cable to one or more cable modems, the Ethernet service is running as a LAN, and every cable modem's Ethernet port is similar to the port on a large Ethernet switch; thus, everyone can talk to one another.

Anecdotal information (in the form of complaints from subscribers to cable modem systems) collected over the past several years reports that subscribers either can see other subscribers' disk drives or printers or that their own personal computers (and printers) have been compromised, or used, in some fashion, against their wishes. In a LAN environment, every station can exchange Ethernet frames with every other station. The most significant difference between the LAN and the residential cable LAN is that the other stations do not belong to the same administration. In a business environment, if you find that another employee is behaving badly over the office Ethernet, you can locate the person and deal with it quickly. In a residential LAN cable modem system, you don't know who the other user is, nor can you conveniently walk up to his or her door in hopes of remedying the problem easily.

NOTE The problem of having access to a neighbor's personal computer over the cable network was described by the folks at Com21 to be the "oops, there goes the neighborhood" (OTGTN) problem.

At this juncture, we want to clear up a misconception: that a subscriber on one cable modem can "sniff" the traffic of another cable modem. This is likely to be true if the system is a legacy dump headend system and if the vendor hasn't fixed the problem. In this case, cable modems look more like repeaters, transferring every package everywhere. In contrast, the intelligent headend controller systems have usually implemented some form of Ethernet switching. Recall from the review course earlier that Ethernet switches forward only unicast packages from a source port to the destination port. All other ports in the system don't see or hear that unicast traffic. In a cable modem system, traffic flow of Ethernet frames is between the individual cable modem's Ethernet interface and the WAN interface in the headend controller. That is, a unicast frame arriving at the WAN interface from the Internet will be forwarded via the cable modem MAC protocol to the individual cable modem corresponding to that unicast MAC address. Conversely, a unicast frame received from a cable modem will only be forwarded to either the WAN interface or to another individual cable modem. This behavior prohibits one cable modem from being able to perform a third-party sniff of the unicast traffic of another cable modem.

Unicast traffic appears to be well protected from sniffing. However, if the headend controller's Ethernet switch is in LAN mode, then broadcast and multicast frames are forwarded to every cable modem. The higher-layer protocols (e.g., IP, IPX, EtherTalk, NetBIOS) use broadcast and multicast techniques to find neighbors on a LAN, and to establish unicast connections between the neighbors. For example, the Address Resolution Protocol (ARP) is used by IP to find the unicast MAC address of another IP station on the same LAN. ARP uses an Ethernet broadcast to initiate the address information exchange. With ARP, an IP station connected to a cable modem can find the unicast MAC address of another IP station on the same cable modem system, if, and only if, the headend controller is in LAN mode.

Fortunately, the DOCSIS standard is an intelligent headend controller-based cable modem system. Unfortunately, it specifies an end-to-end Ethernet service without sufficient specification in the headend controller to limit the OTGTN problem. It is up to the vendors of the CMTS product and the cable operators' deployment and their provisioning of any options to make sure that one subscriber cannot talk directly to another subscriber using the Ethernet service.

A Megabit in Every Pot

One of the promises of cable modem systems is the delivery of a fast Internet connection to the subscriber. But just how fast is fast? Is the fast connection always going to be fast? More often than not, the first users in a cable modem system experience blazing fast speeds. As more users are added to that cable modem system, the original speeds are reduced proportionately. This creates a torrent of "I'm not getting what I paid for!" complaints from users.

NOTE Up-to-date anecdotal postings from cable modem users can be found in the USENET newsgroup comp.dcom.modems.cable. This group provides interesting insight to the minds of cable modem subscribers. The more vocal users generally have an axe to grind and must be taken with a grain of salt. On the other hand, it is worthwhile tracking the themes that consistently run throughout the threads.

In reality, the fast speed anyone should expect falls in a range, from approximately 256Kbps (32KBps) up to about 1Mbps (125KBps). Remember that the download speed reported by some Web browsers is in kilobytes per second (KBps). Multiplying that number by 8, yields kilobits per second (Kbps). Understanding how cable modem MAC protocols share bandwidth is important to solving the problem of how to keep subscribers happy.

Since 1979 and through 1994, high-speed data-over-cable TV networks have borrowed protocol techniques from Ethernet and ALOHA. Not every vendor chose to go this route, but many did. In these systems, cable modems used the CATV network as a replacement for the common LAN coaxial cable. The Ethernet protocol itself didn't work over the propagation delays of residential CATV networks, but the ALOHA and slotted-ALOHA WAN satellite protocols did work, and they could move Ethernet frames over the residential access CATV network.

In these legacy networks, every station had equal access to the broadband LAN, just like an Ethernet LAN. There was no central controller allocating bandwidth, so users got a proportional share of the bandwidth based on how many total users were active at the same time. An Ethernet LAN protocol enabled stations to abuse bandwidth, by taking up more than their fair share . A notable exception to the dumb headend controller class was the cable modem system made by the company LANCity, now part of Arris Interactive, which was discussed in Chapter 1. LANCity's approach was to elect one of the cable modems to be a pacer station, in effect, a central controller for the other modems on the CATV LAN. LANCity created a cable protocol called UNILINK, which allocated bandwidth better than the much simpler ALOHA-based models. Bandwidth allocation in the LANCity system is coarse-grained, but useful for allocating bandwidth compared to a controller-less system. The LANCity system was well respected by the North American cable industry, and in 1996, was selected as the starting point for the development of the MAC protocol in the DOCSIS RFI specification.

Intelligent headend controllers are required for achieving precise bandwidth allocation. The caveat is that vendors of the headend controller needs the foresight to engineer these controls into their product. In addition, they have to make the controls easy for the cable operator to use. The secret of bandwidth allocation is to create a scheduling system in the headend controller that is capable of allocating both downstream and upstream bandwidth on a per-cable modem basis.

Initially, most of the traffic over the cable modem network is generated by subscribers surfing the World Wide Web. The underlying transport protocol for Web browsing is the Transmission Control Protocol (TCP). TCP is a protocol that uses acknowledgment (ACK) packets to confirm the correct reception and sequencing of packets. This creates an end-to-end reliability. When someone is Web browsing, these ACKs flow from the subscriber to a given Web site server. A property of TCP is that if you throttle (rate-limit) the flow of ACKs, the flow of downstream data is proportionately reduced. Therefore, a cable modem system that can rate-limit a cable modem's access to the upstream bandwidth will effectively limit the availability of downstream capacity to that same cable modem. Another motivation for rate-limiting the upstream is that, typically, there is less upstream data-carrying capacity than downstream capacity. The upstream capacity is therefore far more precious a resource, and so must be appropriately shared. Another aspect of controlling the upstream bandwidth is to prevent abusive users from taking more than their fair share.

As explained earlier in the book, the DOCSIS V1.0 specification is chiefly a best-effort system; that is, the specification didn't detail the allocation of bandwidth to and from cable modems. Some vendors have included value-add improvements to their V1.0 CMTS products, enabling bandwidth allocation on a per-modem basis, sometimes called quality-of-service features. In reality, these are bandwidth allocation features. The DOCSIS V1.1 specification adds the necessary support to both the cable modem and the CMTS for more precisely controlling bandwidth allocation from a cable modem, including QoS support for data and voice. When these systems are deployed, cable operators will have a more uniform system for managing bandwidth allocation.

The bandwidth available via the cable modem system is one of the main points of focus when subscribers question the quality of their access. In fact, subscriber access to the Internet is also impacted by the speed of the WAN link that connects the cable operator's headend facility with the next hop toward the Internet. The cable operators and their partner ISPs have deployed a system for providing Internet services to their subscribers. *Bandwidth throttling*, or *choking*, can appear any point in the system where there is insufficient capacity to meet demand. The cable modem system may not be at fault, rather some piece of the system in the backend network.

Allocating Bandwidth Using Pricing Plans

Charging for Internet access today is a lot like eating out. An all-you-can-eat restaurant usually sets an affordable flat price, but limits what is offered on the buffet tables and how often new food is served. Other restaurants charge by the item or set of items, the à la carte approach. If you want the more expensive entree or bottle of wine, you pay more money. Cable Internet service operators, for the most part, have been charging a flat rate for "buffet" Internet service, although some operators charge using the à la carte approach, and offer different-sized bandwidth allocations for different prices.

What's the difference between the two approaches in terms of the socialization of the cable modem service? A flat-rate approach, also called a single price tier, is common to the cable Internet service offered by such providers as Excite@Home and Time Warner's RoadRunner service. For example, in January 2000:

- Excite@Home (www.home.com) was charging from $39.95 to $44.95 a month, depending on the market, at speeds up to "100 times faster than a 28.8Kbps modem." That translates to up to 2.8Mbps to the subscriber.

- RoadRunner (www.rr.com) was charging an average price of $39.95, with varying price per market for "blazing speed," with no actual statement, just a sliding-bar download demonstration of how fast it was compared to ISDN and dial-up 28.8Kbps service.

From either of these offerings, it's hard to determine what bandwidth subscribers are actually going to receive on a moment-to-moment basis for their money. That said, at the time of this writing, there were over a million cable modem subscribers, and most were paying a flat rate.

Another approach to managing bandwidth allocation is to give the subscriber the opportunity to pay more money for more bandwidth. Offering multiple price tiers with multiple bandwidth allocation plans lets the subscribers choose what they will pay for what level of performance. The catch, of course, is that the cable modem equipment must be able to support the various bandwidth tiers that may be offered. Moreover, the prices of the bandwidth tiers have to be well thought out. Once put into service, increasing the price or reducing the allocated bandwidth for a tier would be viewed negatively by subscribers. One advantage of this approach, however, is that the bandwidth allocation mechanisms in the headend controller will produce consistent performance as long as the service tier has not been heavily oversubscribed. If an operator does provide multiple tiers, and if there are subscribers paying for service at each of the tiers, a straightforward analysis demonstrates a better return on investment and increased net present value over a five- to seven-year period. However, there are many factors that go into the cable operator's business plan, and this may or may not be one that influences a multiple-tier approach.

NOTE DSL competition started out with the multiple-tier service approach. For example in January 2000, residents and businesses in the San Francisco Bay Area, DSL price plans were offered in multiple tiers starting at $49/month for 1.5Mbps x 128Kbps ADSL residential service from PacBell (www.pacbell.com) to $499 per month for 1.5Mbps x 1.5Mbps SDSL business service from Concentric (www .concentric.net).

Summary

The major problem with socializing cable modems is creating the customer support structure that will keep services operating smoothly and effectively as perceived by the subscriber. Recent reports state that the biggest challenge facing cable operators is managing the support costs of the cable modem service, and that the cost of support alone can make or break the business.

Cable operators and their ISP partners are exploring new service territory by exposing greater numbers of subscribers to high-speed Internet access. The technology and its reliability are part of the equation. Timely turn-up of service and effective response to problems are part of the socialization process.It is important to deploy a cable modem to meet the expectations, demands really, of the subscribers, without hidden surprises, such as the aforementioned neighborhood LAN problem and the diminishing bandwidth problem.

Using a LAN service model for residential access was a good place to start in the business, but for the longer term, it is inappropriate for a public residential access network, for the reasons stated earlier. If the LAN option is available, it should just be turned off.

The diminishing bandwidth problem is the unfortunate side effect of deploying a cable modem service without first communicating a clear service model to the subscriber, and then enforcing that model with facilities built into the cable modem system. Giving subscribers maximum bandwidth at the outset will cause problems down the road if later the subscribers feel they are getting lower QoS than they believe they were paying for. Ethernet best-effort access with all stations equal was a way to get started in the business. However, having bandwidth allocation policies and multiple service classes is the best way to start out and continue in the business. First, a given class or tier can have its own bandwidth allocation rates and priorities. Second, the enforcement of that tier keeps the performance consistent with the user's expectations. Third, having multiple tiers is a better business model and leads to higher return on investment.

CHAPTER

8

Open Access over Cable

The intent of this chapter is to focus on the important topic of open access, specifically addressing the many technical aspects to its implementation. This chapter also points out the need for a common understanding of the problem space. Currently, there is no single definition of open access. Consequently, when any operator, service provider, or vendor promises to provide open access, a red flag should go up.

NOTE This chapter is based on "Comments on the Technical Ability to Implement Open Access Provisioning via High-Speed Data over Hybrid Fiber-Coaxial Cable Television Systems in the United States," a white paper prepared by Mark Laubach at the request of the White House National Economic Council in May 1999. The original white paper is available from www.inconvenient.net.

As implied by the first paragraph, a lot of controversy surrounds the topic of open access to Internet services over cable television networks. To begin to understand what all the fuss is about, we will first examine what open access is all about and why it is so important to today's rollout of cable modem services.

One camp in this controversy contends that subscribers today can reach any content they want through the private cable system and over the public Internet. This access method has been given a label of *content open access* or *open content access*, as if it were a new feature, when in fact it is nothing more than a new label for the Internet. Internet users have always been able to freely access public applications, and therefore, content, in a nondiscriminatory manner over the network. It is this property of the Internet that has resulted in its current worldwide acceptance and its vitality. The very foundation of the public global Internet comes from the ability users have to globally accessible public applications and content on a nondiscriminatory basis (except for age) and, usually, for a reasonable fee. More important, this property must be preserved as we move forward into the new world of broadband access methods. In short, the concept of content open access is redundant. The focus rightfully belongs on network open access.

Thus, open access as used in this chapter refers specifically to *network* open access, that is, on the capabilities of the network infrastructure itself to provide open access to both subscribers and service providers. For network architecture-savvy individuals, this refers to the architecture and capabilities of the Physical, Data Link, and Network layers of the International Standards Organization (ISO) network model, or the Link and Network layers of the Internet Engineering Task Force (IETF) model used in the construction of the last-mile residential access system and the backend operator and ISP networks that interconnect with the access system.

OPEN ACCESS FOCUS IS ON THE NETWORK The focus of open access is on the capabilities and architecture of the network itself, not on access to applications.

Generally, open access involves the concept of multiple Internet service providers, each simultaneously, but independently, using the same cable TV network to supply service to its customers. Included in this concept is the notion that a subscriber of cable modem services could choose his or her Internet service provider. This concept is not currently supported by the cable modem rollouts in the United States for two main reasons:

- The North American standard specifications for cable modems—that is, the DOCSIS Radio Frequency Interface specification—does not support open access at this time. This is a technical limitation.

- The majority of cable modem subscribers are being serviced by one of the two nationwide cable ISPs, either Excite@Home or Time Warner RoadRunner. Both of these ISPs view their markets as a one-service provider business.

From a subscriber viewpoint, depending on where residents are, this means the cable operator will likely only offer services from a single Internet services provider. For example, an AOL customer, using its dial-up services may also be receiving Internet service from Excite@Home on the cable modem. That subscriber can enjoy a high-speed over-the-Internet connection to AOL through his or her cable modem without any problems, but that subscriber also ends up paying both AOL and Excite@Home for monthly service.

If you are a service provider, a large nationwide ISP, say AOL, you might think it unfair that an incumbent cable ISP might have preferential access to a cable modem-based subscriber, in effect locking you out of highly competitive markets where DSL may not be available.

From a community standpoint, local government officials might want to encourage competition among ISPs for the benefit of driving better price and service for their citizens. They might regard having multiple ISPs over the local cable system as an advantage. Unfortunately, that's not possible right now.

Cable operators argue that their private funds and efforts built the cable system in any market, and because it is "their system," not a publicly regulated system such as the phone company, they are within their business rights to offer the Internet service of their choice.

As you can see, this issue comprises much more than just technology. It is complex, and may have to be sorted out via local and possibly national policy regulations. Nevertheless, it is very useful to understand the technical issues of open access, and that is what this chapter is about.

Defining Ideal Open Access

As already explained, there is no lack of definitions for open access. And that is the problem: No common definition exacerbates the controversy regarding this issue. Therefore, for the purposes of trying to contrast and compare approaches, we will use an open access model based on a set of "ideal" general requirements. To that end, the definitions on page 209 are used in the ideal requirements:

NOTE These requirements do not represent a consensus of opinion of today's open access providers, nor are they meant as an official definition for use by the government or any regulatory agency. They are used here to illuminate and support comparisons of different open access provisioning methods that are discussed in this book.

SKIPPING AHEAD

For those readers not interested in the technical details of open access, this highlights the important points from this chapter:

- Open access provisioning is technically possible in all high-speed data broadband residential and commercial access networks.

- Cable television is not enabled, and open access is difficult due to historical and technical issues.

- Currently, digital subscriber line is enabled, and is extending open access provisioning now.

- Metropolitan area wireless services (e.g., MMDS) have no standard at this time; without guidance it will repeat cable television issues.

- Broadband satellite systems have some open access capabilities.

An open access mandate aimed at short-term (less than three years) availability would generate great problems for the U.S. cable industry, as the technology to support open access would take two to three years to develop and deploy. To date, CableLabs and its member cable operators have not viewed open access as necessary; hence, there is no vendor support planned in customer premises or headend equipment in the foreseeable future.

The initial release of the North American Data Over Cable Service Interface Specification (DOCSIS) Radio Frequency Interface (RFI) (V1.0) specification for cable modems does not directly support open access. The subsequent release (DOCSIS RFI V1.1) does provide lower-layer protocol enhancements that can be used for a version of open access provisioning, but no attention has been paid to open access provisioning in the development of the specifications.

Due to the delays in achieving widespread DOCSIS RFI V1.0 rollout, the industry will move rapidly to deploy V1.1. It is expected that the majority of the deployments toward at the end of 1999 and early 2000 will be either V1.1-certified or V1.0-certified, capable of being software-upgraded to V1.1. Nonupgradeable V1.0 cable modems would continue to operate in V1.0 mode.

The facilities provided by DOCSIS RFI V1.1 could be used to implement *ideal open access* provisioning for cable television networks. However, implementation requirements contained within the RFI specification and other DOCSIS specifications would need to be appropriately updated to document which facilities should be engaged for the open access system, for example, choice of IEEE 802.1p versus ATM. Previously deployed V1.0 cable modems could not participate, and would need to be replaced where open access is needed. Previously deployed V1.1 cable modems may lack software or hardware capabilities required to achieve open access provisioning with a software upgrade; hence, they would have to be replaced where open access is needed. It is also likely that headend Cable Modem Termination Systems (CMTSs) would need to undergo partial hardware upgrade or complete replacement where open access is needed, even to support one open access-provisioned cable modem. It would be possible for an open access CMTS to support open access modems as well as legacy nonopen access modems.

Subscriber. Refers to the residential or commercial end user who is receiving a service (e.g., Internet service, IP dial-tone service, packet voice service, packet video service, etc.) that is delivered over the broadband access network.

Service provider. Refers to the organization or business supplying one or more services to the subscriber.

Broadband access provider. Refers to the owner or operator of the broadband access network last-mile facilities to which subscribers are connected and through which services are exchanged between the subscriber and the service provider.

Broadband last-mile facilities. Refers to one of the following: a DSL, a CATV plant (concentric pair), a fiber-to-the-curb (FTTC) plant, a wireless network, a satellite network, and, in some cases, combinations of these access methods.

The discussions and conclusions of this chapter are made relative to the ideal open access model that is presented in the following subsections. We note that it is possible to implement open access systems that do not meet these requirements but that still might have viable appeal to subscribers and service providers. However, these requirements have been structured to be durable over time, as well as apply to other broadband access networks such as DSL and wireless systems.

Requirement 1: Provider Selection

The technical delivery of a high-speed data broadband access facility to a residential home or commercial site allows subscribers to be provisioned to the service provider of their choice, selected from a set of service providers; for example: high-speed data (i.e., Internet) access and potentially separately for packet voice service provider(s) access. The number of service providers in this set may be from several to upward of several hundred.

The intent of this requirement is to make available to the subscriber more than one service provider option, and to preclude the necessity of changing the broadband access network or subscriber equipment when moving from one service provider to another. Thus, when a broadband access network service is delivered to a subscriber, that subscriber should be able to choose a service provider, where that service provider has made arrangements with the broadband access provider. For example, if three ISPs have arranged to provide service, then the subscriber should be allowed to select from among the three. The same applies to voice and video services.

In addition, each type of service (e.g., data, video, voice) should have its own list of service providers so that the subscriber is not forced to order all types of service from one provider. Note that this is a technical requirement statement only and not a statement of policy.

Requirement 2: Multiple Providers

Extends Requirement 1(R1) to support multiple service providers selected from a set of service providers; the broadband access device (e.g., cable modem) and facility would allow a subscriber to be served by multiple providers. For example, the subscriber might be serviced by his or her employer's IP service provider for in-home telecommuting at the same time he or she pays for an Internet service provider for private nonwork-related Internet access, and, perhaps, a packet voice provider for voice services, with the potential to use a different service provider for each enabled phone service.

This requirement extends the technical capability of requirement R1 to require the broadband access equipment in the subscriber's premise to support multiple service providers of the same type. For example, a subscriber may need two ISPs to provide service to the home, one a general ISP, the other an employer's ISP. For example, a subscriber may need access to two different voice telephony providers, one for personal phone calls, the other provided by the local school system for use with educational programs for children. From a technical standpoint, the number of multiple service providers of the same type might be limited to three or four, but in all cases would be greater than one.

Additionally, this requirement precludes the need to install a second broadband access network to the subscriber's premise for services from a second service provider.

Requirement 3: Ability to Provide

A service provider is technically able to offer service to its customers via any high-speed data broadband access network that reaches that customer. Actual delivery of services will be dependent on a number of factors, including backend network access, access network physical deployment issues, tariffs, quality-of-service needs, franchise rights, settlement fees, and others.

This requirement means that there should be no technical barriers of entry for a service provider to reach its customers over any given broadband access network. At the same time, it recognizes that a connection to a broadband access network is not free, nor is it a right, rather a business relationship between the broadband access network operator and the service provider. Furthermore, any costs should be calculated fairly and applied in a nondiscriminatory manner to all service providers.

Requirement 4: Data Rate Allocation

The broadband access network should support service contracts and provide reserved individual or aggregate data rate to a subscriber or service provider. The allocated rates may be statically provisioned or dynamically changeable through signaling with the subscriber or service provider. The broadband access network system should support a range of data rate allocations that may be contracted between the service provider and the subscriber. For example, Internet data access may offer a best-effort service with contracted minimum and maximum data rate delivery and/or delay agreements, such as 386Kbps or 1.5Mbps full-duplex Internet data service with or without a committed information rate (CIR).

The intent of this requirement is to give broadband access network operators sufficient data rate controls throughout their systems to ensure that subscribers and service providers are receiving their expected and agreed-to allotments. That is, it should be technically possible for the broadband access operator's network to support data rate allocation. The actual amount of such allocations is agreed to as part of the business relationship between the service provider and the operator, and subsequently between the service provider and the subscriber. Once a contract (or other agreement) has been made, the broadband access network will deliver data rates as expected.

Note that subscribers should be permitted to install any type of equipment in their premises as long as it meets the interconnection standards of the broadband access network's subscriber premises equipment. A service provider or broadband access network operator may not deny service on the basis of type or types of equipment belonging to the subscriber, if that equipment meets established interconnection standards, for example, Ethernet 10BaseT for data, RJ11 POTS service for telephones, and so on.

Requirement 5: Quality of Service

The broadband access network should support specific QoS attributes for specific services (e.g., delay, jitter, and error rate), which meet the subscriber's needs of that service; for example, a 64Kbps constant bit rate with low delay and jitter per off-hook packet voice connection while the call is in progress. The QoS required could be statically provisioned or dynamically changeable and negotiable through signaling with the subscriber or service provider. This includes streams invoked in the course of Web browsing that require dynamic QoS.

In the near future, broadband access networks will simultaneously handle mixtures of high-speed data, voice, and video communications. Therefore, in addition to being able to tailor data-rate allocations, the broadband access network must be able to handle the different QoS requirements for the type of service being provided. For example, packet voice telephony has more strict requirements for timely packet delivery, as compared with simple Web browsing. Furthermore, the subscriber's premises equipment, as well as the service provider's connection equipment must be able to support Requirement 2.

Requirement 6: Subscriber Containment

The broadband access network must contain and limit abusive subscribers; that is, a subscriber in one service should not be able to interfere with the services being provided to another subscriber in the same or different service. For example, a large file transfer by one cable modem user should not interfere with the voice call in progress with another cable modem user.

At any given time, individual subscribers will be placing different demands on the broadband access network for the delivery of services. When subscribers attempt to obtain more service—for example, faster data rates—the broadband network should contain the subscribers' service to the contracted rates. Furthermore, other subscribers who are operating within their contracts should not suffer the effect of any other subscriber.

Requirement 7: Provider Containment

The broadband access network must contain and limit abusive service providers; that is, a service provider should not be able to allow its services to interfere with other services or with subscribers of other services.

At any given time, individual service providers will be placing different demands on the broadband access network for the delivery of services. When providers attempt to obtain more service, the broadband network should contain any single provider's service to the contracted rates. Furthermore, other service providers operating within their contracts should not be affected by any other service provider.

Requirement 8: Link Privacy

In the case of shared media or publicly propagated media, high-speed broadband access networks (e.g., cable television, wireless), communications over that media between the subscriber's premises equipment and the headend must employ cryptographic techniques at the data link layer to provide a high degree of privacy for individual subscriber communications. Note level of privacy is intended only to prevent vicarious observation by other parties connected to the same shared media; this is not an end-to-end cryptographic solution.

This requirement is specific to shared media broadband access networks, specifically cable networks and wireless networks. That is, any public medium used by the broadband access network over which the private communications of one subscriber can be vicariously viewed by any other individual (i.e., not an employee of the broadband access operator) should be encrypted over public links on a per-subscriber basis, for individual communications, or on a per-group basis for multicast communications.

Requirement 9: User Content Preservation

User information contained in packets and packet headers exchanged between the subscriber's premises and the service provider are not altered by the broadband access network or the backend network, except as defined by protocol standards and standards of operation of Internet gateways and routers.

This requirement maintains that the content of the digital data packets exchanged between the service provider and the subscriber should not be altered in any nonstandard way by the broadband access network, unless it is specifically provided for in the business agreement between the operator and the service provider, and subsequently disclosed to the subscriber. An example of what might be agreeable is the broadband access network may force a packet of voice data to have a specific IP precedence value in the IP header in order to distinguish that packet from others for QoS support reasons.

Requirement 10: Provider Address Management

The addresses used by the service (e.g., IP addresses for Internet, phone numbers for packet voice, etc.) are managed by the service provider, not by the broadband access network provider.

This requirement gives service providers control of any network addresses used by their service. Specifically, as part of the provisioning and turn-up of service between the provider and subscriber, the subscriber will receive address and configuration information from the service provider, not from the broadband access provider.

Requirement 11: Provider Subscriber Management

Service providers are able to manage their service to the demarcation point associated with the customer premises equipment. For example, ISPs can manage their service delivery through the broadband access network to the cable modem, and be able to troubleshoot to the cable modem Ethernet interface; or a CLEC can manage a voice over cable service to the RJ11 jack in the cable modem.

When subscribers have problems with their service, they should be able to communicate with their service provider, and that provider should be able to monitor and manage customer service connections from the their network through the broadband access network and to the point of service demarcation in the customer's premises. All the subscriber should have to do is call the service provider. Any issues with the broadband access network should be handled via separate communications between the service provider and the broadband operator, on behalf of the subscriber. Furthermore, the broadband access network and the customer's premises must be technically manageable by the service provider on a per-subscriber basis.

Requirement 12: IP Dial-Tone Service

The subscriber has the option of obtaining unblocked unrestricted IP packet exchange for any packet submitted to and/or received from the access network, according to IP protocol standards and Internet standards for routers and gateways. That is, broadband access network and broadband service providers will not block and/or alter IP packets except according to IP routing standards. The subscriber may be subject to contracted data rate allocation restrictions and admission control policies for quality of service. It should be noted that most subscribers will want to take advantage of the services and content provided by the cable operator and/or their ISP; for example, residential subscribers seeking turnkey email, Web-based content, and the like. However, some subscribers will want a plain IP connection (IP dial tone) without additional services and features; for example, experienced subscribers, small businesses, larger commercial establishments, and others.

Most large ISPs create applications and Web browsing environments as an aid to their subscribers. This is done for many reasons, including ease of navigation of the ISP's services, as well as helpful support for less experienced users. However, more technically savvy users may want only a connection to the Internet without all the bells and whistles, and without any specific login encumbrances. In these cases, the subscriber should be able to select IP dial-tone service only. Furthermore, this should be done at less than or equal to normal subscription rates. That is, a subscriber should not be penalized for requesting only IP dial-tone service.

Summarizing Broadband Access Technologies

This section gives a brief overview of the alternative broadband technologies that are in existence today for residential access networks.

Digital Subscriber Line

The varieties of broadband access via digital subscriber line (ADSL, SDSL, G.lite ADSL, etc.) all, technically, support nearly, if not the ideal, open access system. Today's DSL deployments are more or less following the specifications set forth by the ADSL Forum; that is, they are following a standard. The basis for DSL open access support is Asynchronous Transfer Mode (ATM) networking between the subscriber premises equipment and the service provider. ATM virtual circuits are straightforwardly provisioned from the ADSL modem via the broadband access network provider, through the central office and the access network and backend networks, to the service provider. The architecture of DSL and developed technology supports open access from initial deployment.

Fiber to the Curb

Over the past decade, there have been significant developments in fiber-to-the-curb (FTTC) technologies for the delivery of voice, video, and data services to subscribers. However, deployment of this broadband access technology has slowed since early efforts. But it is anticipated that efforts will renew after DSL deployment has reached sufficient penetration. Motivation for moving to FTTC solutions include the timely replacement of aging twisted-pair copper plants, and the need to push more last-mile access bandwidth closer to the subscriber. FTTC architectures are capable of supporting ideal open access provisioning.

Metropolitan Area Wireless

The deployment of high-speed data for Internet access over wireless systems (e.g., MMDS) has been undergoing substantial churn in the past several years. At the time of this writing, both the market demands, service providers, and the technology appear to be better aligned for the next attempt to grow the market.

Currently, the high-speed data over broadband wireless access network environment has no standard, although industry rumors hint that several companies will enter the market in the near future, with adapted systems using the DOCSIS RFI Media Access Control (MAC) protocol. In contrast, Com21 is considering entering the market with a wireless version of its CommUNITY, ATM-based system. Another company, Hybrid Networks, which has been in the market for several years, and has ridden its ups and downs, does not at this time appear to have an ideal open access solution.

In the absence of public or de facto standards and policies, the politicians may select a DOCSIS-based system, thereby perpetuating the same lack of support for open access provisioning as the cable modem specifications. Only a small—and shrinking—window of opportunity exists in which to persuade the wireless market to adopt a more ideal open access posture.

Broadband Satellite

To date, high-speed Internet services via satellite transmission systems have some active deployments; and it is expected that there will be an increasing number of satellite-based deployments over the next several years, including changes in deployment architectures. DirectPC is an example of a satellite-based Internet service for personal computers.

Early satellite deployments provide chiefly high-speed, one-way downstream service (provider to subscriber), using a terrestrial return path. Newer deployments will make use of two-way transmissions. Due to propagation delays and bandwidth requirements per transponder, there will be degrees of scale. It may be possible for satellite systems to support ideal open access provisioning; however, more study is needed in this area.

Cable Television

The CableLabs DOCSIS project has produced a family of coordinated specifications dealing with many aspects of a cable modem access system (see www.cablemodem.com for more information). The most well-known, as explained throughout this book, is the Radio Frequency Interface (RFI) specification, usually referred to as the DOCSIS Specification, DOCSIS V1.0 or DOCSIS V1.1. DOCSIS RFI V1.0 was adopted by the Society of Cable Telecommunications Engineers (SCTE) Data Standards Subcommittee (DSS) as its standard in July 1997. In the fall of that year, it was adopted as the U.S. position to the ITU J.112 recommendation.

Recall that the DOCSIS RFI specification is technically founded on an evolved LANCity-based protocol, with the objective of achieving these attributes: residential, low-cost, off-the-shelf, Internet access, interoperable (base functions) with vendor differentiation. The architecture of the DOCSIS system is a single, large Ethernet-based bridged LAN, with a single ISP service provider. As noted earlier, V1.0 is primarily a best-effort Internet access system; V1.1 adds protocol support and sufficient operation detail to provide dynamic QoS facilities for packet voice services, in addition to packet data services, along with other enhancements such as baseline privacy, multicast support, and more. In addition, V1.1 has packet recognition support for IEEE 802.1p tagged Ethernet frames, to support both priority tagging as well as virtual LAN (VLAN) tagging.

As explained previously, DOCSIS-based systems started to become widely available in the second half of 1999; by the end of that year, in North America, just over a million cable units had been deployed. Prior to this, a number of proprietary cable modem systems were deployed in the United States, from 3Com, ADC, Com21, Hybrid Networks, LANCity (later Bay Networks, then Nortel, now Arris), Motorola, Phasecom, Terayon, Zenith, and others. Of these, Motorola, LANCity/Arris, Com21, and Terayon are the most commonly deployed. Of these, only Com21 system directly supports open access provisioning by use of direct Layer 2 VLAN support and ATM networking (similar to DSL), which more or less comes close to providing the ideal open access system. At this time, there are cable overbuilders (e.g., Knology in southeastern United States) that are using Layer 3 approaches (described later) to provide less than ideal, but workable, open access provisioning.

Focus on the DOCSIS RFI Specification

To most effectively describe open access provisioning techniques using DOCSIS RFI-based cable modem systems, this section has been organized based on the ISO networking layer, starting with the physical RF layer up through applications.

Open Access at Layer 1: The Physical Layer

In the DOCSIS RFI world, the physical layer of the networking stack is provided using RF channels that operate within the RF spectral bandwidth of a cable television network. In the downstream direction (headend transmitter to subscriber receiver) the RF channels are compatible with existing analog modulated television channels. The high-speed data channels are digitally modulated, are 6MHz wide, and have a raw data-carrying capacity of approximately 30Mbps using 64 Quadrature Area Modulation (64 QAM) (with an option to use 40Mbps with 256 QAM modulation in CATV plants that have a cleaner downstream noise environment). A high-speed digital data channel uses the same digital modulation standard as for digital television—that is, MPEG encoding.

However, MPEG's lower layer, called the MPEG Transport Stream, allows for the digital data to be typed: Video has one type, DOCSIS data has another type. The amount of available downstream RF spectrum available to all services (analog video, digital video, data, and others) varies from system to system and cable operator to cable operator. There is no one standard configuration or topology that is followed. In modern systems, new deployments and upgraded systems typically support roughly 750MHz to 860MHz of downstream spectrum, which in turn is subdivided into 6MHz television channels. Some cable plants are already at capacity for television distribution, leaving at most one channel available for digital data. In the best-case scenarios, one or two digital data channels can live in the rolloff region at the high end of the plant's operating bandwidth. Digital data is less sensitive in the rolloff and can provide viable service. However, there is precious little available room at capacity plants. Some cable operators have many tens of MHz available in the downstream, and could potentially support multiple downstream high-speed data RF channels; however, this capability is not universal.

In the upstream direction (subscriber transmitter to headend receiver), the allocated spectrum is from 5MHz to 42MHz (sometimes less than 42MHz). The selection of 5 to 42MHz is fraught with problems due to ingress noise impairments from outside of the cable plant. Unfortunately, this RF spectrum is "dirty," noise-wise, and presents a somewhat difficult environment for digitally modulated signals. As such, a little less than half the band is virtually unusable (except in very clean cable plants), leaving about 15 to 18MHz of spectrum for signals. Due to the inherent noise environment, the type of modulation used for upstream communications is less dense for reasons of robustness. Moreover, RF channels are smaller in spectral width. In DOCSIS, an upstream data channel RF spectral width can be anywhere from 200kHz to 3.2MHz depending on configuration, which is done at deployment time. In terms of data-carrying capacity, a DOCSIS V1.0 and V1.1 channel will operate either at, approximately, 2.5Mbps raw or 5.0Mbps raw in most plants. In cleaner plants, the upstream capacity can be doubled per channel, to a maximum of 10Mbps in 3.2MHz.

NOTE The available RF spectrum in cable plants is highly asymmetric, with potentially up to 10 times more bandwidth in the downstream direction. Unfortunately, this causes upstream bandwidth for high-speed data services to run out before exhausting potential downstream bandwidth for high-speed data channels.

When a DOCSIS Cable Modem Termination System (CMTS) is installed in a headend, one downstream channel is configured, along with one or more upstream channels. Specific configurations, number of channels, and placement of RF channels are determined at installation time.

Open access at Layer 1 means that for each service provider that wants access to the cable network, a separate CMTS and set of downstream and upstream RF channels must be allocated. This approach does not work, because:

- There is insufficient RF bandwidth downstream or upstream to create a single, let alone multiple, high-speed data service for varying numbers of providers.

- FCC regulations require that cable operators must control (operate) and manage all RF transmitters attached to the cable plant so that the plant does not inadvertently radiate unwanted signals into the community. This means that all CMTS devices must be managed and operated by the cable operator. The CMTS design and requirements do not readily enable the divorce of the CMTS operation from the service provider using the equipment.

Conclusion: Open access at Layer 1 is not workable.

Open Access at Layer 2: The Data Link Layer

Layer 2 is called the Data Link Layer or the Media Access Control (MAC) protocol layer; it supports a variety of data link protocols (e.g., Ethernet and the DOCSIS MAC). In DOCSIS RFI V1.0, this layer provides an Ethernet frame-based access protocol, mediated by the DOCSIS MAC. The architectural approach used between the CMTS and all the cable modems is that of a single, large Ethernet-based LAN—that is, a switched/bridged large Ethernet address space supporting a single broadcast domain. As noted numerous times, the bandwidth management practice of DOCSIS V1.0 systems is a best-effort system. There is little to no data rate allocation management, except by vendor initiative; likewise, there is no real QoS management to differentiate services, for example, packet data from packet voice.

DOCSIS V 1.1 adds several important elements that can be used as foundations for open access (although open access did not drive their implementation): packet classification, QoS support, multiple queues/services per cable modem, better support for multicast, and recognition of IEEE 802.1/p frame tagging (VLAN and priority tagging). DOCSIS V1.1 efforts are focused on supporting packet voice with packet data services.

DOCSIS V1.0 provides for an ATM cell as a MAC data packet type; however, neither V1.0 nor V1.1 make use of ATM cells, nor are there any requirements for this in the specifications beyond support of the packet type flag. The DOCSIS RFI was not designed to support ATM service classes; i.e., the combination of bandwidth management and QoS control (delay, jitter, cell loss). Neither is there support for any services over ATM, for example, Ethernet or Point-to-Point Protocol (PPP) over ATM. The use of the ATM packet type and the limited support was left for future development. No vendor offers support for ATM.

The following list reviews the ideal open access requirements and their support by the DOCSIS RFI specification:

Requirement 1: Provider selection. Multiplexing through the Layer 2 space would allow multiple service providers access via shared downstream and upstream data channels. The multiplexing capability at Layer 2 is limited, and can only be accomplished using the IEEE 802.1p VLAN tagging or by exploiting the enhanced multiplexing of ATM. Though DOCSIS V1.1 recognizes the IEEE 802.1p tagging, it omits any specifications or requirements for support of the VLAN operations in the cable modem or the CMTS.

To date, there has been some interest in exploiting only the priority tag field that is part of IEEE 802.1p to aid in packet classification and QoS support. Therefore, initial DOCSIS V1.1 cable modems will not support VLAN tag processing as a standard. VLAN tagging support would allow an Ethernet frame to be tagged and switched accordingly. This has the potential result of either a VLAN per service provider, with all common cable modems sharing the same tag, or of an ATM virtual circuit equivalent in the Ethernet frame, allowing cable modems to directly receive frames from a single provider. Note that the IEEE 802.1p VLAN tagging supports up to 2,048 values, which presents aggregation, scaling, provisioning, and labeling challenges when put into practical use. Efficient processing of Ethernet frame tagging may require hardware enhancements for acceptable packet throughput performance. Leveraging DOCSIS ATM cell transport support would remedy the multiplexing scale issue to be equivalent with DSL multiplexing capability. As mentioned, there are no requirements in DOCSIS for any services over ATM transport, leaving it vendor-dependent at this time.

Requirement 2: Multiple providers. The DOCSIS architecture is a single-provider service at Layer 2. With IEEE 802.1p extensions, it would be possible to extend to multiple service providers, but that would likely quickly exhaust the VLAN tagging space. Leveraging DOCSIS ATM cell transport support would remedy this, but, again, there is no requirements support in DOCSIS for any services over the ATM transport, leaving it vendor-dependent at this time.

Requirement 3: Provisioning capability. The DOCSIS CMTS would have to be able to provision and perform packet switching, based on a Layer 2 tag between its WAN interface and all the cable modems the CMTS supports (1K to 3K cable modems). Service providers could be connected to individual subscriber cable modems or connected to groups of cable modems within the limits of the IEEE 802.1p tagging. However, given the 2K VLAN tag identifier space, the service providers' equipment would have to be collocated near a CMTS if the number of subscribers for that provider became large. An ATM-based approach would provide more multiplexing address space and would allow service providers to be connected with individual subscribers in just about any configuration. But there have been no requirements for CMTSs to support tagging or ATM for service provider separation.

Requirements 4 through 7: Data rate allocation, QoS, subscriber containment, and provider containment. The additional facilities in DOCSIS V1.1 support these needs from a Layer 2 protocol and management standpoint. Actual support would vary by vendor implementation.

Requirement 8: Link privacy. DOCSIS supports link encryption as an option. Cable operators would need to enable that option in their deployments.

Requirement 9: Content preservation. In DOCSIS RFI V1.0 and V1.1, Ethernet frames (Layer 2 packets) are not altered by the DOCSIS MAC during exchanges between the cable modem and the CMTS. If the cable modem or the CMTS embodies a Layer 3 IP routing facility (or similar facility) based on vendor value-adds, the Ethernet frames exchanged is altered or discarded; but the Ethernet data, the user data contained within the Ethernet packet (typically an IP packet), is not. These operations are normal for Ethernet switches and IP routers. Thus, though the subscriber data contained within the IP packet is unaltered, the IP packet header may undergo expected changes as per IP standards and router and gateway standards.

With the Layer 2 Ethernet tagging approach, IEEE 802.1p allows for Ethernet headers to be extended with tagging information. Inserting, altering, or removing a tag would change the subscriber's Ethernet packet, but according to standards. With a Layer 2 ATM approach, the Ethernet packet could be exchanged unaltered between the subscriber's cable modem and the service provider. (Note that there are many variations for Layer 2 multiplexing approaches, some of which would preserve the subscriber's Layer 2 packet completely, others that would modify the packet according to defined standards and procedures. In either scenario, with Layer 2 processing, the subscriber's IP packet would remain unaltered.)

Requirement 10: Provider address management. For Layer 2 Ethernet addresses, the standards dictate that the vendor build a MAC hardware address into each Ethernet controller. Service providers do not manage or administrate Layer 2 Ethernet addresses. Internet protocols have been designed for vendor assignment of Layer 2 Ethernet addresses. ATM addresses—for example, virtual path identifiers (VPIs) and virtual circuit identifiers (VCIs)—are managed over each segment of the ATM path, such as between ATM switches. ATM addressing does not require that a service provider be in control of all VPI/VCI assignments between it and the subscriber, only that there be an end-to-end connection established between subscriber and provider.

Requirement 11: Provider subscriber management. There are no provisions in the DOCSIS architecture for the cable modem Layer 2 service to be managed by anyone other than the single ISP.

Requirement 12: IP Dial-tone service. This service is independent of Layer 2 service.

Summary of Layer 2 Open Access

DOCSIS V1.0 cable modems do not provide sufficient support for ideal open access provisioning at Layer 2. DOCSIS V1.1 offers additional support that can be exploited for ideal open access at Layer 2, provided that the specification is expanded and enhanced. It is not clear that Layer 2 Ethernet tagging solutions would scale as needed to support numerous service providers and numerous subscribers. ATM cell transport is the most flexible method, as demonstrated by DSL services; however, while ATM cell transport is provided for in DOCSIS, there is no support for ATM networking or for defined services; nor are there specifications and requirements at this time for its use. In addition, DOCSIS was not optimized for ATM networking. The issues at the CMTS are unexplored at this time. Without the support of written additions to the DOCSIS specifications, specific functions would be vendor-dependent. Therefore, any DOCSIS V1.1 modems deployed prior to open access support may need to be replaced, simply because they may not be software-upgradeable to an open access modem.

It would be possible for an open access Ethernet tag-processing CMTS to simultaneously support open access-enabled and nonopen access-enabled modems, with the caveat that the nonenabled modems could continue to interoperate only with the incumbent Layer 2 provider.

Open Access at Layer 3: The Network Layer

Internet Protocol Techniques Layer 3 is called the Networking Layer; it supports the IP and the Address Resolution Protocol (ARP). The DOCSIS RFI system has been optimized for the transport of IP packets. DOCSIS is principally a Layer 1 and Layer 2 service. The specifications call for rich assortment of Ethernet, IP, TCP, and UDP packet filtering, making the DOCSIS cable modem aware of Layer 3 and Layer 4 packets. In DOCSIS RFI V1.0, these filters are used principally to provision a given cable modem for packet access rights into the network. DOCSIS RFI V1.1 adds filters, including packet classification filters that are essential for QoS support. The cable operator and/or service provider control these filters in each cable modem. Said differently, a DOCSIS RFI V1.0 and V1.1 cable modem is a Layer 2 switched Ethernet service with Layer 3 and Layer 4 packet-filtering awareness. The specification stops there however; different vendors will augment their cable modem's functionality with one or more Layer 3 services, such as IP routing, specialized routing, tunneling, virtual private networking (VPN), Point-to-Point Protocol (PPP), and applications services, such as voice-over-IP (VoIP).

Recall that the DOCSIS RFI creates a switched Ethernet service to support a single Ethernet segment at Layer 2 and, essentially, a single large IP subnetwork at Layer 3, with a single provider administering IP addresses. There are no facilities in the specifications for providing open access provisioning—that is, multiple Ethernet segments, multiple IP subnetworks, or multiple address administration. There are Layer 3 open access solutions that, to varying degrees, meet the ideal requirements. A few operators are already implementing these solutions to provide open access support.

There are two general classes of Layer 3 solutions: specialized IP routing (forwarding) and tunneling, described in the following two subsections.

Specialized IP Routing

Specialized IP routing encompasses known techniques such as source address-based routing, proxy ARP, policy-based routing, and others. For source addressed-based routing, the cable operator administers IP addresses for the subscriber's home computing equipment, but also maintains special source-based routes for each subscriber, routing packets to/from his or her assigned home IP address(es) to the designated ISP. Additional home IP address assignments (e.g., for multiple personal computers) are taken from the same service provider address space. A large IP address space is subnetworked into smaller IP address space allocations, where each allocation is dedicated to a specific ISP. Backend routing in the service provider's network directs packets from the home to the ISP via the source address, rather than the traditional destination address.

The support of source addressed-based routing in the DOCSIS CMTS and the cable modem is transparent only if the vendor has provided a Layer 2 service; the CMTS doesn't see Layer 3 routing. In general, Layer 3 routing techniques are essentially transparent to Layer 2 devices, even with sophisticated DOCSIS packet filtering. If, however, the CMTS or cable modem supports any Layer 3 routing intelligence, then that vendor's products either must ship addressed-based routing-aware or must be upgraded as such. This may or may not involve a hardware upgrade and/or replacement.

DOCSIS QoS for subscriber services/applications is possible; QoS can still be achieved over the CATV network. In the cable operator's backend network, QoS is determined by vendor support in the various equipment. Any vendor support for specialized routing is outside the scope of the current DOCSIS specifications. (Note that for specialized routing, cable operators have to design and select appropriate IP routing technology to support their deployment model. Currently deployed backend technology may not directly support specialized routing for open access. Furthermore, supporting multiple service providers via the same cable modem is problematic for specialized routing techniques, as the cable modem must support multiple IP subnetworks. Usually, they support one IP subnetwork, though it is technically possible to implement support for multiple IP subnetworks in the cable modem, if required by an update specification. A more detailed examination of source address based routing is presented at the end of this chapter.)

Proxy ARP can be used by the cable modem, CMTS, and/or headend router to preferentially reroute IP packets to a preferred router port (provider), based on Ethernet MAC address, IP source or destination address, or other mechanisms. The effect is to transparently steer IP and ARP implementations to support semi-intelligent service provider provisioning. That said, support for this type of provisioning could impact the cable modem, CMTS, or vendor headend router, depending on vendor implementation. For example, a cable modem with IP router functionality might be more affected than a cable modem Ethernet bridge. It is not clear that these mechanisms can provide differentiated services for QoS or multiple-service provider provisioning in the cable modem. More study is needed in this area to explore capabilities.

Policy-based routing, just beginning to emerge at this time, is an augmentation of normal routing forwarding rules to include routing decisions based on addresses and packet classification criteria. Early indications are that it may have merit for open access. For example, policies could be established to route QoS-sensitive packets on separate links from best-effort packets. However, more study is needed in this area to explore capabilities.

NOTE Proof that specialized routing can provide access from a subscriber to a single ISP of his or her choice exists. Knology (www.knology.com) is exploiting address-based routing techniques (and likely other supplemental techniques) to connect subscribers with either MindSpring or other ISPs. Details on the Knology solution were not available at the time of this writing, but in general it can be said that the system operates with specialized routers at the headend and possibly with customized software in the cable modems. It is believed the solution's source addressed-based routing approach can be wrapped around any cable modem system to produce a workable, but less than the ideal, open access provisioning system. The solution may be transportable to other cable operators.

Tunneling

The term tunneling, as used in this chapter, refers to a mechanism by which to tunnel IP packets through another protocol, such as IP, PPP, Point-to-Point Tunneling Protocol (PPTP), Layer 2 Tunneling Protocol (L2TP), or IP Security (IPsec) for Virtual Private Networking (VPN) support. With the general form of tunneling, the IP address of the end of the tunnel within the DOCSIS cable modem is administered by the cable service provider, while the IP addresses that flow through the tunnel are administered by the service provider. This model assumes that, for each service, the cable modem would create a tunnel between itself and a remote access server maintained by the service provider. This tunnel would run transparently through the CMTS and any intervening routing and switching equipment until it reached the service provider. The cable modem would be aware of which IP addresses assigned should be moved through which tunnel.

Technically, it is possible for a single cable modem to support multiple tunnel endpoints by leveraging an extension of its DOCSIS packet-classification filters. This also allows voice traffic to be segregated into a different tunnel from other QoS traffic, for example. There are several different tunneling protocols, each with its own distinctions. The one undesirable effect of tunneling is that it forces all tunneled packets to have the same QoS, thereby requiring different tunnels to be established for different QoS needs even if the endpoints of the tunnels are to the same service provider. DOCSIS does not specify any requirements for tunneling in the cable modem, leaving it to the vendor to value-add support. The best implementation would be for the cable modem to be the endpoint of the tunnels, because the cable modem has direct knowledge of QoS requirements and packet classifications to support QoS. In addition, tunneling itself as well as tunneling with encryption, requires more processing power in the cable modem than with the base DOCSIS system. This suggests that the cable modem would have to be replaced to support multiple-service provider provisioning via tunnels.

VPN technology is becoming increasingly popular for telecommuters, because work-at-home employees can benefit from high-speed access over the Internet to their corporate VPN firewall. In these cases, corporate MIS departments manage any security configurations (cryptographic keys, logins, passwords) and local IP address assignments. If extended beyond corporate telecommuting, VPN and/or other cryptographic authorization techniques can be used for access to service providers. This enhanced level would require software and hardware processing beyond that of the

DOCSIS specification. [Note, at this time, VPN facilities are often being deployed with software in personal computing equipment or via specialized appliances placed between the subscriber computing equipment and the cable modem. A future natural migration for external VPN support is into the broadband access mediation device, for example, the cable modem. At this time, there is no mandatory or even a suggested implementation of a Layer 3 IP signaling protocol that could be used to communicate with the DOCSIS system. Hence, QoS interaction between the DOCSIS system elements (CMTS and cable modem) and other routers in the network is up to individual vendors.]

CableLabs' PacketCable project is focusing on packet voice and video over cable data systems, specifically on DOCSIS RFI V1.1 implementations. The PacketCable effort is driving QoS signaling protocols for use in voice call setup and teardown. Possibly, in the future, this may be extensible to Layer 3 open access provisioning implementations. Some believe that vendors will be implementing the IETF Reservation Protocol (RSVP) in their CMTS, allowing QoS signaling exchanges with other RSVP aware routers. It is too soon to tell precisely where all the efforts are headed; however, some signaling protocol will be available in the future to interconnect the CMTS with the backend network in a meaningful QoS manner.

Probably, requirements for signaling will emerge first from a PacketCable specification requirement, as opposed to directly from a future DOCSIS RFI requirement.

Requirement 1: Service provider selection. Source address-based routing, policy routing, and tunneling mechanisms provide a method of allowing subscribers to be connected to a service provider of their choice. DOCSIS does not specify either mechanism.

Requirement 2: Multiple providers. With the current DOCSIS specification, source address-based routing appears suited to provisioning only a single service provider per cable modem. Policy-based routing appears capable of provisioning a single service provider per QoS type per cable modem. Software and hardware enhancements would likely be needed to support multiple service providers via a single cable modem; for example, the cable modem might need to be augmented to support specialized routing or tunneling. Policy-based routing and tunneling could support multiple providers and the capability to differentiate/route various services to different providers—for example, packet voice to a voice provider or Internet access to an ISP. Tunneling must be done via vendor software or hardware cable modem extensions or external boxes.

Requirement 3: Provisioning Capability. Source address-based routing and policy-based routing must be done in conjunction with the cable operator and/or service provider administering IP addresses for the cable network. Tunneling approaches without QoS support are independent of cable data IP address administration. QoS-aware tunneling must be done in conjunction with the cable operator, the CMTS, and cable modem management. That is, tunnels containing QoS-sensitive packets must be identified to the cable backend infrastructure to receive proper priority. Technically, either solution is workable to varying degrees of the ideal.

Requirement 4: Data rate allocation. This feature follows directly when dynamic QoS and signaling are universally supported and coupled to the DOCSIS Layer 2 facilities. Absent that, any data rate allocation support, dynamic or static, has to come from vendor value-add implementations.

Requirement 5: Quality of service. Without QoS signaling, Layer 3 approaches require static QoS provisioning of the CMTS and/or cable modem as required and as provided for by individual vendors. At some point in the future, QoS signaling will be available for IP, and will likely be implemented in CMTS and/or cable modems as a requirement for PacketCable packet voice services. At that time, QoS signaling support would be in place for open access provisioning. Some vendors may have provided sufficient management and control capability to allow some QoS to be statically provisioned.

Requirement 6: Subscriber containment. This requirement relies directly on DOCSIS RFI Layer 2 facilities and the CMTS's ability to manage cable modem bandwidth appropriately for a subscriber's access to the network.

Requirement 7: Provider containment. At Layer 3, the CMTS will have to be software- and, possibly, hardware-upgraded to manage downstream and/or upstream bandwidth per service provider. In the absence of or in addition to CMTS functionality, provider containment would be performed where the service provider connects with the cable operator's backend network.

Requirement 8: Link encryption. This requirement is not an issue at Layer 3, except to mention that Layer 3 packets will be transparently encrypted on a per-cable modem basis over the DOCSIS RF channels.

Requirement 9: Content preservation. Specialized routing techniques will alter the headers of IP packets that traverse the cable operator's network between the cable modem and the service provider. Tunneling approaches preserve the IP packet header that was placed into the tunnel at the cable modem. When open access is provided at Layer 2, subscriber data contained within the IP packet is unaltered; however, the IP packet header may undergo changes per IP and router and gateway standards.

Requirement 10: Provider address management. Source address-based routing techniques require that the cable operator and the ISP managing the CMTS, cable modems, and DHCP server control the IP address space for cable modems and the subscriber's personal computer equipment. Policy-based routing should allow for the outside service provider to coordinate address allocations with the cable operator and cable ISP. For tunneling techniques, the subscriber-side tunnel endpoint address is in a space administered by cable operator and/or associated cable ISP; the actual addresses that flow through the tunnel are managed by the service provider to which the tunnel is connected on the backend-side of the network.

Requirement 11: Provider subscriber management. There are no provisions in the DOCSIS architecture for the cable modem Layer 3 service to be managed by anyone other than the single ISP.

Requirement 12: IP Dial-tone service. There are no provisions in the DOCSIS RFI specifications for altering IP packets in general. However, QoS requirements and packet classification at the CMTS and cable modem may require that certain fields of the IP header be altered due to results of certain packet classification rules and subsequent processing.

Summary of Layer 3 Open Access

DOCSIS RFI specifications at Layer 3 do not support ideal open access, due to the single-provider architecture of the DOCSIS system and Layer 3 and Layer 2. DOCSIS RFI V1.1 does provide facilities that can be exploited for ideal open access solutions, but additional design work must be done and requirements added before ideal open access can be supported by the DOCSIS standard.

There are specialized routing and tunneling techniques that support workable open access solutions, but they are less than ideal. These techniques could be extended, however, for improved solutions, but that would require enhancements at Layer 2 for ideal open access.

Technical Observations

Clearly, the cable system *can* technically support ideal open access provisioning, as proven by the Com21 CommUNITY cable modem system that is a nearly ideal open access system. That said, the DOCSIS standards developed by the North American cable industry do not support ideal open access. Reengineering ideal open access into the DOCSIS system at Layers 2 and 3 is possible, but not in the short term. As such, to date, DOCSIS-compliant products being shipped, and subsequently widely deployed, will not be capable of providing ideal open access provisioning within the DOCSIS system itself.

In the short-term, techniques such as specialized routing and tunneling can be used to augment a DOCSIS system to allow a broadband access provider to provision IP addresses so as to preferentially route packets to and from a subscriber-selected service provider. Such a system is workable, but may not support all the requirements of the ideal open access system. Further developments in IP signaling for data rate allocation and quality-of-service support will improve as vendors implement standard Layer 3 signaling—when available.

For the longer term, the DOCSIS RFI V1.1 specification has fundamental facilities necessary for enabling ideal open access provision. But these need to be further developed, then implemented and tested. Unfortunately, sufficient motivation currently does not exist within the cable operator community to actively pursue enhancement of the specifications to achieve an ideal open access system. However, it could be mandated, that, for example, in three to five years, high-speed data-over-cable systems must support ideal open access provisioning. Updating the applicable DOCSIS suite of specifications would be necessary, and one or more technical solutions would have to be adopted. IEEE 802.1p VLAN tagging support is useful, but it has less scaling potential than ATM. DOCSIS could make use of its ATM cell transport capability, to achieve the same scale and level of ideal open access as the DSL solution, but the DOCSIS system was not designed to optimally handle ATM, hence there would be a drop in data channel efficiency.

Augmenting the DOCSIS specifications to support ideal open access would require a substantial effort, probably taking six months to a year from the time the cable industry becomes motivated to direct CableLabs and vendor authors to update the specifications. Following an approved specification it would take approximately 18 months before multiple certified vendors were active in the marketplace. So, even if the motivation were there today, it would be mid-2002 before DOCSIS-based open access cable modems and CMTSs were available. Between now and that hypothetical time, there would be close to several million cable modems deployed, most DOCSIS V1.1, some DOCSIS V1.0, and others DOCSIS V1.2 (the balance between DOCSIS V1.1 and V1.2 will be determined when it is determined whether V1.2 is optional or mandatory).

If open access were mandated to launch, say, sometime in late 2002 or early 2003, there would be several million cable modems and tens of thousands of CMTSs deployed, with subscribers owning the cable modem; so if they desired open access facilities, the cable modem would have to be replaced. In cable plants, where open access was already enabled, the CMTSs would need to be upgraded and/or replaced. The backend networks would need to be expanded and improved, at significant additional cost, to support exchanges between multiple service providers and their subscribers. (Note: In contrast, such a backend network would be in place for DSL access networks in that time frame.) Subscribers who had legacy DOCSIS cable modems, but who didn't want open access, could coexist on the same CMTS and RF channels as DOCSIS cable modems that did support open access provisioning—in which case, the CMTS would have to support open access provisioning. Nonopen access cable modems would get service from either a default service provider or, if specialized routing or tunneling were employed, a service provider of the subscriber's choice. Subscribers who required the features of a cable modem to support ideal open access provisioning would need to replace their legacy cable modem with a new one. This would be similar to buying a feature-enhanced cellular phone for use with the same cellular provider.

Providing separate downstream RF channels in the cable plant to different service providers is not workable, as discussed previously, due to the lack of availability of sufficient downstream or upstream channels. Theoretically, it is possible to reserve a future channel for open access-capable systems or, perhaps, to convert a local must-carry video channel for use as a local must-carry open access channel for operation of cable modem equipment that does support ideal open access. In this case, multiple subscribers and providers could adequately use that equipment to the limits of performance offered by that equipment and the configured downstream and upstream channels. In practice, however, this would not be possible on all cable systems because of local plant capacity issues in either the downstream or upstream spectrum. Technically, it would be possible to convert a must-carry local television channel to a must-carry open access cable modem channel in the downstream direction, but the upstream spectrum still might not be available.

It is important to point out at this juncture that the cable industry is rapidly moving toward digital video distribution. For example, TCI has made great headway turning up new digital TV services. Digital video is contained in a digital video channel that is 6MHz wide, which is the same as analog. The difference is that a digitized 6MHz channel contains multiple video programs. Said differently, converting analog channels to digital channels takes up between one-fourth to one-sixth the RF spectrum as the same number of analog TV channels. The number of TV channels supported per digital RF channel is variable, depending on quality of delivered video and delivered format. Upcoming HDTV systems will likely have one video program per digital RF channel, while NTSC formats may have from four to six or more video programs. Converting from analog to video may release downstream RF spectrum for other uses, but not in all cases; hence, it might not be subject to universal mandate. More study is necessary here to understand if, in the future, downstream RF space for open access channels could be provided. Upstream RF channel allocation is still problematic! If the space is available, technically it is possible to operate multiple CMTSs in the same cable plant, allowing open access cable modems to be provisioned on the RF channels associated with open access CMTSs, while one (or more) legacy CMTS (nonopen access cable) supports legacy cable modems.

Open access provisioning could leverage the existing DOCSIS V1.1 specification and subsequent specification(s). Technically speaking, if another specification or standard were selected for ideal open access support, the preceding observation regarding multiple CMTSs would become standard practice in cable plants. Where one (or more) CMTS would be present to provide legacy DOCSIS support, the other non-DOCSIS CMTSs would be supporting open access to non-DOCSIS open access cable modems.

Technical Cost Considerations

In general, Internet architecture has always been open access, in that it allows any subscriber (client) to connect to any service provider (server) via the IP and the other higher-layer Internet protocols (e.g., TCP, UDP, etc.). Supporting numerous subscribers are numerous ISPs, which have deployed large server "farms" and backend networks to support their customers. Subscribers today chiefly use dial-up modems over legacy POTS systems, with the subscriber bearing the cost of the phone call, and the service provider bearing the cost of providing local dial-up access to the subscriber. The phone system provides the individual connection between subscriber and service provider. The telephone company gains revenues from calls made by subscribers and from revenues gained from ISP connections to remote access servers (e.g., primary rate ISDN, T1, T3, etc.). Subscribers simply select their ISP, then, after authorization has been set up, call a specified phone number.

In the DSL model, the technical architecture is open access from the start. It moves service provider equipment directly into the local telephone central office (CO) or directly connects it to a CO (e.g., via an ATM network). Access to the copper local loop requires an exchange of payment (settlement), either from the subscriber to the local phone company, with a separate payment for ISP access, or a single payment to an ISP; in the latter case, the ISP pays the local phone operator, in part, for rent of the subscriber's copper pair wire that is carrying the high-speed signals. The revenue model changes somewhat from the dial-up POTS network, but the local wire provider gains revenue from the additional high-speed data services. The revenues are used for expansion, upgrade, and maintenance of twisted-pair plants and other distribution technology in support of high-speed services.

In the cable environment, cable operators have begun to deploy high-speed data over cable equipment (CMTSs, or the equivalent, and cable modems) and to construct servers and backend networks. In most cases, the size of the servers and the capacity of the backend networks have been balanced for deploying a single ISP service for the subscribers. Cable operators indicate that their revenue models are leaner than other broadband access solutions, and are carefully balanced between cost of capital technology and cost to support that technology and customers. By mandating open access, cable operators would be required to install additional new and/or upgraded open access capable routers, to offer support for multiple high-speed interconnections to connect a headend with each service provider desiring access, and to provide the local maintenance needed to support the additional equipment and high-speed interconnects.

Another factor is that there are technical limitations as to how many service providers can be connected through a given headend. Practical limits may top out at several dozen to several hundred ISPs. In contrast, there are several thousand ISPs in the United States. The costs associated with technical upgrades and support would roughly scale with the number of ISPs connecting through the headend; in short, open access provisioning for high-speed data-over-cable services is not free. A short-term mandate for open access would come with severe costs implications for existing high-speed data-over-cable services, with respect to a cable operator readjusting/adapting for new technology and new support, let alone the costs associated with upgrading subscriber cable modems. If open access were mandated in the future, say three to five years, vendors would likely be motivated to design for open access support in later generations of technology. As discussed previously, it would take about two and a half to three years from that point to bring open access into widespread deployment. A lengthier time frame would allow operators to gradually enhance and deploy required technology. However, any technology upgrade or its support would still require a revenue stream to pay for the enhancement and deployment. It is apparent that a revenue exchange similar to that for DSL would be needed, one where service providers pay their way for connection to a headend and for support of subscribers.

Detailing Source Address-Based Routing

We discussed source address-based routing earlier, in the subsection titled "Open Access at Layer 3: The Network Layer" on page 223. This open access technique is being widely considered today. Recall that it is a non-traditional way of routing I P packets from router to router by looking at the source address of the IP packet rather than at the destination address. This approach cannot route packets from a particular host or site to a specific destination, for example, from a subscriber's home to an arbitrary ISP. On the surface, source address-based routing appears to have some benefits, which, some argue, are sufficient to provide *reasonable open access*. But a closer examination of the technique leads to a recommendation that, at best, it be considered a very short-term interim solution.

The apparent benefits include the following:

- Could work with any DOCSIS CMTS-equipped system, including the installed base of DOCSIS 1.0 CMTS equipment and DOCSIS 1.0 cable modems.

- At least, provides a mechanism to enable subscriber service provider selection, including allowing subscribers to receive services from an ISP of their choice from a list of participating service providers.

- Appears to support packet VoIP flow separation in a DOCSIS 1.1 environment.

The problems associated with this approach are more numerous:

- *For the system to work, the cable operator would have to own and partition a large IP subnetwork address space.* Essentially, this would mean carving out a portion of the address tree for each service provider and for every potential subscriber. The only suitable block of IP addresses for this comes from using the net-10 private address space. This partitioning would be done on an operator-by-operator basis, and all cable operators would probably choose their own method for carving up the address space. The cable operator might be able to accept blocks of globally routable addresses from each ISP, but the mechanisms to support this could be cumbersome for some cable operators. (Note: For DSL services, ISPs already have large blocks of globally routable addresses.) In sum, the nature of the cable environment precludes ISPs being able to make assignments out of their address pools.

■ *Management and assignment of addresses within this block would continue to be assigned and managed by the cable operator.* Any participating ISP would have to develop a mechanism of communicating user address changes as subscribers add/drop the service. No standard mechanism is in place to support this type of interaction between ISPs and the central cable operator address management system. This would lead to ad hoc solutions by the various cable operators. Moreover, based on the one service provider model of the DOCSIS architecture, it is not possible for the service provider to provide IP addresses to the subscriber directly.

■ *The one-service-provider DOCSIS architecture enforces what the cable industry calls a "walled garden" approach to servicing (read: owning) the customer.* The source address-based technique, which allocates private IP addresses, merely replicates walled-garden approaches. Subscriber may be free to move from one garden to the next, but they are entrapped within the constraints of the entire system, as well as by the services offered in each garden.

■ *In the DOCSIS system only the cable modem can be managed from one management system, that is, the cable operator's.* Participating ISPs may not have access to the cable modem itself, thereby interfering with their ability to provide a first-tier, one-stop phone call for managing customer support issues. At this time, there is no standard mechanism for enabling an ISP to manage to the cable modem. This may lead to ad hoc solutions by individual cable operators. The ability of the ISP to manage to the subscriber service demarcation point is a fundamental requirement of public network open access systems. Anecdotal evidence from DSL networks suggests that there are problems when ISPs must work with the DSL equipment provider that manages the DSLAM. These problems result in longer turn-around times to remedy subscriber complaints, such as lack of service. In comparison, the walled garden approach of the cable networks, from the individual ISP view, seems to be a more complicated management infrastructure. This suggests that the same customer support issues would surface in the source address-based routing approach, and to a greater degree for cable systems. This would be unacceptable to the ISP and the cable operator; lengthier customer service response times directly reduce already slim revenues, and, ultimately, could lead to the failure of a business venture. Customer support costs are critical to any ISP and last-mile access operator.

■ *When subscribers are allocated net-10 private addresses, they are in reality disconnected from the public Internet global address space, and are allowed to access it only based on the proxy service facilities of the particular ISP on an application-by-application basis.* This is similar to what happens with firewall and application proxy services used within corporations today. The employees' computers cannot be accessed directly from the Internet, period. Employees can access the public content of the Internet—to Web surf, use email, and so on—but only under the specific authorization and control of their IT departments and the chief information office (CIO). Though acceptable in a corporate environment, this type of private architecture (which is very similar to what is being proposed for source address-based networks for cable access for public residential access) would be unacceptable.

■ *For a public open access solution to effectively meet the needs of subscribers, and to ensure the development of future services and economies, it is critically important that each subscriber have his or her choice whether to and how to be connected directly to the public global Internet.* The walled garden approach as just discussed directly impedes these requirements. Future services and economies are under development in the areas of immersive family communications, Internet security management, and general home Web and communication servers. It is vital that a subscriber be able to connect to any upcoming service from anywhere in the Internet. For example, (1) from his or her workplace, a user should be able to log in to the home server, wave hi to the spouse and baby using packet voice and video services, then set the VCR; (2) from home, a couple should be able to call their parents located anywhere on the Internet to set up a video conference call; (3) a subscriber's home security firm should be able to periodically check the security system's alarms and video cameras for routine monitoring. The source address-based system effectively breaks from the traditional public Internet open network access approach by restricting inbound (to subscriber) reachability only from within the same walled garden. General access initiated from anywhere on the globally routable Internet can only be done via application proxy servers provided by the ISP. This is problematic, as server placement is controlled by the ISP; moreover, a separate proxy server is needed per application service. As new services are developed, a subscriber's access to these services is directly controlled by the ISP, not by the subscriber. In effect, the subscriber is no longer free to use any Internet application service because the ISP is in direct control.

- *There is no clear QoS support for the entire system interconnection between subscribers and ISPs.* More diligence is needed here, following the ideal requirements presented earlier in this chapter: specifically QoS for differentiating services, such as voice from file transfer, providing ISP containment, or providing appropriate service guarantees to the subscriber.

- *In the past, when source address-based routing techniques were used with Layer 2 bridging techniques, the industry found that scaling to larger networks produced severe performance problems.* This gave momentum to using Layer 3 destination address-based routing approaches. The introduction of source-based routing techniques into Layer 3 will likely cause problems in regard to ability to scale the system to many subscribers and many ISPs, thus making it impractical for larger systems.

- *Subscribers will begin to tailor their home Internet connection to suit many needs.* Some of these needs will require residential broadband access solutions to truly be always on. This is especially important for home security access systems as well as primary line voice-over-cable solutions in the future. To achieve a high degree of availability, the cable operator and ISP must avoid single point of failure topologies as much as possible. The traditional destination-based routing of the Internet does provide a degree of redundancy, because in a well-connected network, routers can quickly find alternative forward paths to the destination. However, combining source address-based reverse routing into a redundant architecture will cause the same problems that source address-based Layer 2 bridging experienced in redundant architectures. In short, it just won't work.

Observations

As stated at the beginning of this section, the source address-based routing technique that allocates private, nonglobally routable addresses should be considered a very short-term interim solution. True, when globally routable addresses are assigned, the situation improves, but such deployments must be compared against the ideal open access model to determine which requirements have been met.

> **NOTE** At best, the source based routing technique that allocates private non-globally routable addresses should be considered a very short-term interim solution.

Clearly, the source-based routing approach, using private IP address space(s), prevents the subscribers from being able to use any public Internet application they choose. Rather, the ISP of the particular walled garden, which is in direct control, arbitrarily decides to which Internet-initiated services a subscriber has access. This is, essentially, a private intranet approach, and one that directly infringes on the foundation philosophy of the public global Internet, which has led to its worldwide acceptance and growth. The United States must continue to bolster Internet vitality; to that end, it must encourage public open access approaches that give subscribers the freedom to both access and provide services from their home, and when and how they choose to do so, as well as to be able to choose their ISP.

APPLICATION TO WIRELESS FIXED POINT NETWORKS

On July 13, 2000 ADC Telecommunications Inc., Conexant Systems Inc., Gigabit Wireless Inc., Intel Corp., Nortel Networks Inc., and Vyyo announced jointly the formation of the Wireless DSL Consortium stating:

> *In order to provide a quick-start solution in this year, the consortium members embraced the Data-Over-Cable Service Interface Specification (DOCSIS), with enhancements compensating for media access control and physical layers to support wireless operations.*

Three terms used in this announcement are disturbing, with regard to open access in the wireless fixed-point market: *quick start*, *this year*, and *DOCSIS*. Using DOCSIS as it is specified today will only cause this wireless effort to repeat history, essentially condemning the wireless market to the same open access restrictions as suffered by DOCSIS over cable. Any heads-down, quick-start initiative will have no time to design the support and services necessary to properly enable network open access. Consequently, wireless server providers will be put into the same awkward situations, resulting in legal disputes between cable operators and the public that is demanding open access.

It is relevant to note here that the public switched telephone network and dial-up modem architecture enables tens of millions of subscribers to access the Internet. The phone network itself does not constrain what is communicated over outgoing or incoming calls, nor to which ISP calls are made. This same open network philosophy should be enforced, regardless of whether the communications are provided via phone line, cable network, digital subscriber line, or wireless.

Summary

The goal for this chapter was twofold: to define ideal open access provisioning and to review the technical capabilities of the current DOCSIS cable modem specifications to meet the ideal open access requirements in the U.S. cable TV broadband access environment. Various approaches and alternatives were discussed, which included an in-depth look at source address-based routing.

A short-term mandate for open access provisioning over cable systems would cause immediate technical and cost hardships for U.S. cable operators (the current and future DOCSIS RFI specifications do not support open access directly; however, DOCSIS RFI V1.1 does provide fundamental facilities that could be exploited for open access). Most cable operators' high-speed data over cable and backend servers and networks have been designed and optimized for a single ISP. Forcing these systems to support open access provisioning would impose technical costs for new capital equipment and support.

Certain specialized routing and tunneling techniques used by some cable operators do provide workable solutions, but they fall short of ideal open access provisioning. For example, these techniques may rely on customized software from select vendors that is not generally available. These techniques are being applied to cable modem systems, independent of the cable modem system; that is, they can work with both DOCSIS-based or proprietary-based cable modem systems. In some cases, a vendor's cable modem may need a software or hardware update to work. Tunneling techniques also have merit, but they impact the cable modem directly, and will take time to implement. Either solution can be developed to better couple with upcoming data rate allocation and QoS capabilities of DOCSIS V1.1 systems.

A three- to five-year mandate should be sufficient for the U.S. cable industry and associated vendors to develop and upgrade the DOCSIS specifications and products to support ideal open access. However, any cable modem systems deployed between now and then would not support ideal open access, and significant costs are associated with upgrading legacy technology. That said, given sufficient planning, open access-capable cable modems could be deployed on the same upgraded CMTSs that support legacy cable modems. There are other broadband access network methods being used in the United States, with some methods in place today (e.g., DSL) and others under development or in the early stages of deployment: wireless, satellite, FTTC, but the wireless and satellite methods lack open access provisioning requirements and standards.

It is worth observing that all broadband access systems *could* share the same ideal open access provisioning goals, thereby providing a consistent service offering to subscribers, regardless of broadband access method.

What's Next?

As noted at the beginning of this chapter, in the United States, there is no common definition of open access. The first step, therefore, would be for an appropriate organization to develop such a description, in both technical and layperson terminology. The layperson's definition should convey the viability of open access absent Internet technology geared to professionals. Either the Federal Communications Commission (FCC) or the Federal Trade Commission (FTC) might be the government body to take on this task. A working definition would go a long way toward encouraging vendors and operators to comply with the requirements, and would postpone or preclude any regulatory action on behalf of the public.

Once a definition for open access exists, the next appropriate step would be to design support into the various standards and specifications for broadband residential access equipment. ATM is well suited as a Layer 2 open access implementation technology due to its inherent large address space and packet-labeling capabilities; that is, there is sufficient multiplexing power in the ATM cell header to support the needs of open access and QoS.

As noted, the DOCSIS protocol was not engineered to carry ATM cells efficiently. In fact, if ATM were to be mandated, the DOCSIS protocol would have to be completely reengineered from the physical layer on up. There is another pseudo-Layer 2 protocol called the Multi-Protocol Labeling Service (MPLS) that could be used in conjunction with IP to create a large address space, similar to that of ATM. Should open access enhancement be undertaken for DOCSIS, MPLS support directly in the cable modem would provide the basis for meeting all the open access requirements identified in this chapter.

The policy-based routing technique is emerging in routing products today, and appears to have some merit in regard to implementing an open access system. However, more study is needed to determine whether these systems can meet the needs of both subscribers and service providers.

The bottom line on open access over cable is that the industry should not implement an overly complex system, one that will be difficult to support. Rising customer support costs for a single fixed monthly subscription plan can consume any profits. If it is too difficult for the cable operator and participating ISPs to manage a new open access system, the customer support costs will go up. Care must be taken to balance costs with profitability.

Speaking of costs, allocating CPE IP addresses from globally routable allocations is less expensive than the private address allocation of the rubber-stamped walled garden approach. With the walled garden approach, extra servers are required to do application proxy management as well as conversion from private to global address space. As new services are added, these tasks require support personnel to maintain and update. With global IP address assignment, these extra servers or personnel are not needed. This suggests that pricing for global access would be less than for walled garden access.

The Vulnerability of the Home Computer Caused by the Always-on Connection

The deployment of residential broadband networks will make it possible for the millions of home personal computers deployed in North America and around the world to be continuously connected to the global Internet 24/7. Always-on is a feature of the new broadband access technology, including cable modem systems, DSL systems, wireless data systems, and so on. This chapter addresses the impact of the always-on home Internet connection as it increases the vulnerability of home computing equipment and, subsequently, threat to electronic commerce and telecommuting in the United States.

The home personal computer is much more susceptible to intrusion attacks via an always-on connection as compared to traditional dial-up modem access. Once compromised, the clear side of any cryptographically protected transaction is vulnerable to tampering; consequently, that vulnerability undermines all consumer electronic commerce and workplace telecommuting services. Moreover, it invites malicious indulgence. Education of the public at large, and particularly the home computer user is the fundamental first step to countering this problem. Awareness must be backed up by the availability of viable hardware, software, and cryptographic solutions to invasion.

SKIPPING AHEAD

For those readers who prefer to forgo the technical details of this topic, the following summarizes the salient points of this chapter:

- Users demand the always-on feature of cable modems and DSL for continuous access to the Internet. This feature makes home computer open to and accessible from everyone on the Internet, including hackers and other malicious users located anywhere in the world.

- Application and operating system software on the home computer are notoriously prone to security defects and virus infection, making uninvited access easy.

- Once a system has been compromised, electronic commerce transactions from the home, as well as workplace telecommuting communications, become easy targets for Internet criminals or voyeuristic intruders.

- Effective countermeasures to intrusion include public education, in conjunction with software and hardware solutions, which include embedded on-board strong cryptographic support in the home computer.

DIRECT THREAT TO ELECTRONIC COMMERCE   The widespread use of the always-on feature is a direct threat to electronic commerce.

Overview

Globally, the telecommunications infrastructure is undergoing a sea change, brought about by the widespread deployment of high-speed broadband Internet access to the home. This change is being fueled by the competition between the cable TV and telephone industries as they race to capture the home-based customer, with offers of next-generation services, which include, but are not limited to high-speed Internet services, and video and telephone services. The cable TV industry aims to deploy its service using advanced cable modem technology. The telephone industry is planning for mass residential deployment armed with a variety of digital subscriber line (DSL) technologies. Also, emerging mobile and fixed-point wireless technologies will be rolling out in major U.S. markets starting in late 2000.

Though fundamentally different, cable modem and DSL technologies are very similar in that they deliver high-speed services to the subscriber.

Using either technology, the residential user receives high-speed Internet access and, soon, telephony services. High speed Internet access marks an evolutionary advancement over traditional dial-up Internet services for two main reasons:

- Access speeds are typically above 128 thousand bits per second (kbps) to over a million bits per second (Mbps) depending on technology, service provider, and subscriber choice. The maximum dial-up speed is at most 56kbps. This represents a 2 to 20 times and beyond speed improvement over traditional telephone dial-up services.

- A broadband access connection is always available, does not use a telephone voice (modem) line, and is usually available at a flat rate for unlimited use. In contrast, a dial-up connection ties up a voice phone line for the duration of the access; each connection takes time to establish; and either the phone line or the service provide sets time-based usage limits.

The always-on high-speed connection is very attractive to consumers. It puts the World Wide Web at their fingertips, on demand, without the wait. Several services take advantage of always-on connections, including stock quote services and the popular instant message and friend location services of AOL and Microsoft Network. For telecommuters, the immediacy of Internet access at home rivals that found at the office.

The treatment of the always-on Internet connection for the workplace and the home is vastly different. Since the emergence of the Internet in the mid-1980s, companies have been aware of the danger of intrusions via the Internet, thus have been facing the issues of data privacy. Today, sophisticated firewall and virtual private networking (VPN) technologies supplement Internet connections for many companies across North America. The market for products in this space is growing at a tremendous rate, with much more attention being paid to VPNs, higher-functionality firewalls, and intrusion detection.

Any IS manager CIO in any company across America that is connected to the Internet understands that the computers, hence the information, in their workplace are vulnerable to intrusion from the outside, either by direct access over the Internet or by virus infection. The software applications and operating systems of most companies fall prey to bugs, features, or oversights in application design. To manage a computer platform, specifically, to be able to defend against and/or "disinfect" a compromised computer, sound administrative practices, education, and common sense, are required. IS managers recognize that they need to stop the threats as close as possible to their inbound Internet connection, through use of fire-walls. They are all familiar with available software solutions, such as virus protection and other utilities. In short, the bottom line is that after initial installation (when it is assumed a system is "clean"), today, there is no way to guarantee that a computer system or its software won't become com-promised one way or another

Naturally, IS managers must do whatever they can to protect their com-pany's confidential information from intrusion. And VPN technology is emerging as one way to guarantee privacy of data sent through the public Internet, whether it be from business to business, one company location to another, or from a telecommuter working at home. In the latter case, using VPN technology, the telecommuter accesses the company network as though he or she were at the corporate site. This usually permits open access to the same number of machines within the company. However, what the telecommuter doesn't have at home is an IS department. Thus, most telecommuters, unless they are highly techno-savvy, leave them-selves open to potential abuse. Fortunately, public awareness of privacy and confidentiality concerns is helping to motivate home users to learn to protect their systems and their data. Still, more education is needed.

Home Computer Vulnerability

A broadband access system provides high-speed two-way Internet access to and from a subscriber's home. In many cases, the IP address assigned to the home computer is allocated from the globally routable Internet address space. This gives subscribers the best access model for any ser-vices and applications that they want to access.

The obvious downside of such a globally routable address is that other Internet users around can attempt to make a connection to that IP address. This is true of any broadband access system, whether it be cable, DSL, wireless, or satellite. Cable systems are criticized for being less secure than other broadband systems, but a modern cable modem system that is properly administered is no less secure than any other broadband access system. Recall from Chapter 5 that the DOCSIS system includes Baseline Privacy to encrypt data transmitted over the shared media RF links. This protects privacy of data sent over the cable. In Chapter 7 we examined the topic of Ethernet LANs and cable systems. Administratively, the "oops, there goes the neighborhood" problem can be remedied easily, too. This puts cable modems systems on par with the other broadband access systems with respect to home vulnerability.

Threats

Threats to the home computer fall into two broad categories, externally initiated and internally initiated:

- *Externally initiated threats are those attempted from outside the home and directed at the home computer.* Usually these threats come from hackers exploring the Internet simply for the purpose of finding exploitable computers. Hackers find opportunities in file-sharing and print-sharing software that is turned on, and in applications providing network services with known vulnerabilities.

- *Internally initiated threats are initiated from the home computer itself.* Threats in this category include various viruses (that, for example, inject a so-called Trojan horse process, which permits external invasion) and compromised applications and operating systems. Sometimes, the human user unwittingly enables invasion, by making an operator error or by visiting a pirate Web site that hacks in through the HyperText Transport Protocol (HTTP) used by the World Wide Web to exploit a problem. To date, the most infamous virus is the I Love You virus that infected thousands of computers worldwide in early 2000. Naïve users who download software from the Internet may introduce Trojan horses that hurt themselves and possibly others, as in distributed denial of service attacks.

Any successful hacker attempt can cause one or more of the following problems:

- Loss of privacy
- Loss of money, often in the form of credit card theft
- Loss of property
- Loss of time and money to correct the problem
- Loss of confidence in using the Internet
- Loss of Identity!!!

Countermeasures

Countermeasures come in two forms: hardware and software. The hardware form is a box that sits between the home computer and the broadband access connection (see Figure 9.1). It may be a firewall appliance, a dedicated device, or a personal computer running a firewall or application proxy security system.

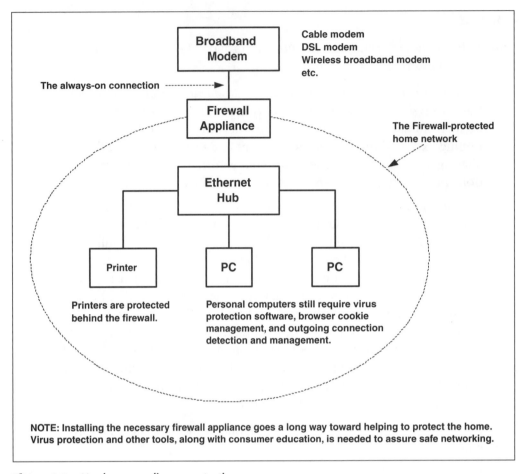

Figure 9.1   Hardware appliance protection.

The purpose of a hardware countermeasure is to make it really difficult for externally initiated connections to reach anywhere on the home network. Hardware appliances are very effective as far as they go, but they are not a complete remedy.

Software countermeasures include virus protection, antihacker, firewall, incoming and outgoing network connection monitoring, cookie management, and other programs. Many vendors today offer such software. Though these products are good, any software solution is only as effective as the user's knowledge of proper use, the integrity of the operating system (OS), and the integrity of the personal computer hardware and basic I/O system (BIOS).

Once the OS software has been compromised, the effectiveness of any software protection mechanism is nullified; thereafter, any application is

---

ELECTRONIC COMMERCE VULNERABILITY

Today, most efforts to ensure the safety of electronic commerce transactions focus on business-to-business (B2B) exchanges, ignoring to a great degree the problem these transactions cause to the home computer user. This is a mistake. As the Internet, in particular the Web, extends its reach to more millions of people, conducting business online will become more prevalent, both B2B, as well as business to consumer.

All communications over the World Wide Web will be based on the Secure Sockets Layer (SSL) cryptographic protocol with no less than 128-bit encryption. This means that the information sent over the Internet will be relatively secure. The key is the word "relatively"; the endpoints of these connections, most notably the Web browser on the user's computer will still be "in the clear," that is, allowing clear passage to hackers or viruses. If such attacks become more common, consumers will eventually lose confidence and respond by not using the systems, to the detriment of both businesses and consumers.

---

at risk, including the clear side of a secure Web transaction. And once the hardware BIOS has been compromised, the entire computer is at risk. The key is to, one, protect the OS and BIOS; two, learn to detect if and when intrusions have been made; and, three, learn to contain any problems. These are not easy tasks with today's computers, although efforts industry-wide are underway to improve this situation.

ELECTRONIC COMMERCE IS AT RISK Any content presented on the so-called clear side of any secure e-commerce connection is, in fact, insecure. The key to ensuring safe e-commerce transactions in the future is to close the door on intrusion at these points.

Possible Cryptographic Solutions

The major problem of protecting against home computer vulnerability is that, to date, there is no mechanism for ensuring that the software running on the computer is the software that is meant to be running on the computer. By that we mean that we take it on faith that the BIOS, OS, and applications are the same as those originally shipped by the vendor, when in fact, as soon at they are put to use, they have become vulnerable to bugs, viruses, and human invasion.

Among cryptographic protection mechanisms are those that enable electronic signatures to be applied to data, such as text and application programs. Any cryptographic signature can be checked in a straightforward manner to provide some level of assurance that the information sent by the vendor arrives in an untampered state.

There is still no mechanism for authorizing software to run on a computer other than just installing it. In the future, hardware-based cryptography must be built into the motherboard.

Closed Operating Systems

Another source of vulnerability are so-called closed operating systems where it is impossible to see the actual code and what it is doing. In response, today, open source code and the Linux operation system are gaining widespread attention and popularity. It may be a short period of time before the public demands to be able to see operating code, as a form of security assurance.

Summary

Linking a personal computer to the public, globally routable, Internet is like leaving the front door of ones home open on a busy city street. Sooner or later, someone will invade one's privacy. The first step to reduce the vulnerability of the home computer is to better educate both the lay and professional populations to the problems inherent in the always-on feature of broadband access. Once aware, people can more readily and successfully protect themselves in regard to their online communications and transactions.

In the real world, we have many mechanisms for securing our homes: locks, electronic security systems, not to mention laws and police, all of which give us some measures of safely. In the virtual world, on the Internet, there are no parallel measures. To invoke that level of safety, users must be informed of simple procedures that need to be followed when using the always-on connection. In the long term, online ethics will have to be taught as a matter of course in schools, in the same way we are socialized to the issues of personal privacy in our homes.

People must also be taught practical methods for protecting the home computer, including how to use firewalls and virus and connection-detection software, then how to monitor those devices. Finally, the most rigorous and effective mechanisms *must* involve the use of computer-based hardware cryptographic systems to validate OS, BIOS, and application software.

Leading-Edge Topics in Broadband Communications

Once restricted to educational institutions and government entities, it appears now we are well on the way to connecting every home in the world to the Internet. This expansion is fueling growth in other industries as well. For example, the communications and entertainment industries are undergoing their own evolutions prompted by the interactive nature of computer programming. The old video-only set-top box is evolving to a gateway into the digital world, accessible from the home entertainment center. A movement is underway that will send the home broadband interface to the outside of the house or to just inside the house and grow it into a multifunction home gateway. Likewise, the home network will undergo significant changes. As dial-up modems give way to high-speed home networks, everything in the house will be connected; and when away from home, people will be able to connect back to home for almost any purpose.

All of this points to continuing growth of the global Internet, ultimately testing IPv4. Will it be able to meet processing and address translation challenges, especially if the cable and other industries proceed with private network walled garden approaches, as discussed in Chapter 8? This chapter looks into this vital question by providing a short introduction to these topic areas, and asks another important question: Who's in charge?

The intent of this chapter is to raise awareness by asking such questions about the future of telecommunications.

The OpenCable Project

In Chapter 5, we briefly mentioned another CableLabs' activity called the OpenCable project. Similar to DOCSIS (in fact, fueled by the success of the DOCSIS), this project is focused on the next-generation digital set-top terminals that will be interoperable across cable systems in North America. OpenCable is on the fast track at CableLabs, as it strives to meet a number of goals for its own specification process:

- Support of integrated environments for broadcast services (analog and digital), as well as real-time interactive services, including voice telephony, video, high-speed data, and other on-demand services.

- Foundation on open standards, computing, and network architectures to promote interoperability. Availability of software, hardware, and intellectual property at fair and reasonable costs.

- Support of portability and availability in retail channels. OpenCable will provide for point-of-deployment (POD) decisions for network, security, and operator-programmed user interfaces. This means that cable operators will have control over these issues for systems deployed within their networks.

- Renewable and replaceable core encryption system included in the POD module, meaning that both the security keys as well as the encryption algorithms will be contained within the POD module. If the system is compromised, the operator can replace/reprogram POD modules with the fix, without requiring the disposal/replacement of the set-top terminal.

- Interactive program guide.

- Migration path from unidirectional to bidirectional networks and from broadcast to real-time interactive services.

- Efficient bandwidth allocation through the use of MPEG2; high-order modulation systems (e.g., 64 QAM and 256 QAM); optimized network capacity; resource-efficient applications.

Key to the OpenCable project is the separation of the terminal components from the Point-of-Deployment (POD) module, which is a plug-in module that tailors the operation of the set-top terminal to the MSO's services. The POD module has a defined interface, which has been specified in the document "OpenCable HOST-POD Interface Specification," number IS-POD-131-INT01-991027POD. Functions will include conditional access (CA) facilities, copy protection mechanisms, scrambling system, out-of-band (OOB) signaling, as well as cable-ready service operation for applications such as:

- Emergency alert system (EAS)
- Interactive program guide (IPG)
- Impulse pay-per-view (IPPV)
- Video on demand (VOD)
- Interactive services, for example, email, games, and so on

Figure 10.1 shows the high-level internal architecture of a sample Open-Cable set-top terminal, which includes a DOCSIS CM and the POD module. All two-way-capable OpenCable terminals will have two downstream digital receivers: one for digital video, one for DOCSIS downstream. Each channel will have its own tuner. The POD module will share the upstream DOCSIS channels for its operation. OpenCable boxes will also have an OOB downstream data channel reception capability. In this example, the OOB channel is used by the POD module for conditional access messages, freeing the DOCSIS modem to provide high-speed data services to applications running on the CPU. The set-top terminal will likely have an IEEE 1394 Firewire network interface, and may or may not have an Ethernet interface.

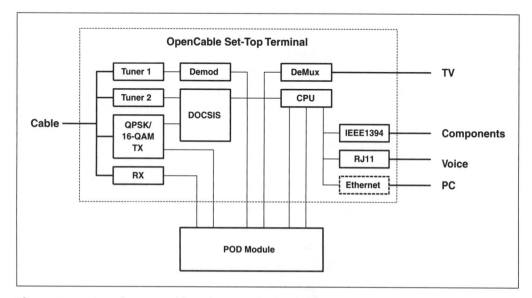

Figure 10.1   Sample OpenCable set-top terminal with DOCSIS.

Note that because an OpenCable set-top terminal will provide two-way high-speed data network services to an Ethernet port or IEEE 1394 port, as well as voice telephony services, the set-top terminal and the DOCSIS cable modem may be on a collision course, raising such questions as: Where will the home Ethernet be located? Where will the new telephone jacks be located? The answers will probably become clear in the market as consumers choose which capabilities they want in which box, and where in the home to put them.

THE FUTURE CONFLICT BETWEEN CABLE MODEMS AND FUTURE SET-TOP TERMINALS Set-top terminals are TV-centric; cable modems are not. Home computer use generally centers in the den (or other such space) or home office. Phones may or may not already be located near the TV; therefore, consumers will have to decide which box to buy when they both support Ethernet and/or voice services and learn how to rewire the house.

Residential Gateways

There is a growing interest to move the cable modem from the interior of the house (e.g., from the den) to just inside or on the outside wall of the house, then to turn it into a general-purpose gateway. Such packaging is called a *residential gateway*, and it is the focus of a great deal of attention because it offers several key benefits:

- Terminates all broadband services delivered over the media, for example, cable network, DSL network, wireless, fiber, and so on.

- Provides a network operator-side and a subscriber-side, much like today's existing telephone subscriber/network interfaces (SNIs). Operators will be able to manage to their side of the gateway. In today's telephone networks, the SNI is the box that establishes the demarcation between the telephone operator's network and the home phone wiring.

- When outside the house, the operator can perform predictive and reactive maintenance without requiring access to the home.

- Provides multiple application/service slots, so that customers can add new services themselves by installing another telephone line card or set-top terminal.

- New services will likely require just a phone call to the service provider; no home visit required.

There are several motivations for creating a residential gateway product:

- It's important to have a single box for all services, rather than a separate box for each service, for RJ11 phone, wireless phone, video, data, security, and so on.

- Operators are becoming more concerned about providing high-quality, reliable service. When a residential gateway is outside the house, system monitoring and management may alert operators to upcoming module failures, as well enabling them to troubleshoot to their side of the gateway.

- Advances in home networking and other high-speed interactive services show no signs of slowing down. Therefore, the consumer will need, want, a single-box approach to support emerging applications, yet not have to throw out old boxes (e.g., CMs). The consumer will also want support for multiple applications via one approach.

The success of two-way high-speed cable modem services, together with the push for modern digital set-top boxes, has fueled the movement to residential gateways. Probably, these gateways will be part of the next generation of home networking connectivity services provided by broadband residential access networks.

As mentioned in the previous section, there is a conflict coming between next-generation set-top terminals and cable modems causing customer confusion as to which to buy. This conflict has the potential to be compounded if another high-speed interactive service were to be deployed over cable, one that had a different location centricity, such as home security systems or power and appliance monitoring. Residential gateways could solve the location problem by linking all services to a common network operator-supported point of entry into the home.

THE COMING OF RESIDENTIAL GATEWAYS Residential gateways will no doubt be part of the evolutionary process of interfacing the home to the high-speed digital interactive future. They solve the problem of competing in-home service locations by linking all services to the same network operator-managed point of entry.

The Explosion of Home Networks

Not too long ago, the only networking home computer users had to deal with was the dial-up phone line and maybe a printer cable. Today, it's not that simple. The number of interconnection options has significantly increased, including the following:

- Ethernet WAN: cable modems, DSL, fixed-point wireless
- Ethernet LAN: switches, routers, and hubs; 10/100Mbps; Ethernet over power lines and phone lines
- Universal serial bus (USB)
- IEEE 1394 (FireWire)
- Wireless WAN: Metricom Ricochet, cell phone interconnects, and others
- Wireless LAN: IEEE 802.11b, Apple Airport, and others
- A number of other appliances, such as integrated Web/email/file servers and firewall boxes

It is also important to mention in this discussion the impact that the availability of low-cost computers has on this market; that is, not unlike what happened with television sets, soon most homes will have more than one computer. Companies are acting to keep pace; for example, in 1999, Apple Computer started shipping its iBook laptop with wireless Airport (IEEE 802.11b) support, and at a substantial savings from earlier in the year.

Figure 10.2 depicts how a household that uses all the interconnection technologies mentioned might be hooked up. A DSL line provides the connection to the Internet with a Ricochet modem as a backup. The home network is wired as a 10/100Mbps, and connects a UNIX server for Web and email, a PC, some Macintoshes, in fact all home computers, a printer, and a wireless hub. A USB connects slower-speed peripherals to the PC and Macs. Firewire is used for an extra hard drive and CDROM writer connection off one of the Macs. That's a lot of different interconnection technologies!

What's Next?

On the near horizon we see numerous wireless technologies for the home network, including:

- Ongoing surge of IEEE 802.11b type products
- Emerging products, such as the cellular phone-centric Bluetooth RF (www.bluetooth.com) technology and the pending emergence of HomeRF (www.homerf.org)

- Home phoneline networks based on HomePNA (www.homepna.org)

- Potential for using the home powerline system as a network (www.homeplug.com)

In short, the network infrastructure of the home will begin to rival that of businesses both in scale and speed.

From a box perspective, more and more home appliances will begin to "get the Net," for example, microwaves, refrigerators, clocks, entertainment devices, TVs, VCRs, ReplayTV (www.replaytv.com) or TiVo (www.tivo.com) boxes, game stations, and the like. Home security products will go wireless, and will add features such as video and audio pickup capability. The cellular phone-centric wireless will interconnect with the home wireless.

From a services perspective, the home will become more interactive. Packet voice and video services will become commonplace, and will be

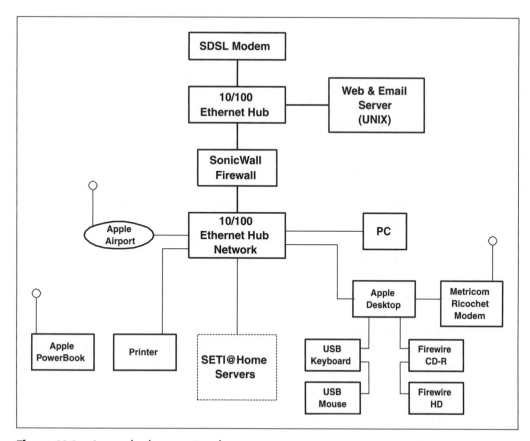

Figure 10.2   A complex home network.

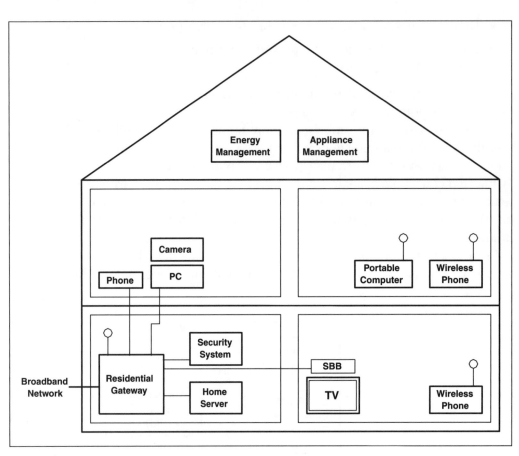

Figure 10.3 The well-connected home of the future.

used for enhancing communications within the family unit. Remote service management will become more commonplace, such as predictive appliance repair and home security monitoring. At-home patients will be able to receive a better quality of care through interactive monitoring by their doctors. The list goes on.

Figure 10.3 shows the home of the future, with the networks coming together at the residential gateway. The home server provides support for incoming connections, such as Web, email, packet voice and video, as well as a gateway control device for managing the home network. Potentially, a home security server will be managed by an electronic security service provider.

Still, this setup doesn't answer all questions or resolve all issues, including security, privacy, how to manufacturer all the devices for user-friendly plug-and-play, and others.

> **NOTE** In Figure 10.3, the set-top terminal is referred to as a *set-back box* (SBB). It is expected that the residential gateway will assume the functionality for managing the broadband communication interfaces as well as the DOCSIS CM functions, while the SBB takes care of the remaining features: presentation, navigation, and so on.

The Future of IPv4

Recall that at the beginning of the chapter we asked the question: Will IPv4 be able to meet the needs of the continuing growth of the global Internet? The short answer is no. In Chapter 8 we stated that using private nonglobally routable net-10 IP addresses would eventually lead to a problem whereby the home was not reachable from the Internet. In light of the growth of the home network as just discussed, this issue is particularly critical. Why? The IPv4 address is 32 bits long, allowing for 4,294,967,296 possible allocations; however, they are grouped into classes (chunks)—A, B, C, and D—which limits how they can be allocated. Routing in IPv4 is well coupled to the value of the IP address itself. As more IP addresses are consumed with broadband access to the home services and wireless cell phone applications, the risk is that address space could be exhausted or that service providers might be forced to assign private net-10 addresses to their customers. Either scenario directly restricts the growth of the home network and services.

Fortunately, the IETF took a long view, and designed a new protocol called IP Version 6 (IPv6). IPv6 solves the address space problems by specifying an address length of 128 bits, and loosens the tight tie between addresses and routing. IPv6 provides for straightforward mapping between IPv6 and IPv4 addresses, and can even work for private net-10 addresses. IPv6 can either be converted at a border gateway into IPv4 space or be tunneled through IPv4. Figure 10.4 illustrates these two methods.

> **NOTE** The term net-10 refers to one of the address spaces which has been reserved by the IETF for intra-enterprise communications only. That is, without any intention to directly connect to other enterprises or the Internet itself. The complete descriptions of private non-globally routable address spaces are documented in the IETF RFC1918 document "Address Allocation for Private Internets."

IPv6 has other advantages as well, including built-in support for multicast, IP security (IPsec), flow control, QoS, and mobility. Thus, if the broadband

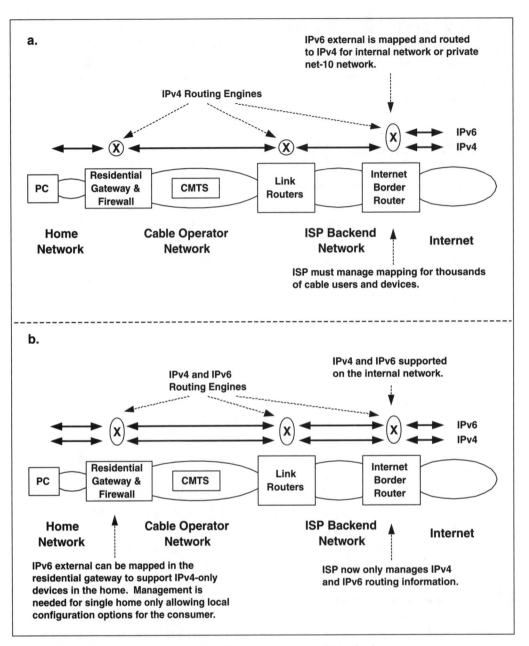

Figure 10.4 IPv6 meets IPv4, (a) at the border router and (b) in the home.

access network were IPv6 aware, a home user on the road would be able to connect to his or her home server regardless of the IPv4 addresses along the way. In addition, the user would be able to have automatic end-to-home privacy, through IPv6's use of IPsec.

Unfortunately, to date, few vendors have made their IPv4 products IPv6-capable, and it will take a number of years to roll out IPv6 support. The sooner the better. However, and this isn't trivial, there is still a lot of work to do making applications IPv6 capable.

Summary

Each topic in this chapter presented the problems or conflicts between old and new technologies. To summarize:

- *Next-generation set-top terminal versus cable modem:* Which owns the Ethernet and RJ11 jack for telephony?

- *Residential gateway versus cable modem or set-top terminal.* Which will be the broadband interface to the home network?

- *Growth and demand in home networks and applications outpacing provider ability to supply interactive services to millions of homes.* Who will decide which and how many protocols will be used in the home? Another standards group or a fast-moving company's de facto standard?

- *IPv4 versus IPv6.* Will IPv6 gain acceptance before deployment hits the wall?

A less-obvious question raised by the first three topics is: Who will wire up the 100 million houses and multiple dwelling units in the United States? If residential gateway deployment lags too far behind cable modem and set-top box deployment, how will the newly rewired homes be rewired yet again when the more powerful and appropriate gateway moves to, say, the garage?

NOTE It is beyond the scope of this chapter to offer an in-depth discussion of the difficulty—impossibility really—of regulatory activity keeping pace with technological developments. In the past, before a regulated carrier could roll out new services, the local or state public utilities commission had to approve new tariffs for the services, as well as marketing trials and the like. This suggests that it will take longer for these new technologies to become comfortably "socialized," that is, reduced to one or a few practical approaches.

The mass deployment of home networking solutions will be successful only when the components become widely available off the shelf of local electronics retailers. However, in the future, it will take longer than an afternoon to get all the new home networking equipment working, and the danger is that it will be far more complicated than it should be. More choices and more standards will probably mean more questions, problems, frustrations, and for the short term at least, the message is: caveat emptor.

For Further Information

For more information about public OpenCable specifications, visit the project Web site at www.opencable.com.

Information about the Open Services Gateway Initiative can be found on the World Wide Web at www.osgi.org.

CHAPTER

11

Converging Video, Voice, and High-Speed Data

The advent of new services moves the need for additional switching or routing *fabric* beyond the capacity of a typical headend, which, traditionally, consisted of equipment focused strictly on the broadcast of analog video and audio signals (see Figure 11.1). With the introduction of new services and technologies (high-speed data, circuit-switched telephony, Internet telephony, and digital video and audio), most companies respond by creating a separate business entity; they don't consider leveraging the same network switching or routing fabric. Consequently, floor space becomes exhausted by the deployment of separate switching or routing fabric to support each of these service types.

The Concept of Shared Fabric

The DOCSIS platform uses MPEG2-TS framing, and the DOCSIS CM will exist in every two-way OpenCable set-top terminal, so the potential exists that future CMTSs will be able to switch digital video as well as high-speed data. DOCSIS can then offer a converged platform that enables a single fabric solution to support the transport of these services over a single net-

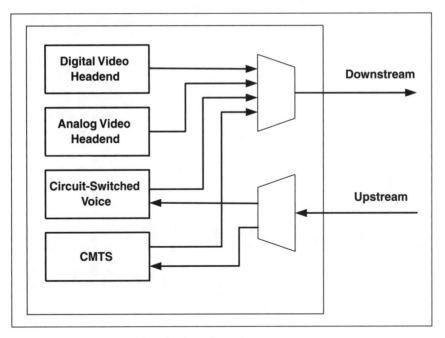

Figure 11.1 Traditional headend configuration.

work infrastructure. This gives rise to the term *shared fabric*, which will be used in this chapter to describe both switching and routing technology.

If the notion of a shared fabric is not considered, the migration of dedicated fabric can be costly, even potentially fatal to a new business unit, because it will be difficult to achieve the desired return on investment (ROI) within the targeted time frame. For cable operators to take advantage of the existing infrastructure, as they have in the past, the multisystem operator (MSO) must consider how to create a shared-fabric infrastructure that enables the incremental addition of new applications and services. Such an infrastructure precludes the use of dedicated fabric for each service or application; the key is to use a shared fabric for all services.

But even after determining that the shared-fabric approach makes economic sense, the question arises as to which protocols to use. DOCSIS is an appropriate starting point for the analysis of this question, because it incorporates MPEG Transport Stream framing. MPEG is used for digital video and audio, and therefore, two major applications are considered directly.

The situation begs for a networking device that could carry traditional analog programs, digital video programs, expanded video services, voice services, high-speed data, and any other service that might emerge in the future. The solution will have to involve a common protocol and transport layer that is capable of efficiently delivering all of the various information types.

The purpose of this chapter is to assess possible network constructs for transitioning from the traditional cable network to a DOCSIS-based infrastructure that combines to support evolving services. The assessment will include quality of service, flexibility, scalability, and robustness or supportability of an overall cable infrastructure for data, voice, and video.

Transitioning from the Traditional Cable Network to a DOCSIS-Based Infrastructure

Cable companies recognize that digital networks afford major new revenue opportunities and increase the value proposition of a 6MHz slot. Some operators see a lucrative market for video-on-demand; others recognize huge sales potential from entertainment gaming applications; and many anticipate that voice-over-IP will add to the corporate bottom line. But how should a cable business move forward into these new areas? What are the best methods for adding these services? What is the most cost-effective way to transition away from existing analog networks?

SWITCHING/ROUTING A critical element for introducing new services is to ensure they do not also introduce network elements that can be used only by that single service. Switching or routing is one such element that must be shared among all new services.

Traditionally, launching a new service meant installing equipment specific to the service offering, and maintaining separate delivery systems, all within the spectrum of a cable system, for example, 550 or 750MHz. For example, an operator planning to move into digital video would typically install an MPEG or statistical multiplexer that would take the digitized video and output it in MPEG transport. But in addition to installing the multiplexer, the company also had to decide how to reallocate the spectrum to accommodate the digital transport, which required sacrificing some number of analog channels to digital transmission. Without a comprehensive plan for allocating programming within the spectrum, this could be a daunting task.

In many cable systems, analog programming contracts require access to the entire base of subscribers; or they do not provide for migration to digital. To satisfy the first requires a digital set-top terminal (STT) at each television or dual carriage. In many businesses, analog video accounts for 99 percent of the current revenues, making that decision complex. It requires fixing bandwidth based on predetermined traffic patterns and speculative service adoption rates.

Fortunately, new technologies and communication protocol standards are making possible the migration to digital over a single transport infrastructure, one that handles both analog and digital traffic and can dynamically adjust to accommodate changing traffic loads. The goal is to migrate to an all-digital spectrum that dynamically allocates bandwidth to whatever service needs it. The enabling technology includes the implementation of a CMTS that supports transmission of IP packets over an MPEG transport construct. By evolving to this unified architecture, cable companies can make use of existing structures, minimize new equipment investments, and secure the technical flexibility to rapidly prototype new service offerings and optimally exploit market opportunities at a small incremental cost, compared to the original separate mode systems.

The Motivation of Multimedia Applications

By their nature, multimedia applications incorporate some combination of audio, data, graphics, voice, and video content; more often now, new services require interactive capabilities as well. Though it is impossible to predict which applications will become popular in any given market, some of the most promising include:

- Voice
- Video entertainment
- Internet information and entertainment
- Enterprise communications (intranets, extranets)

To support the broadest set of applications, and to offer the greatest revenue potential, a multimedia-enabled infrastructure must also support interactive services and audio, data, graphics, voice, and video applications that converge in a single transport protocol.

These applications can be categorized into three major subgroups: video, high-speed data, and voice. The typical headend requires an analog headend, digital headend, circuit switch, and CMTS to route or switch and combine for transport over the cable infrastructure. The cost of each system, and the incremental cost to the network with low market penetration for several years, raises the risk for the cable operator; and so these costs are difficult to justify. Therefore, though introducing new services is necessary for cable, because many of these new services require incremental or dramatic changes to the infrastructure, a critical factor is that these new services *not* be limited to use by a single service.

That's where the value of the shared fabric comes in: Shared fabric enables multiple services to be offered over a single switch *without* imposing a heavy capital investment. Thus, rapid prototyping of new services can be undertaken without investing large amounts of capital.

Prior to the advent of these new applications and services, those in the cable industry were focused on the challenges of broadcasting analog video and on optimizing networks for the delivery of this service. This mind-set precluded operators pursuing new opportunities. With the transition from broadcast analog video to multiple services, cable operators must learn to optimize the network to support the delivery of an array of new options. The notion of shared fabric can be applied to the rest of the infrastructure, as well.

Network Requirements for Multimedia and Interactivity

A number of technical challenges are related to developing a network infrastructure. The network structure must be robust, to ensure consumer access; flexible, to support the transmission requirements of a wide range of applications; and transparent to the consumer. To meet these objectives, an infrastructure has to adhere to the following requirements:

   Bidirectional functionality. Eventually, most multimedia applications will require interactive capabilities. These services require bidirectional functionality (downstream and upstream spectrum) and some form of switching and control. The switching or routing solution may be as simple as using multiplexers or a router.

   Most cable systems will enable the return path. Downstream signals can exist in available spectrum on a subsplit system from 54MHz to as high as 1GHz—although 750MHz is typically the upper boundary on most systems. The return path typically is limited to 5 to 42MHz, and is the limiting factor on the overall infrastructure. There are also midsplit and high-split implementations, but they require additional distribution equipment.

   A passive coaxial network design would also provide additional upstream spectrum per subscriber, because the number of subscribers per node is smaller. This approach enables dynamic alloca-tion of spectrum for upstream requirements. Because the amplifier defines how spectrum is allocated on the coaxial portion of the cable infrastructure, the elimination of the amplifier provides the means to manage bandwidth, either on a transaction or demand basis, con-trolled by the CMTS.

Quality of service management. IP telephony applications must be able to manage QoS, to ensure that appropriate priorities and band-width are available for lifeline services. DOCSIS V1.1 specifies the QoS needed to support voice-over-IP and other over-the-cable services.

The network must support peak and nonpeak, real-time and nonreal-time traffic, without blocking or contention. The other challenge is to avoid significant overhead associated with the protocol usage for delivery of traffic over the network. With multiple services delivered over a single infrastructure, traffic management can occur at the CMTS or be controlled at the ingress points using RSVP resources for scheduling services and bandwidth.

Security/privacy. The HFC topology is a shared infrastructure at the coaxial cable level. Recall from Chapter 5 that DOCSIS specifies Baseline Privacy Interface Plus (BPI+), for security between the CMTS and the cable modem. Several hardware- or software-based approaches can be implemented. These include customer-owned encryption or a scheme inherent to the cable infrastructure, such as conditional access for video content or movies. Additional security will be required, such as end-to-end security from the corporate office to the employee's home.

With the transport of voice, data, and video applications over this shared infrastructure, a more robust, renewable security system is necessary. The cable industry has long supported proprietary condi-tional access or security systems as methods of protecting the content delivered over the network. The challenge for cable in the future will be to create an open security model, such as the security specified in the original DOCSIS specifications, which was a renewable system. However, because of the complexity of the security system and the singular focus on data, the security system was not supported, and DOCSIS gravitated to BPI+, which offers a lower degree of security. The original intent of the DOCSIS security was based on the need for a single, renewable security system that could be changed *on the fly*, if attacked, for voice, data and digital video applications, without requiring replacement of the cable modem. Whether the algorithm defined in the original DOCSIS security specification is optimal, or another is preferred, the notion of a single, integrated renewable security system ultimately offers the network provider with control over hacking and piracy.

Some may conclude that a renewable security model exists in the form of the point of deployment (POD) module. But though the POD module solves an attack on the existing security system, it does not address security for high-speed data and voice over IP, nor does it offer an economical solution for security. Another shortfall of the POD is that it addresses only the digital set-top terminal, not the head-end. A more robust solution would be to adopt the DVB simulcrypt interface which permits different decoders with different conditional access methods to decode different groups of channels from different service providers. Simulcrypt is a method of addressing renewable security that focuses on an open interface at the headend and a removable, renewable security module at the digital set-top. This model can be extended to DOCSIS, although an embedded security system that is open and renewable is typically more secure.

Bandwidth and throughput requirements. Most multimedia applications, today, are asymmetric in their bandwidth requirements in that the downstream bandwidth requirement typically exceeds the upstream requirement. Initially, a few channels may handle the demand, but as the demand increases a plan must be developed to increase upstream capacities. This can be accomplished by reducing node size or implementing more efficient compression algorithms.

Most current applications require average downstream throughput of 2 to 4Mbps. On the return path, bandwidth requirements are much lower, ranging from 300bps to 1.5Mbps. Ethernet applications over cable requiring 10Mbps throughput are available within a 6MHz channel. A system operator may choose to limit access to bandwidth (e.g., 128Kbps to manage user expectations); however, ultimately, competitive pressures will require support of higher data rates.

Performance and reliability. Fiber-optic facilities have yielded the largest improvement in performance and network reliability in cable infrastructures. Also, as fiber migrates further down into the infrastructure, improvements are realized. This is largely a result of the reduction in the number of active components—amplifiers and line extenders—in the network. Many existing network designs provide for no more than four amplifiers and two line extenders in a cascade to any one home. Newer designs seek to entirely eliminate the active components on the coaxial plant, and add a low-noise amplifier at the residential unit.

Network management. Multimedia applications demand effective network management. Traditional approaches to maintenance are not reliable enough to support most multimedia applications. New approaches, using neural networking techniques, can detect a faulty amplifier before the failure actually occurs. For example, the practice of removing an amplifier from service to test its integrity cannot be tolerated. The passive coaxial network makes it easier for the cable operator to eliminate active components and to introduce an automated, dynamic approach to network management from a centralized facility, such as the regional hub. This leads to quality improvements and operating cost economies.

Convergence around the CMTS will likely result in a paradigm shift to a unified management system across multiple services, using an SNMP-based solution that offers fault detection and performance monitoring. In the future, network management will need to support other functions, such as relational databases.

Jitter and buffers. The delivery of MPEG2 and MPEG4 in a DOCSIS construct requires buffers at the endpoints in the network to manage jitter introduced from the public-switched telephone network (PSTN) and IP networks.

Hierarchic mass storage. Transport exceeds the processing capabilities of most computer systems. For video and game applications, bandwidth can also be a scarce commodity, requiring storage at the home. The variability between speed of transport and processing will necessitate some form of storage at national distributors, at regional hubs, headends, and the home. In order to minimize the cost of mass storage systems, a hierarchical storage capability can be deployed to manage and optimize scarcity of bandwidth in the infrastructure. Several solutions exist between the STT and the consumer electronics device to manage traffic over the network.

Economics will generally determine where mass storage resides in the network. Operators may implement a hierarchical approach with distributed storage devices in the form of video servers located at the regional hub, the headend, the fiber hub or node, and even in the residence. The option of the consumer owning mass storage can reduce the MSO's capital investment in the network, and increase flexibility for network operators.

Mass storage may include a standalone device resident between the digital STT and the consumer electronics platform—a television, VCR, or an embedded hard disk drive within the digital STT. The size of storage varies from approximately 14 to 28GB, or 14 to 30 hours of programming.

HIERARCHIC STORAGE Operators may implement a hierarchical approach with distributed storage devices in the form of video servers located at the regional hub, the headend, the fiber hub or node, and even in the residence.

Latency. Applications, such as games or video on demand, are sensitive to delays incurred over the network or in a server complex. Mapping MPEG2 digital video into IP, and IP into an MPEG packet, may cause delay.

Network power. For lifeline telephony services, network power is essential. Whether power is derived from the network or from batteries in the home, a source of backup power is a requirement in the event of a commercial power outage.

Impulse noise. Under consideration are advanced physical layer solutions that mitigate the noise introduced into the network from the home, primarily, on the return path. These solutions are based on time domain multiple access (TDMA) and code division multiple access (CDMA) approaches. However, with the wide deployment of fiber into local distribution, the need for advanced physical layer solutions may not be necessary because of smaller nodes sizes; for example, 500 home-passed nodes split four ways. For topologies incorporating fiber to the mini-fiber node that serves fewer than 75 to 125 homes passed, advanced multiple access methods are of little value. When the size of fiber nodes is routinely 500 HHP or less, the capabilities of the existing DOCSIS V1.1 PHY are more than sufficient to handle any noise issues in the distribution network.

ADEQUACY OF DOCSIS V1.1 UPSTREAM PHY As more interactive services are delivered to the home, the cable operator will follow a procedure of splitting fiber nodes to scale the data-carrying capacity of the system. When the node size falls below 500 HHP, the DOCSIS V1.1 PHY specification is more than adequate to handle impulse noise issues.

Existing Network Architecture

For some time, cable operators have been upgrading from the traditional coaxial-based systems to hybrid networks of fiber and coaxial infrastructure. Recall from Chapter 2 that both designs deliver predominantly analog signals. Fiber offers improvements in system performance and reliability through its low-loss, increased-passband characteristics and the significant reduction in the number of required active components. Overall, fiber greatly increases downstream passband capability. (Deployment of fiber further into the cable infrastructure results in smaller nodes and the elimination of trunk amplifiers. However, without the addition of new services, the generation of new revenues is not absolute.)

MPEG TRANSPORT DOCSIS uses the MPEG Transport Stream packet as the multiplexing construct for delivering IP-Ethernet-over-MPEG packets over a cable network infrastructure.

In hybrid fiber-coax systems, fiber cables connect a headend to fiber hubs in a distributed topology in either a ring or star configuration serving 64 fiber nodes, or 32,000 homes passed. These hubs feed fiber up to 64 fiber nodes that serve 500 homes passed. A fiber mini-node deployment enables fiber to 10 to 20 homes passed. The connections between the headend and the fiber hubs and the hub-to-hub interconnection uses a counter-rotating fiber ring that offers true physical route diversity.

As cable MSOs upgrade and introduce fiber, the networks are also expanding to carry other signals— high-speed data, voice—and the spectrum is extending into higher frequency ranges.

Converting or augmenting networks to carry digital signals offers great advantages for expanding network bandwidth: In North America, each 6MHz slot can carry from 8 to 12 digital program signals, compared with a single analog signal. Because of the inhibiting costs of converting an entire cable network from analog to digital, cable operators typically add digital headends to the network and divide the spectrum to allocate passbands to the new digital programs (see Figure 11.2). This scheme is still costly because it duplicates headends, and it requires that the traditional analog segment of the business sacrifice a portion of its programming spectrum. Until the new digital services actually generate healthy revenues, these overhead costs will severely impact the company's bottom line.

The existing underlining protocols that enable the convergence of these service types to a single fabric are the DOCSIS and MPEG standards. The

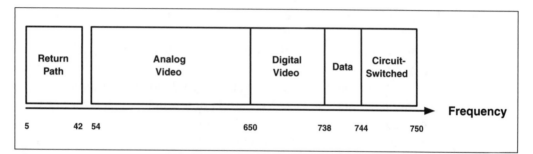

Figure 11.2   Spectrum allocation for discrete implementation of voice, data, digital, and analog video.

manner in which DOCSIS multiplexes packets through the MPEG2 Transport Stream frame offers a single transport protocol for delivering digital video, voice-over-IP, and high-speed data services. So why are there four separate systems—analog video, digital video, circuit-switched, and a CMTS—when one will suffice? Switching all services through a CMTS represents a dramatic departure and potentially strands a significant amount of investment. Instead of new services struggling to survive with penetrations of 3 to 5 percent, consider being able to rapidly prototype services without changing the network equipment. Instead of four different systems, companies could employ a single fabric based on DOCSIS.

A Next-Generation Architecture

In a typical cable system today, separate systems exists for voice, data, and video applications. As examples: a circuit switch is used to support voice; an analog headend exists, by definition, for analog programming; a digital headend is used for compressed, digital video; and a CMTS supports high-speed data applications. Not only are separate systems used, but, typically, separate business units and human resources are aggregated to support each application or service. Separate systems for voice, data, and video result in independent billing and security systems, as well. Moreover, each of these systems occupies separate floor space.

To introduce new services to an existing customer base, cable companies have been increasing the equipment and complexity of the existing network architectures while leveraging all of the existing broadcast, multicast, switching, or routing fabric. The results of this incremental approach include high start-up costs and increased management costs. The incremental approach also introduces technical challenges and costs for in-home interfacing and service access.

Clearly, today's network infrastructure is capable of carrying a broad spectrum of combined signals. The situation begs for a networking device that can carry traditional analog programs, digital video programs, expanded video services such as VOD and conferencing, voice services, high-speed data, and any other service that might emerge in the future. The solution requires a common protocol and transport layer capable of efficiently delivering all of the various information types.

The next-generation network achieves additional bandwidth through the conversion of the infrastructure from analog to digital, and the use of IP mapped into DOCSIS. Digital enables the cable operator to map 8 to 12 programming choices into a single 6MHz slot, hence increasing the value of each 6MHz slot. DOCSIS offers a method of more efficiently utilizing the bandwidth available in a 6MHz slot.

With the introduction of the DOCSIS standards, it is possible to migrate the analog headend to a digital headend (see Figure 11.3), map digital video into MPEG packets, transport IP in DOCSIS and circuit-switched voice as voice-over-IP—all using DOCSIS as the underlying protocol.

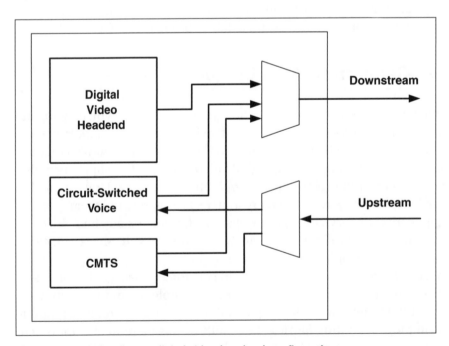

Figure 11.3 Migration to digital video headend configuration.

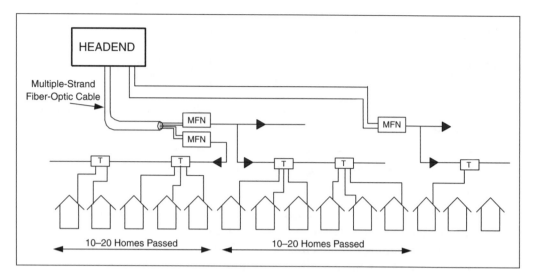

Figure 11.4 Mini-fiber node topology.

Voice-over-IP is accomplished through segmentation, fragmentation, and concatenation of the MPEG packet and the addition of quality of service.

Migration of fiber from a fiber node to a fiber mini-node serving areas of 10 to 20 homes passed can be more easily justified through the elimination of costly equipment at the fiber hub and fiber node, even at the mini-node capabilities that an all-IP delivery protocol can offer (see Figure 11.4). The adoption of digital and IP over DOCSIS enables the latter benefit to be achieved.

A DOCSIS packet is MPEG-encapsulated (or A DOCSIS packet encapsulates an IP packet in MPEG). The same MPEG construct is also in use for digital video, and the foundation for voice over IP, which enables efficient delivery of multiple services. If all-analog video were converted to digital, then transported in IP, one broadcast/switching or routing fabric could be used for all traffic.

By transitioning all traffic to DOCSIS, the headend configuration can be greatly simplified. Instead of the existing analog headend, digital headend, circuit switcher, and CMTS, the headend architecture may be consolidated to a single CMTS that can be used to deliver interleaved video, voice, and data services to the common existing broadcast/switching or routing fabric. While the CMTS currently supports access to a single 6MHz slot, ultimately the CMTS will support multiple 6MHz slots.

A common protocol and transport construct would greatly affect spectrum allocation (see Figure 11.5). Currently, existing analog programming

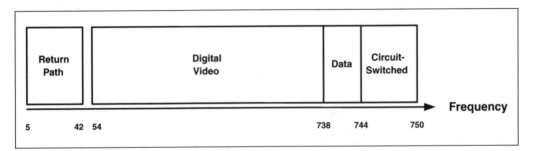

Figure 11.5   Spectrum allocation for migration from analog to digital video.

and new services are both restricted to a fixed number of 6MHz slots. Even with a move to digital services, and the resulting increase to as many as 10 programming choices in a single 6MHz slot, peak traffic in any one service area raises the risk of bottlenecks.

With the DOCSIS construct and the use of a single infrastructure for all traffic, the spectrum can be handled in a different fashion. At any point in time, 6MHz slots can be allocated where needed with no fixed frequency ranges or limits on the number of slots for any particular service. The full spectrum can be made available in a manner that complements the revenue streams; and the inefficiencies of dedicated or fixed programming can be eliminated.

Many new companies are starting up in the consumer electronics market, and the resulting offerings of in-home solutions are expected to increase dramatically in coming years. A common networking infrastructure encourages the development of standard in-home interfacing options, and will accelerate the proliferation of affordable, intelligent devices for the consumer. The cable modem in this scenario will serve as the network interface unit (NIU) to the home. The NIU will serve as the interface to multiple cable modems and digital STT or set-back devices within the home, or will be embedded in the consumer electronics platform or personal computer made possible by the CMTS-based headend architecture.

By eliminating the need for numerous and complex headend configurations, companies reduce the costs of delivering data to the infrastructure. CMTS products can be located where needed, simplifying the management of the overall infrastructure. Many of the functions that are currently duplicated at each analog/digital headend can then be moved up a level in the network hierarchy with highly centralized regional functions. A single, centralized back-office configuration can manage bigger regions. This next-generation back office will replace numerous, distributed headend systems with one implementation, which can support:

- Conditional access systems (CAS)
- CMTS
- Circuit switches (existing phone system access solutions until the public networks transition to IP)
- Game modem pools
- Billing systems
- MPEG or statistical multiplexers
- VOD servers
- Analog video (off-the-air or from other sources)
- Caching
- File servers
- Fast Ethernet switches
- Gatekeeper functionality
- Gateways
- Advertisement insertion

In addition to the fact that many functions can be centralized at a higher level for reduced equipment costs and simplified management, the new IP/DOCSIS infrastructure also enables the placement of intelligence further downstream. For example, in-home intelligent devices could be designed to control the downloading of advertising that is tailored to the homeowner's buying history. The CMTS and cable modem connection support the placement of a variety of devices with intelligence where they can best accomplish revenue goals and achieve consumer satisfaction (see Figure 11.6).

Previous efforts have focused on MPEG mapped into IP packets. These efforts have failed to gain the momentum needed to serve as a single protocol for transporting voice, data, and video applications. With the advent of DOCSIS, IP over DOCSIS has enabled not only high-speed data, but voice-over-IP and digital video over DOCSIS.

The key enabling hardware elements are the CMTS and the cable modem, combined with the use of routers deployed at the hub to route traffic to the various fiber nodes. These system components are based on standards that serve as the platform for DOCSIS.

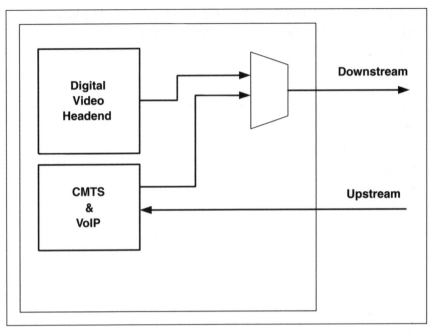

Figure 11.6   Migration from circuit-switched to VoIP configuration.

Benefits of the DOCSIS-MPEG Solution

The collapse of the traditional headend architecture into a distributed network of CMTS devices results in far-reaching benefits for the individual cable providers and the industry as a whole. Today, the logistics and start-up costs for introducing a new service demand costly planning and implementations, because each new service can translate into additional infrastructure capital expenditures. With a move to IP over DOCSIS across the entire network infrastructure, cable operators can:

- Reduce the incremental cost to introduce a new service using the same broadcast/switching or routing fabric and the same CMTS delivery system as existing services.

- Bundle more services, thereby improving the company's competitive advantage.

- Lower maintenance costs thanks to the less-complex architecture and the many centralized functions that were previously duplicated at each headend.

A common infrastructure that is capable of transmitting any data type gives cable companies the opportunity to inexpensively and rapidly prototype new services or deploy new services on a limited or test basis. New services do not require any changes to the headend equipment, network equipment, or NIU; therefore, companies can quickly introduce the new services to customers. Introduction cycles are also shortened because a new service does not require the design or availability of a new delivery system (customized servers or devices).

The CMTS/CM network and the IP-over-Ethernet-over-MPEG transport construct defined by DOCSIS V1.0 and V1.1 give cable MSOs the flexibility to maximally place intelligence to meet business goals while ensuring customer satisfaction. With game services, for example, the game servers can be centralized so that costly duplication of servers can be avoided while still covering a large region. The IP-over-DOCSIS ITU-T J.112 standards based on MPEG transport promise to efficiently support a broad range of application architectures, both centralized and distributed.

By supporting dynamic allocation of the spectrum based on real-time traffic requirements, the DOCSIS over MPEG infrastructure makes optimal use of bandwidth (see Figure 11.7). With more bandwidth available, not only can cable companies introduce more services and reach more homes with any given infrastructure, they can guarantee various levels of service and evolve to a pricing structure based on QoS.

Convergence of the various service types enables simplification of the shared-fabric network infrastructure and to back-office functions such as billing systems, network management, QoS, signaling, security, scalability, and bandwidth management. For example, with four separate service types, integration of billing is far more complex, and typically results in a single, fixed billing scheme to accommodate the combination of services. With a single network fabric, a cable operator will eventually be capable of

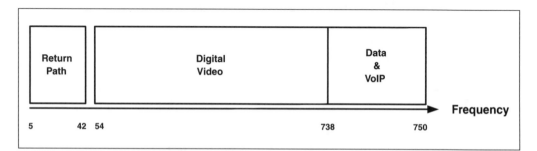

Figure 11.7   Spectrum allocation for migration from circuit-switched voice to packet voice.

offering both fixed- and variable-rate billing based on usage. Similar benefits exist for each of the other functions mentioned.

A single network fabric also enables further degrees of integration at the
interfaces. For example, the WAN interface and CMTS can be integrated
into a single-edge device with a common interface, like a bus or crossbar
switch.

The DOCSIS-based network allows large and small cable operators, with
large and small systems alike, to offer a common set of services. The challenge with many of these new services and technologies has been that
many small and medium operators cannot offer the full suite of services
that many of the large cable operators currently deploy. A single fabric
provides a scalable approach for offering a full complement of services
without an investment in multiple discrete systems.

A Single Transmission Protocol: DOCSIS

The final stage of integration is based on the notion that digital video and
high-speed data are integrated into the same underlying transport protocol—MPEG packets—as illustrated in Figure 11.8. This construct enables

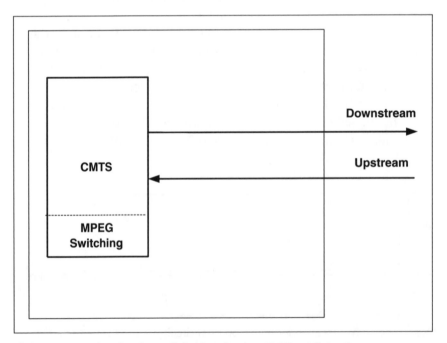

Figure 11.8 Migration from digital headend to CMTS configuration.

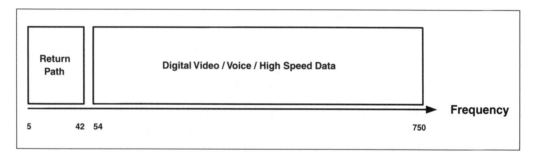

Figure 11.9   Spectrum allocation for integrated voice, data, and video.

a single fabric, the CMTS, for switching or routing voice, data, and video at the headend and throughout the network in a single transmission protocol. The use of a single transmission protocol also reduces complexity at the fiber hub because the only functionality at the hub is a router. This integration results in a spectrum allocation, as shown in Figure 11.9. The spectrum allocated for each application can be used separately or combined. The allocation of 738 to 750MHz remains the same, or could be reduced to a single 6MHz slot, initially.

The use of the CMTS as the primary network element enables the cable operator to manage a wide range of services within the network without high incremental costs. Advanced services can coexist with core services without a high incremental cost. With the growth of services, such as high-speed data or IP voice, the operator can use the same fabric to incrementally expand these new services without the risk of stranding capital investments. The same human resource used to manage the video can support the data or the voice, since the CMTS is the single element that aggregates all the services at the headend.

Initially, this is not practical. The cost of deploying cable modems as NIUs in every home, along with a digital set-back device for every television, is too high. The alternative is to migrate to the DOCSIS platform by allocating a portion of the spectrum and/or applications to this platform, and, over time, migrate to an all-digital DOCSIS platform.

Companies can allocate 650 to 750MHz to the DOCSIS platform, including the conversion of circuit-switched voice to IP telephony using DOCSIS V1.1, high-speed data, and digital video on demand. Video-on-demand service requires a digital STT. The content for video on demand consists of film and NTSC video. Games and other latency-sensitive programming can be added in future migrations. This gradual migration enables the cable operator to carry analog and digital programming from the outset and, eventually, to migrate to a DOCSIS platform that occupies the entire spectrum.

This example applies to a 750MHz system; however, the same migration can be applied for a 450 or 550MHz system.

Changes to the network would include the following:

Back Office. Simplification to a CMTS results in a new back office, and enables the cable operator to move this functionality one level higher in the hierarchy, to a regional headend facility.

CMTS. The use of a CMTS allows the cable MSO to manage various versions of DOCSIS with a common backplane and separate line cards. As IP telephony roles evolve, a CMTS can support DOCSIS V1.0 and V1.1 without the need for separate systems. The CMTS offers the cable operator the capability of supporting multiple service types through a single switching or routing fabric.

Initially, the integrated CMTS fabric is likely to include two segments, one that switches or routes high-speed data and VoIP, and the other MPEG2 digital video; both would be mapped to the underlying MPEG transport.

The CMTS will likely evolve to an edge device that supports the DOCSIS high-speed interface on the WAN side and the traditional CMTS function on the local distribution side, interconnected by a crossbar switch or bus-type functionality.

Hub. The functions of a host digital terminal, high-speed data, public educational and government (PEG), analog and digital headend, and so on, in the hub are simplified because the only functionality that resides at the hub consists of a router, some storage, and possibly local advertisements for insertion. The remaining functionality is migrated to the headend or higher in the network infrastructure.

NIU. The NIU is, effectively, a first-generation residential gateway, referred to in some deployments as a broadband terminal interface (BTI.) It reduces complexity over the network. The NIU with an integrated cable modem and IEEE 1394 (firewire) interface offers the capability of supporting consumer electronics and computer devices with embedded digital STTs and cable modems to exist in a more simplified format. The digital STT may become less complex with more of the functionality embedded with the television platform.

Set-back device. In a typical STT, the STT consists of three major components: a network interface, STT core, and subscriber interface. In an integrated solution, the cable modem in the residential gateway serves as the network interface function; hence, the STT becomes a set-back device without network interface functionality. The output of a cable modem-based NIU is probably a digital video interface (DVI) or possibly an IEEE 1394 interface that supports bandwidth for voice, data, and video applications. Because the cable modem does not perform the functions of an STT, a set-back device is required at each television or is embedded within every consumer electronics device. The digital set-back device will likely need to have buffers to support jitter and time stamp derived in an IP network.

Summary

As cable companies strive to reach more homes and attract more customers, the cable MSO that can offer more services while reducing the costs of expanding its subscriber base will have the competitive advantage. By evolving existing network infrastructures to a common IP-over-DOCSIS protocol, companies can more rapidly and economically introduce new services, while preserving investments in existing equipment and the physical wiring connecting to subscriber homes. DOCSIS and MPEG standards can address all of the information transmission requirements today and in the future, and will enhance the overall revenue-generating opportunities in the cable industry. This approach optimizes the cable infrastructure for new services and allows the efficient, dynamic allocation of bandwidth across services.

Glossary

10BaseT. The IEEE 802.3 international standard specification for 10Mbps Ethernet over unshielded twisted pair (UTP).

100BaseT. The IEEE 802.3 international standard for Fast Ethernet 100Mbps over Category 5 (Cat5) UTP.

ANSI. American National Standards Institute. An umbrella standards organization in the United States. The Institute for Electrical and Electronic Engineers (IEEE) and the Society of Telecommunications Engineers (SCTE) are ANSI sanctioned standards organizations.

ARP. Address Resolution Protocol. A protocol of the IETF for converting network addresses to 48-bit addresses.

ATM. Asynchronous Transfer Mode networking. A protocol and networking technology for the transmission of a variety of digital signals using uniform 53-byte cells.

BPI. In DOCSIS, the Baseline Privacy Interface. BPI defines MAC layer security services for DOCSIS CMTS to CM communications. The goals of BPI are to provide cable modem users with data privacy across the cable networks and to provide to cable operators the ability to prevent unauthorized access to MAC services.

Broadband access provider. The owner or operator of the broadband access network's last-mile facilities, to which subscribers are connected and through which services are exchanged between the subscriber and the service provider.

Broadcast address. A predefined destination address that denotes the set of all data network service access points.

CATV. Community Antenna Television. Initially used to describe a cable network; today it refers to any cable or hybrid fiber and cable system used to deliver video signals to a community.

Channel. A specific frequency allocation within the RF spectrum, specified by channel width in hertz (cycles per second) and by center frequency.

CLEC. Competitive local exchange carrier. A service operator who provides alternative telephone and/or data services to the user in place of the traditional local telephone company, often using wireless services.

CM. Cable modem. The device in the home that connects to the cable network and provides a high-speed data connection and/or a telephone connection to the subscriber.

CMCI. Cable Modem to CPE Interface. The network or input/output interface on a cable modem that connects to the subscriber's home network or computer. Examples are Ethernet 10BaseT and Universal Serial Bus (USB) interfaces.

CMTS. Cable Modem Termination System. A generic term referring to the intelligent controller in a cable modem system.

CMTS-NSI. In DOCSIS, the interface between a CMTS and the equipment on its network side.

CODEC. Abbreviation of coder/decoder; refers to a device that converts between digital and analog signals. For example, a telephony voice CODEC takes analog speech signals from a telephone handset and converts it to a digital stream of bytes and vice versa.

Codeword. A unit or block of protected data used by a forward error correction (FEC) process.

CPE. Customer premises equipment. A term used to describe devices in the home which connect to a network connection.

CRC. Cyclic redundancy check. A suffix of one or more bytes appended to a packet or a portion of a packet that is calculated using the same algorithm by both the sender and receiver of a packet of data. A receiver detects if there is a bit error in the packet if the calculated CRC value is different than the transmitted CRC value.

Data link layer. Layer 2 in the Open Systems Interconnection (OSI) architecture; the layer that provides services to transfer data over the transmission link between open systems. Also called the MAC layer.

DAVIC. Digital Audio Video Council. An industrial council which developed digital video and cable modem specifications from September 1994 through 1999. The output of DAVIC fed mostly into European standards for set-top box interface standards as well as cable modem standards.

dBmV. Decibel relative to one millivolt. A measure of RF power.

DHCP. Dynamic Host Configuration Protocol. An Internet protocol used for automatically assigning IP addresses.

Diplex filter. A common bidirectional device used in CATV. It has three RF connectors: One *sees* the entire combined upstream and downstream frequency range, a second *sees* only the upstream frequencies, the third *sees* only the downstream frequencies.

Distribution hub. A location in a cable television network that performs the functions of a headend for customers in its immediate area, and that receives some or all of its television program material from a *master headend* or *regional headend* in the same metropolitan or regional area.

Distribution network. The last-mile network of transmission cables, amplifiers, repeaters, optical equipment, and power equipment, which supply and maintain the transmission of signals between the service provider and the subscriber. For CATV plants, this is the collection of coaxial cables, fiber-optic equipment, power supplies, splitters, taps, amplifiers, and so on, used for the transmission of television and high-speed data and voice signals between the CATV headend and all the homes in the serving area. For DSL networks, it is the collection of twisted-pair cables, amplifiers, repeaters, remote terminals, and so on, used to connect the telephone central office (TCO) with residential and business subscribers.

DOCSIS. Data over Cable Service Interface Specification. Refers to the ITU-T J.112 Annex B standard for cable modem systems.

Downstream. The direction from the headend toward the subscriber.

Drop cable. Coaxial cable that connects to a residence or service location from a directional coupler (tap) on the nearest coaxial feeder cable.

DSL. Digital subscriber line. A technology to send high speed data over existing telephone copper pair lines, i.e. ordinary phone lines to homes and businesses.

EH or EHDR. In DOCSIS, an Extender Header.

EIA. Electronic Industries Alliance.

End user. An individual, organization, or telecommunications system that accesses the network in order to communicate via the services provided by the network. Also, the entity that pays for cable service.

Errored second. A one-second interval containing at least one bit error.

EtherTalk. A specification developed by Apple Computer that provides the AppleTalk protocol over Ethernet networks.

FCC. Federal Communications Commission. The government body that governs and regulates communications within the United States.

FCS. Frame CheckSum. *See* CRC.

FEC. Forward error correction. The operation of placing one or more bytes appended to the end of or a portion of a packet which allows the receiver to both detect and correct bit errors that may have been introduced in the packet during the transmission process from sender to receiver.

Feeder network. The system of feeder coaxial cables that connect neighborhoods to the trunk cable or fiber node.

Fiber node. A point of interface between an optical fiber trunk and the coaxial distribution feeder network.

Forward channel. *See* Downstream.

Guard time. The minimum time allocated between bursts in the upstream, referenced from the symbol center of the last symbol of a burst to the symbol center of the first symbol of the following burst. A symbol is a collection of some number of data bits that are transmitted together.

HBI. Home Box Internet. A term used to convey the upcoming ubiquity of Internet services to the home via cable networks as a metaphor to the success that the Home Box Office premium channel brought to cable pay TV programming and the rapid acceptance of cable TV in the United States.

HBO. Home Box Office. The first premium pay TV channel offered by cable operators in the late 1970s.

HDTV. High-definition television. Television with significantly more picture information (resolution) than that provided by a good NTSC or PAL standard television image. The term HDTV embodies many resolutions; however, it implies about twice the resolution in both vertical and horizontal directions; i.e., wide aspect ratio.

Headend. In most cable systems, the point of origin for subscriber video signals.

HHP. Households passed. A figure of merit used to describe the size of a cable network or a portion of a cable network by indicating the number of residential homes passed by the physical cable.

HRC. Harmonically related carriers. A system used to synchronize the timing of all downstream video carried on a cable network.

ICMP. Internet Control Message Protocol. Used by IP entities to communicate management and control information between themselves.

IE. Information element. In DOCSIS, the fields that make up a MAP and define individual grants, deferred grants, and so on.

IEEE. Institute of Electrical and Electronic Engineers. An international standards body located within the United States and sanctioned by ANSI.

IETF. Internet Engineering Task Force. An international standards body located within the United States that produces protocol standards for the world-wide Internet.

IGMP. Internet Group Management Protocol. A management protocol exchanged between IP entities which is used to facilitate multicast group membership.

IKE. Internet key exchange. A key management mechanism used to negotiate and derive keys for security associations in IPsec.

IP. Internet Protocol. The foundation network layer protocol of the Internet.

IPPV. Impulse pay-per-view.

IPsec. IP Security. The collection of IETF protocols for protecting IP packets with encryption and authentication.

ISDN. Integrated Services Digital Network. A digital telephone system designed to handle data and voice.

ISO. International Organization for Standardization. An international standards body, commonly known as the International Standards Organization.

ISP. Internet service provider. Generic term used to describe a company or organization which provides its customers with access to the Internet. Access may be via any method, including dial-up, DSL, cable modems, or wireless.

ISUP. ISDN user part. A protocol within SS7 used for call-signaling within an SS7 network.

IUC. Interval usage code. A field in MAPs and UCDs to link burst profiles to grants.

LAN. Local area network. A series of connected equipment that are linked together via a common physical network in a limited geographic area such as a home, office, or campus.

LLC. Logical link control. In IEEE LAN/MAN standards, in a local area network (LAN) or a metropolitan area network (MAN), that part of the protocol that governs the assembling of data link layer frames and their exchange between data stations, independent of how the transmission medium is shared. In IEEE specifications, the LLC is a sublayer above the MAC sublayer.

MAC. Media access control. *See* Data link layer.

MAN. Metropolitan area network. A series of connected communications equipment that are linked together via a common network in a metropolitan area such as a small town, city, or region.

MAP. Bandwidth Allocation Message. The MAC Management message used by the CMTS to allocate transmission opportunities to CMs.

MCNS. Multimedia Cable Network System. The private company that launched the DOCSIS specification. This term has faded in use, replaced by DOCSIS.

MGCP. Media Gateway Control Protocol. A protocol used within the Voice-over-IP protocol suite.

MIB. Management information base. Used in network management, the MIB defines the information that is accessed via an SNMP interface.

Mid-split. A frequency division scheme that allows bidirectional traffic on a single coaxial cable. Reverse path signals come to the headend from 5 to 112MHz. Forward path signals go from the headend from 120MHz to the upper frequency limit.

Minislot. In general, an interval of time allocated in multiples of 6.25 μsec by the CMTS to assign bandwidth on an upstream channel.

Modem. Modulator/demodulator. The generic term for a device which converts digital data for the purposes of communicating to and from an analog transmission link.

MPEG. Moving Picture Experts Group. A standards body that develops specifications for digital, compressed moving pictures and associated audio.

MSO. Multiple systems operator. A cable operator that operates in multiple markets.

MTA. Multimedia Terminal Adapter. In PacketCable, the device that connects to the consumer's legacy telephone and interfaces to the Packet-Cable network.

NCTA. The National Cable Television Association is the cable industry's major trade association. Founded in 1952, NCTA's primary mission is to provide its members with a strong national presence by providing a single, unified voice on issues affecting the cable industry.

Network management. The functions related to the control of data link layer and physical layer resources and their stations across the data network supported by the hybrid fiber/coax system.

NIC. Network interface card. A generic name for an interface card which is installed within a computer for the purpose of providing a connection to a LAN.

NTSC. National Television Systems Committee. The committee that defined the analog color television broadcast standard used today in North America.

OSI. Open Systems Interconnection. A framework of ISO standards for communication among different systems made by various vendors.

OSS. Operations support system. Another term for network management.

OUI. Organizationally unique identifier. A three-octet IEEE assigned identifier that can be used to generate universal LAN MAC addresses and protocol identifiers per ANSI/IEEE Std 802 for use in local and metropolitan area network applications.

PAL. Phase alternating line. An analog video standard used in Europe and throughout the world.

PHS. Payload header suppression. A DOCSIS facility which allows repetitive information in a packet header to be remembered at the receiver and to be deleted from actual transmissions, thereby improving channel efficiency.

PHY. Physical layer. Layer 1 in the Open System Interconnection (OSI) architecture; the layer that provides services to transmit bits or groups of bits over a transmission link between open systems and that entails electrical, mechanical, and handshaking procedures.

PID. Program identifier. A unique integer value used to identify elementary streams of a program in an MPEG2 Transport Stream.

PMD. Physical media-dependent sublayer. A sublayer of the physical layer that is responsible for connecting to the physical media type, including electrically and mechanically.

PPV. Pay-per-view. The cable TV network services where customers pay a fee to watch a program, such as a movie.

QAM. Quadrature Amplitude Modulation. A digital modulation method in which the value of a symbol consisting of multiple bits is represented by amplitude and phase states of a transmission carrier.

QoS. Quality of service. The method by which a packet switching or transmission system can give priority to data packets appropriate to the end-to-end application needs. For example, scheduling and transmitting voice packets in preference to Web browsing file download.

QPSK. Quadrature Phase Shift Keying. A digital modulation method in which the state of a two-bit symbol is represented by one of four possible phase states.

RADIUS. Remote Access Dial-In User Service, as defined in RFC2138 and RFC2139. A client/server protocol which provides network access authentication and configuration services.

RC4. A variable-length stream cipher used to encrypt media traffic in PacketCable.

RF. Radio frequency.

RFC. Request for Comments. Technical policy documents issued by the IETF and accessible on the Web.

RFI. Radio Frequency Interface. A DOCSIS term for the system's MAC and PHY specification for the over-the-cable communications protocol between a CMTS and CM.

SECAM. Système Électronique Couleur avec Mémoire. An analog video standard used in France and some parts of Russia.

Service flow. A DOCSIS MAC-layer transport service that provides unidirectional transport of packets from the upper-layer service entity to the RF. Also, shapes polices and prioritizes traffic according to QoS traffic parameters defined for the flow.

Service provider. In this book, the organization or business supplying one or more services to subscribers over the broadband access network.

SFID. Service flow identifier. In DOCSIS, an identifier assigned to a service flow by the CMTS.

SID. Service identifier. An identifier assigned by the CMTS to the CM. The SID is used to allocate bandwidth on the upstream channel.

SNMP. Simple Network Management Protocol. The open network management system protocol of preference in the Internet. The standard is described in IETF RFC-1157.

SONET. Synchronous Optical Network. A standard for high-speed digital transmission over fiber optic networks which is used in the United States.

SS7. Signaling System 7 protocol. Developed for out-of-band call-signaling within the PSTN.

Subscriber. The residential or commercial end user receiving a service or services (e.g., Internet service, IP dial-tone service, packet voice service, packet video service, etc.) delivered over the broadband access network.

Subsplit or Low Split. A frequency division scheme that allows bidirectional traffic on a single coaxial cable. Reverse path signals come to the headend from 5 to 42MHz. Forward path signals go from the headend from 50 or 54MHz to the upper frequency limit.

TCAP. Transaction Capabilities Application Protocol. A protocol within the SS7 stack used for performing remote database transactions with a signaling control point.

TCP. Transmission Control Protocol. The transport layer protocol of the Internet.

TFTP. Trivial File Transfer Protocol. An Internet protocol for transferring files without requiring user names and passwords typically used for automatic downloads of data and software.

Timetick. In DOCSIS, the 6.25 µsec time interval used as a reference for minislot size and timing.

TLV. Type/length/value. In a protocol, a means of communicating information using preassigned variables referenced by type. The variables can be variable length, for example, strings of text.

Transport stream. In MPEG2, a packet-based method of multiplexing one or more digital video and audio streams that have one or more independent time bases into a single stream.

Trunk cable. Cables that carry the signal from the headend to groups of subscribers. The cables can be either coaxial or fiber, depending on the design of the system.

UCD. Upstream Channel Descriptor. In DOCSIS, the MAC Management Message used to communicate the characteristics of the upstream physical layer to the cable modems.

Upstream. The direction from the subscriber location toward the headend.

USB. Universal serial bus. A high-speed external serial interface standard which provides extended input/output services for connection peripherals to computers, such as a keyboard, mouse, speaker, printer, or scanner.

WAN. Wide area network. A series of connected communications equipment that are linked together via a common network in a very large geographic area such as a state. WANs will frequently cross state boundaries.

Index